A WORLD THAT WORKS

TOES Books

The Other Economic Summit (TOES) is a forum for the presentation, discussion, and advocacy of the economic ideas and practices upon which a more just and sustainable society can be built—"an economics as if people mattered."

TOES/USA is part of an international network of independent but cooperating initiatives. Those active in TOES/USA are convinced that promising and constructive alternatives are being developed and implemented all over the globe. An economics constrained by respect for the natural world and human dignity *is* possible. It is the goal of TOES to promote its further conceptualization and to encourage its elaboration in practice.

TOES Books are an initiative of TOES/USA. These books do not represent a TOES position on issues on the TOES agenda but rather seek to further dialogue on and increase understanding of those issues.

A WORLD THAT WORKS

Building Blocks for a Just and Sustainable Society

Edited by Trent Schroyer

A TOES Book

The Bootstrap Press
New York

Published by The Bootstrap Press, an imprint of the Intermediate Technology Group of North America, Suite 3C, 777 United Nations Plaza, New York, NY 10017 (Tel/Fax: 800-316-2739).

ISBN 0-942850-38-6

Cover design by Warren Hurley
Formatted and typeset by Peggy Hurley
Printed in the United States of America

Contents

Preface

TOES (The Other Economic Summit) is an international forum for the presentation, discussion and advocacy of the economic ideas and practices upon which a more just and sustainable society can be built—"an economics as if people mattered," in E. F. Schumacher's classic formulation.

But TOES is more than just an international forum for alternative economic ideas and practices, as the making of this book demonstrates so vividly. It is a truly voluntary movement without paid staff or infrastructure to speak of (except what it can beg, borrow or steal from established institutions with which those most active in TOES are associated). It has no continuity, reconstituting itself every seven years with the rotation of the G-7 Economic Summit; yet it has a history.

What makes it possible for such a non-organization to accomplish a feat like producing this book is a shared conviction that an economics constrained by respect for the natural world and human dignity *is* possible. It is this sense of communion, rarely articulated but omnipresent, that moves all of us to rally around such an unlikely banner as TOES—and the collective task of producing *A World that Works*.

Trent Schroyer, the moving spirit behind this book, calls this spontaneous resistence to global capitalism imposed from above "Cosmopolitan Localism," echoing Wolfgang Sachs in the *Development Dictionary.* "Cosmopolitan Localism" is different from parochial isolationism which advocates of global capitalism typically characterize those who resist globalization of harboring. Instead, it involves the search for different ways of nurturing local communities while linking them to wider connections and new approaches to producing real wealth, creating real sustainability and furthering real international security. These three concerns constitute the core of the program of TOES/97 in Denver and the strands that, woven together, make up the tapestry of this book.

These same strands connect TOES/97 with its predecessors, which have been held every year—with one or two exceptions—since the first TOES was organized in London in 1984 to provide a stage for presentation and discussion of alternatives to the official agenda of the heads of the Group of Seven leading industrialized country governments at their Economic Summit—derisively labeled "The *Other* Other Economic Summit" by the London TOES participants! (TOES/84 was not, however, the first alternative event at a G-7 Economic Summit; that distinction belongs to the Popular Summit in Ottawa in 1981.)

While a number of TOES Books have been published over the years, this is the first attempt to produce an anthology geared to issues being addressed and presentations made at a TOES gathering. But it is in no sense a proceedings volume. It rather seeks to frame some of those issues and help set the stage for debate at TOES and beyond on how to build a more just and sustainable future.

It is certainly not the last word on the three core themes of the book. We look forward to critical feedback on what appears in these pages, perhaps leading to future TOES anthologies to frame other key issues or extend the debate on these themes.

Nor do the views expressed here reflect TOES' position on any of the issues addressed in the book. The TOES practice in dealing with this situation is set forth in the statement on TOES and TOES Books facing the title page.

Anthologies are by their nature collective endeavors, and this book is surely no exception. We want, first of all, to thank those who contributed essays and ideas, often on very short notice. A number of those active in organizing TOES/97 in Denver also played important roles by helping to identify possible pieces for the anthology, including Winifred Armstrong, Romesh Diwan, Susan Hunt, Larry Martin and Ward Morehouse.

The Bootstrap Press team worked overtime to produce this book in an incredibly short period of time. Peggy Hurley did the typesetting, Cynthia T. Morehouse was the copy editor, and Judi Rizzi, Teena DiNota and Carol Marino played important supporting roles.

Trent Schroyer, who has played a major role in conceptualizing the program for TOES/97, was also the intellectual godfather of this book.

Amid numerous personal and professional distractions, he pushed himself the extra mile and then some to finish *A World that Works* in record time.

But he was not alone in pushing himself to meet an uncompromising deadline. In the final days before the book was due at the printer, Cynthia Morehouse and Peggy Hurley, especially the latter, worked around the clock to get the job done. Without their extraordinary effort, this book would never have made it to Denver.

Because of the time pressures under which this book was produced, it will inevitably contain imperfections. We beg our readers' indulgence. We also seek the understanding of some of the authors whose contributions had to be shortened in order to keep the total volume within manageable bounds. There was simply not enough time to clear the final edited versions with them. The editorial team working on the book takes collective responsiblity for the end result.

Each TOES gathering over the past dozen years has helped to make history by demonstrating that there are viable alternative ideas and practices to the economic globalization that is enveloping the world and the promotion of which constitutes the central agenda for the G-7. We hope that *A World that Works* will make still more history by giving increased visibility to the building blocks of a just and sustainable society presented in its pages and added momentum for their embrace.

Ward Morehouse
TOES/USA Chair, 1996-97

May 1997

Introduction

Working Alternatives for a World that Works

Trent Schroyer *

As the millennium approaches, a spontaneous social order is emerging that can appropriately be called "Cosmopolitan Localism."[1] As a metaphor it refers both to new ways of revitalizing and protecting local communities while participating in wider associations to check the growing domination of economic globalization. Cosmopolitan Localism involves new approaches to evaluating real wealth, creating real sustainability and promoting real International Security and Peace—as the three parts of this anthology record.

These working alternatives emerge from socio-cultural resistances to the structural violence of global capitalism. "Structural violence" is control of policy and people from external decision centers that systematically exclude local voices and interests while disvaluing their socio-cultural forms, stocks of knowledge and nature-culture interactions. As communities turn to regenerating their local economies, they are also learning to widen the influence of people-to-people organizations and the creation of new forms of consultation, partnerships and consensus-building from the grassroots up. What we are documenting here are the

---

* The author, editor of this volume, is Professor of Sociology-Philosophy at Ramapo College of New Jersey, Mahway, NJ 07430 (e-mail: tschroyer@igc.apc.org) and TOES/97 Program Coordinator.

"Other" globalization movements, the "Other" economic cultures and
the "Other" paths to a "World that Works."

Collecting and Connecting the Other Economics for a World that Works

Susan George has noted that the great untold story of the 1980s is
how the people at the bottom, impacted by the massive redistribution of
wealth from the poor regions of the South to the North, have managed
to survive.[2] How these peoples have actually survived and how they
have resisted the forces of globalization, regimes of accumulation and
colonizing forms of regulation is a source for alternative futures and
social orders that is mined here. Collecting and connecting these resistances to global capitalism is our task.

The laboratory for the future is out there in thousands of "experiments." Our focus is the innovative learning that is done by people and
people's organizations. But we are not primarily trying to create an
"alternative economics," as a new variation of economic rationalism
that will improve market decision-making. We want to bring together
the mosaic of successful alternatives that forms the basis for working
alternatives to economic globalization.

No one can theoretically deduce the rules for a just and sustainable
economics that reconciles the complexity of diverse regions, nation-
states and international orders; therefore, we are collecting and connecting innovations at the level of practice by people focusing on improving their lives and sustaining their habitats. This is a wider and
more participatory approach than trying to fuse a "new economics."
Precisely because economics avoids dealing with institutional orders,
or aligned forms of cultural and social transformation that change institutional orders, this approach is less about formal economics and more
about "substantive," or democratic people's economics.[3]

This is not mere rhetoric; there are two entirely different senses of
the word "economic."[4] Formal economics derives from the systematic
objectifications of measureable scarcity and constructs logics of economizing action. Substantive economics focuses on the actual processes
of material provisioning that depart from particular historical contexts
of subsistence and social forms of cooperation. Where formal economics develops "universal," quantifiable concepts, substantive economics
must always proceed immanently and historically, since the ways that
people provision themselves, and socially institutionalize these provi-

sioning processes, differ. One is defined by the methodological criteria of formal economic concept formation and the other departs from actual historical and institutional contexts and focuses on the technical-institutional problems of socio-economic life.

The mission of TOES/97 is to identify and promote substantive models of what people are doing to strengthen and support emerging social solidarities, viable popular movements and new socio-economic experiments. By focusing on "the other" (i.e.,traditional communities, community-based economies, the innovations of the "poor"), we become advocates supporting those who are forging their own paths of "development" in opposition to the G-7's policies. An "other economics" requires sensitivity to regionally unique economic livelihoods, bioregions and forms of people-to-people associations. It also involves promoting the networking of people's organizations to pressure governments to overcome their support for unjust and corrupt political regimes everywhere. This continues support for the reform of the destructive operations of the Bretton Woods institutions and will increasingly center on the acts of piracy and other irresponsible actions of transnational corporations.

Substantive research into the "other economics" and people's initiatives for peace and justice increases the likelihood of change because it diffuses experimental social innovations as it fosters wider participation. For example, how regions actually sustain existing forms of security while experimenting with mixed economies, rather than risking an all-out growth strategy, are models for alternatives to neo-liberal economic integration. Similarly, looking at how traditional communities evaluate real wealth based on funds of local knowledge that are systematically disvalued by applied economics yields alternative models of cultural self-restraint that are useful for promoting more sustainable consumption patterns everywhere.

From Cosmopolitan Localism to a People's World Order

To promote an open society internationally, we have to secure open access to information and participation in due process at every level of governance. But in truly open processes, people question not only the market interventions imposed on them, but also the undiscussed normative frames that justify these interventions.[5] Again this is resisting the official progress story of social evolution and includes questioning

Westernizing models of economic development, appropriateness of in-dustrialization of agriculture and knowledge production, the necessity of Western technology transfers and militarizations and so forth. All of these taken-for-granted institutional and cultural frames foreclose in-novations of "the other," more culturally based paths to a sustainable world.

Collecting innovations for working alternatives, as well as strate-gies for wider networking of people's organizations, is also a discovery of new norms that represent the common good for a just and sustain-able world. For example, recent United Nations Conferences have le-gitimated the norm of inclusion of civil societies into global/local plan-ning mechanisms in ways that opens up a social consensus-building process. This process can be used by local, regional and international participations and partnerships to intervene into top-down policies. Many networks advocate the principle of subsidiarity, which holds that tasks should be handled at the most decentralized or lowest level they can be effectively and democratically managed. But this multi-leveled norma-tive discourse requires a distinction between governmental regimes, i.e., nation-states and corporate rule, often exercised through the state as agent, on the one hand, and governance at wider levels of normative order on the other. The latter phenomenon begins to reveal how Cosmo-politan Localism also implies a people's world order.[6]

Cosmopolitan Localism requires three things as essential for peace and prosperity—namely, the regeneration of communities, unilateral self-restraint and the dialogue of civilizations.[7] These norms, and others mentioned in the commentary on an ethics of sustainability at the end of chapter seven, can be used as the sinews for a people's world order. But acheiving a unity-in-diversity of globalizing and regionalizing processes will require more open and cooperative processes and there are many obstacles to this end.

For example, at the Earth Summit non-governmental organizations (NGOs)[8] from every region came together and constituted a loosely integrated social world that refused in its final sessions to give itself a determinate political form. As one of the final global forum papers indicated, "international NGOs could keep themselves together only by remaining apart."[9] This "failure" permits an insight into how to unify regional and transnational processes.

The refusal to form a standing executive action unit was consistent with the intention to allow the regional networks to consolidate them-selves in interactive ways. The stalemate was an expression of a movement that wants to resist central executive authority until the regional integrations are more explicit and have more autonomy.[10] The resistance expressed in those final days at the end of the Earth Summit reveals the priority of creating greater participation as a necessary precondition for realizing the real meaning of wealth, sustainability with justice and truly equitable international security and peace. Only through the widening and empowerment of more regional people's organizations can the monitoring and implementing of global/local norms and local autonomy be protected from the gathering momentum of global neo-liberalism.

There is also need to strengthen the international level of governance as well as the local, a dual agenda sometimes not sufficiently stressed. The complex society that surrounds and penetrates all social worlds today will not go away or be rendered harmless by socio-cultural resistance. Other levels of discourse and counter-organization are essential to transform a globalizing world. All opportunities for participation in norm articulation for wider goverance structures are essential. They can provide alternatives to the dominant de-normativizing regulations, such as "free trade." These regulations impose higher order "universalizing" rules on localities in ways that undermine the social commons and cooperative associations. It is essential to expose how these imposed "universalizing" rules undermine norms of cooperation and consensus-building and distort interaction processes essential for articulating a cross-sectorial consensus.

Recognition of this people's world order requires another historical frame than the dominant "progress" story which sees "humanity" as struggling against nature and ignorance for "liberation." In this scenario, peace comes from development, and any blockage results in rebellion and frustrations that then become ungovernable. A more traditional story is that peace derives from the establishment and practice of justice between peoples, their commons, cultures and institutions. Hence Ivan Illich's analysis of why is it is essential to delink peace and development outlines the cultural conditions essential for peace[11] and implies that a people's world order is rooted in regional norms of hospitality and reciprocity—the means and ends essential for the ongoing dialogue of civilizations.

This then is the context for the present TOES book—an attempt to give concrete representation to Cosmopolitan Localism and a People's World Order within the framework of the TOES program in Denver in June 1997. That framework and this book are organized around three themes—real wealth, real sustainability and real international peace and security. The guiding criterion in making selections for the anthology has been whether they suggest actionable critiques and working alternatives to the G-7-imposed order. Chapters are introduced by commentaries which challenge the theoretical assumptions behind G-7 policies and the policies themselves.

We hope that TOES/97, of which this volume is an integral part, will facilitate greater integration of local/regional issues with wider national and transnational networks of people's organizations. We are concerned that such groups in the United States often distinguish themselves by not being able to create cross-sectorial networks that work together, but by a "star system" that leads to competition for grants and recognition but not to cooperation. Our hope is that TOES will contribute to forming new approaches to networking that will be more effective in moving forward with the agenda for building a just and sustainable future.

Notes

1. The idea of a "cosmopolitan localism"—or a post-modern communitarianism—have been expressed by voices assembled in Wolfgang Sachs, ed., *The Development Dictionary: A Guide to Knowledge as Power* (London: Zed Books,1992). This collection contextualizes the technical terms of the "age of development" (e.g., development, market, planning, population, progress, poverty, standard of living, etc.) by showing how they originated in Western institutional contexts that are now historically outdated. After four decades of failed development and a growing redistribution of wealth from poorer to richer countries, it is time to seek another kind of socio-economic knowledge.

2. In the introduction to her *A Fate Worse Than Debt*, New York: Grove Weidenfeld, 1988.

3. The framework for this approach has been developed in Trent Schroyer, "Karl Polanyi's Post-Marxist Critical Theory," published in *The Legacy of Karl Polanyi: Market, State and Society at the End of the Twentieth Century*, edited by M.Mendell and D.Salee, New York: St. Martin's Press,1991. The effort to combine critical

theory and a participatory action framework is found in Trent Schroyer "Research Programs from the Other Economic Summits (TOES)," published in *Dialectical Anthropology* 17:355-390 (1992).

4. Karl Polanyi's contrast of substantive and formal economics, developed in his *The Livelihood of Man* (New York: Academic Press, 1977), has created wide discussion in economic anthropology, but this discussion has not gone far enough. Whereas formal economizing logics refer wise use of insufficient means to a hierarchy of preferences, material-substantive economic action is oriented to the livelihood ends defined by custom, tradition or chosen norms. Scarcity determines economic action only where insufficiency of means defines the ends itself; otherwise the allocations of means occur in ways defined relevant by normative ends. Substantive economics is not about theoretical reason, but refers to the search for "practical and productive" reason (in Aristotle's terms)—that is, for "what works" in creating and crafting new practices that will change the institutional rules of the game away from the logic of wealth creation as the only goal.

5. George Soros has recently argued that the capitalist threat to an "open society" today is the excessive individualism implicit in the abstract rationalism of economic theory, especially where it presents itself as a formal naturalistic science capable of certitude. He is especially careful to point out that technical success is not the same as what is right; normative arrangements require open processes of dialogue and discourse: George Soros "The Capitalist Threat" in *The Atlantic Monthy,* February 1997, pp. 45-58.

6. See J. N. Rosenau and E. Czempiel, *Governance Without Government: Order and Change in World Politics,* NewYork: Cambridge Univerity Press,1992, pp. 4ff.

7. Wolfgang Sachs, ed., *The Development Dictionary, op. cit.,* p. 113.

8. "Non-governmental organizations" (NGOs) is the official U.N. term, but this can be taken to imply that these organizations are not concerned or involved in governance. For this reason, we should call them "people's organizations."

9. Quoted in the Global Forum newspaper, *Terra Viva,* June 15, 1992.

10. What it also means is that it is premature, even inappropriate, to
    talk about a "global civil society." It is more appropriate to talk
    about "regional civil societies" and these are not necessarily going
    to mirror Western utilitarian individualism because there are di-
    verse ways of relating person, culture and social institutions. Hence
    theorizing about the universalization of "civil society "is another
    Eurocentric theory construction that imputes Western historical ex-
    periences as if they were essential steps in human and social devel-
    opment. In any imputation of universalizing social theory, an in-
    quiry into the appropriateness of the theory for the experiences and
    institutions interpreted by theory constructions is essential. This
    inquiry eventually requires the consent of those interpreted. In the
    introduction to *Theory and Practice* (Boston: Beacon, 1973), Jürgen
    Habermas has suggested that between the level of valid theory and
    prudent political strategies, there is a mediating sphere where the
    organization of enlightenment processes requires insight into spe-
    cific contexts.

11. See Illich's essay "The Delinking of Peace and Development" in
    Alternatives, Vol.VIII, Spring 1982 .

Part One

Does Globalization Work
for the Benefit of All?

Chapter 1: Critiques of the G-7's Globalization Strategy

Is globalization the hope for humanity? Or is globalization the final solution for the transnationalistic capitalistic interests, for whom democracy is a source of uncertainty and must be made secondary to the goal of material wealth creation? How we deal with this dilemma defines the nature of the present and our orientations to possible futures. This discourse has to be sharpened because it constitutes the most crucial existential question of our time. Put simply, which story are we in? Globalization as the material salvation of humanity? Or globalization as the final solution for the out-of-control, money-making system that is eating up both the earth and human communities? The American dream of consumer affluence as the end of the human satisfaction is an active element in this quandary, and the possibility that it cannot be univeralized (i.e., "globalized") has been reconsidered by those aspiring to "progress." These quandaries of globalization have received little, or no, recognition in the daily media. To sharpen these issues is our task.

The June 28th, 1996, Lyon Summit Economic Communique of the G-7 is entitled "Making a Success of Globalization for the Benefit of All." Globalization is presented as providing great opportunites for the future for all countries, especially its unprecedented expansion of investment and trade, rapid dissemination of information and technological innovation.[1] But these benefits will not be realized unless countries adjust to increased competition and adapt to international institutional structures and liberalization of markets. In short, the communique admits these benefits will not be realized unless countries accept the structural and socio-cultural transformations that are essential for entering into "economic interdependence."

Michel Chossudovsky's essay that follows on page 8 argues that globalization sets up a vicious cycle in which financial internationalization undermines the options of the states and national economies as well as weakening democratic potentials in civil societies. The overall result of the restructuring of over 100 countries has effectively been a globalization of poverty that is intensified as the same structural cycle is reactivated by the consequences of forced extensions of trade liberalization and foreign investment regimes. The more indicators of increasing debt and deeper socio-economic dislocations appear, the more the official strategy is aggressive ratcheting up of the globalization process by implementing more powerful mechanisms for removing any type of social protection.

Ratcheting Up the Globalization Process: Extending Free Trade & Investment

These grim realities of forced globalization are counter-intuitive to people who have always assumed that nation-states and communities are the locus for the politically acceptable social protections of land, labor and money. But the dynamics of forced globalization has gone far beyond what most people have yet recognized and therefore some brief interpretations that bring out the new ratcheting up of the globalization process since 1994 follows. Kevin Watkins' "Goods for Some Are Bad for Others" succinctly describes the gobal differences and impacts of the worldwide GATT arrangements which were given fresh impetus at the first meeting of the World Trade Organization in December of 1996. Scott Nova and Michelle Sforza-Roderick's "Worse than NAFTA" points out how the new Mutilateral Agreement on Investment, now being finalized by the OECD countries, has the potential to rule out any kind of alternative development by national and regional communities by empowering investors above all others' interests. These radical extensions of globalization are the final solution for those who see any kind of resistance to free trade-driven development as a block to the global experiment in utopian capitalism.

The "Other" Globalization Movement

Nonetheless there are also counter trends to this G-7 sponsored structural juggernaut. Whereever affected communities recognize the losses that these restructurings in the name of economic growth and development bring, there emerges spontaneous resistance and "working alternatives." Surveying some of these dissenting voices and counter-models, Susan Hunt's "On the Costs of Economic Globalization" is an interpretive account of what is lost in the globalization process, brought to a focus by the International Forum on Globalization's efforts to create public "teach-ins" on these issues. Recording stories of domination and resistance to globalization from many regions suggests a second counter-globalization process is occurring, one that is symbolized by the claim that the only true universal is the local.

In this spirit, Richard Falk claims there are two forms of globalization today; the first is the modernist one promoted by the G-7. The second form is "post-modernist" and recognizes we are in a world where nation-states have changed their roles and where Third World experiments in self-reliance are constituting unique working alternatives to the forced creation of Westernized commerical civil societies.[2] While Falk presents his discussion of the two globalizations as a discourse of the realists with the "utopians," the viewpoints presented in this anthology of "A World that Works"suggest we should reverse these terms and see the "realism" of globalization as a "utopian capitalism" that cannot be realized without destroying human communty, the earth and world peace.

The interrelations of these two movements of global social change today are not adequately understood and it is probably a mistake to think they can now be theoretically comprehended in some grand theory of the World Order or the "Clash of Civilizations." At this moment, the voices of the "other" (the non-modern, non-Western, "poor") have to be heard, viewpoints recorded and "other" world interpretations considered. Gathering "alternative" stories and cognitive viewpoints about the double movement of globalization , and especially local-regional cultural experiments in "development," brings into focus a different perspective on the reality of globalization.

Falk also argues that the second type of globalization is actually rooted in an existential ethical choice—a recognition of a post-Nuremberg obligation for all world citizens to choose solidarity with the poor and to take human suffering seriously. This ethical view on the "globalization" is echoed by voices who are now asserting that the realities of globalization are best viewed as a new holocaust in the making.

Thus Ward Morehouse evokes "the right to be human" as being denied by corporate decision-making. That decision-making undermines the human "right to development," protected by international law and United Nations-generated conventions. Because the power of transnational corporations enables them to evade the normative restraints of national and international governance, documentation of inhuman acts against humanity is essential to inform a people's transnational public discourse. As Herman Daly has stated in *Beyond Growth:*

> Transnational corporations have escaped the national obligations of community by becoming international, and since there is as yet no international community they have escaped from community obligations altogether. Globalism does not serve community—it is just individualism writ large.[3]

The second form of globalization is therefore both an affirmation of local communities and a recognition that this requires a cosmopolitan public participation too. Steps to the coming together of publics that anticipate a world community have been initiated by International people's tribunals that have documented crimes against humanity by the G-7 sponsored" Structural Adjustment" programs. (See the chapter below, "What Is Real Democracy.") More people's tribunals documenting the crimes against humanity by corporations are now being planned, as Ward Morehouse's essay describes.

Introducing the above issues is the function of this chapter, but we are mainly concerned in the following chapters to show that there is a mosaic of working alternatives to globalization. Intrinsic to these working alternatives are emergent associations that point forward to how to widen the scope of democratic discourse within each country by recognizing new linkages that represent issues transcending every nation-state's boundaries. We will show that the issues of international justice and inclusive democracy go beyond the interests represented in the G-7's support for globalization, but we are also concerned with documenting that there is emerging a people's world order agenda that is the working alternative to globalization internationally: in short, "A World that Works."

Notes

1   "News and Views from the Lyon Summit" can be accessed on the worldwide web at http://www.g7lyon.gouv.fr/US/map/fil/fil.html.

2   Richard Falk, *Explorations at the Edge of Time: The Prospects for World Order,* Philadelphia: Temple University Press, 1992.

3   Herman Daly, *Beyond Growth: The Economics of Sustainable Development,* Boston: Beacon Press, 1996, p. 148.

The G-7 Policy Agenda
Creates Global Poverty

*Michel Chossudovsky**

The first part of this text contains an overview of the global economic crisis focusing on issues of debt and macro-economic reform. The second part consists of a critical review and assessment of the Halifax G-7 Summit Communique.

The Globalization of Poverty

At the dawn of the 21st century, the global economy is at a dangerous cross-roads. In the developing world, the process of economic restructuring has led to famine and the brutal impoverishment of large sectors of the population while contributing to the "thirdworldization" of the countries of the former Eastern block.

Since the early 1980s, the macro-economic stabilization and structural adjustment programs imposed by the IMF and the World Bank on developing countries (as a condition for the renegotiation of their external debt) have led to the impoverishment of hundreds of millions of people. Contrary to the spirit of the Bretton Woods agreement, which was predicated on "economic reconstruction" and stability of major

*Professor of Economics, Faculty of Social Sciences, University of Ottawa. Copyright by Michel Chossudovsky, Ottawa 1995. Author can be contacted at chosso@acadvml.uottawa.ca; tel: 1-613-7892051; fax: 1-613-7892050.

exchange rates, the structural adjustment program has largely contributed to destabilizing national currencies and ruining the economies of developing countries.

GLOBAL DEBT

In the developing world, the burden of the external debt has reached 1.9 trillion dollars: entire countries have been destabilized as a consequence of the collapse of national currencies, often resulting in the outbreak of social strife, ethnic conflicts and civil war.

The restructuring of the world economy under the guidance of the Washington-based international financial institutions increasingly denies individual developing countries the possibility of building a national economy. The internationalization of macro-economic policy transforms countries into open economic territories and national economies into "reserves" of cheap labor and natural resources. The restructuring of individual nations weakens the State, industry for the internal market is undermined, national enterprises are pushed into bankruptcy.

Moreover, these reforms—when applied simultaneously in more than 100 countries—are conducive to a "globalization of poverty," a process that undermines human livelihood and destroys civil society in the South, the East and the North. Internal purchasing power has collapsed, famines have erupted, health clinics and schools have been closed down, hundreds of millions of children have been denied the right to primary education. In all major regions of the developing world, the economic reforms have been conducive to a resurgence of infectious diseases, including tuberculosis, malaria and cholera.

STRUCTURAL ADJUSTMENT IN THE DEVELOPED COUNTRIES

Since the early 1990s, the macro-economic reforms adopted in the OECD countries contain many of the essential ingredients of the "structural adjustment program" applied in the Third World and Eastern Europe. These macro-economic reforms have been conducive to the accumulation of large public debts.

Since the early 1980s, the private debts of large corporations and commercial banks have been conveniently erased and transformed into public debt. This process of "debt conversion" is a central feature of the crisis: business and bank losses have systematically been transferred to the State. During the merger boom of the late 1980s, the burden of corporate losses was shifted to the State through the acquisition of bankrupt enterprises. The latter could then be closed down and written off as tax losses. In turn, the non-performing loans of the large commercial banks were routinely written off and transformed into pretax losses. The "rescue packages" for troubled corporations and commercial banks are largely based on the same principle of shifting the burden of corporate debts onto the State Treasury.

In turn, the many State subsidies and corporate "handouts," rather than stimulating job creation, were routinely used by large corporations to finance their mergers, introduce labor-saving technology and relocate production to the Third World. Not only were the costs associated with corporate restructuring borne by the State, public spending directly contributed to increased concentration of ownership and a significant contraction of the industrial workforce. In turn, the string of bankruptcies of small- and medium-sized enterprises and lay-offs of workers (who were also tax payers) were conducive to a significant contraction in State revenues.

In the group of OECD countries, public debts have increased beyond bounds (currently in excess of 13 trillion dollars).[1] Ironically, the very process of "reimbursing this global debt" has been conducive to its enlargement through the systematic creation of new debts. In the U.S., which is by far the largest debtor nation, the public debt increased fivefold during the Reagan-Bush era. It is currently of the order of 4.9 trillion dollars.[2]

A vicious circle had been set in motion. The recipients of government hand-outs had become the State's creditors. The bonds and treasury bills issued by the Treasury to fund big business had been acquired by banks and financial institutions, which were simultaneously the recipients of State subsidies. An absurd situation: the State was "financing its own indebtedness," government hand-outs were being recycled toward the purchase of public debt. The government was being squeezed between business groups lobbying for subsidies on the one hand and its financial creditors on the other hand. And because a large portion of the public debt was held by private banking and financial institutions, the latter were also able to pressure governments for an increased command over public resources.

The debt crisis had also triggered the development of a highly regressive tax system, which also contributed to the enlargement of the public debt. While corporate taxes were curtailed,[3] the new tax revenues appropriated from the (lower and middle) salaried population (including the value added taxes) were recycled toward the servicing of the public debt. While the State was collecting taxes from its citizens, "a tribute" was being paid by the State to big business in the form of hand-outs and subsidies.

CAPITAL FLIGHT

In turn, spurted by the new banking technologies, the flight of corporate profits to offshore banking havens in the Bahamas, Switzerland, the Channel Islands, Luxembourg and so forth contributed to the further exacerbation of the fiscal crisis. The Cayman Islands, a British Crown colony in the Caribbean, for instance, is the fifth largest banking center in the world (in terms of the size of its deposits, most of which are by dummy or anonymous companies).[4] The enlargement of the budget deficit in the U.S. bears a direct relationship to massive tax evasion and the flight of unreported corporate profits. In turn, large amounts of money deposited in the Cayman Islands and the Bahamas (part of which is controlled by criminal organizations) are used to fund business investments in the U.S.

UNDER THE POLITICAL TUTELAGE OF THE CREDITORS

The debts of parastatal enterprises, public utilities, state, provincial and municipal government's are carefully categorized and "rated" by financial markets (e.g., Moody's and Standard and Poor ratings). Moreover, ministers of finance are increasingly expected to report to the large investment houses and commercial banks. Moody's downgrading of Sweden's sovereign debt rating in January was instrumental in the decision of the minority Social Democratic government to curtail core welfare programs, including child allowances and unemployment insurance benefits. Similarly, Moody's credit rating of Canada's public debt was a major factor in the adoption of massive cuts in social programs and layoffs by the Canadian Minister of Finance in February. In the U.S., the controversial balanced budget amendment, narrowly defeated in the Senate in March 1995, would have entrenched the rights of the State's creditors in the U.S. Constitution.

CRISIS OF THE STATE

In the West, the democratic system has been steered into a quandary: those elected to high office increasingly act as bureaucrats. The State's creditors have become the depositaries of real political power operating discretely in the background. In turn, a uniform political ideology has unfolded. A consensus on macro-economic reform extends across the political spectrum.

A new global financial environment has also unfolded: the wave of corporate mergers of the late 1980s paved the way for the consolidation of a new generation of financiers clustered around the merchant banks, the institutional investors, the stock brokerage firms, and the large insurance companies. In this process, commercial banking functions have coalesced with those of the investment banks and stock brokers.

While these "money managers" play a powerful role on financial markets, they are, however, increasingly removed from entrepreneurial functions in the real economy. Their activities, which escape State regulation, include speculative transactions in commodity futures and derivatives and the manipulation of currency markets. Major financial actors are routinely involved in "hot money deposits" in the emerging markets of Latin America and Southeast Asia, not to mention money laundering and the development of specialized "private banks" that advise wealthy clients in the many offshore banking havens. The daily turnover of foreign exchange transactions is of the order of one trillion dollars a day of which only 15 percent corresponds to actual commodity trade and capital flows.

Within this global financial web, money transits at high speed from one banking haven to the next in the intangible form of electronic transfers. "Legal" and "illegal" business activities have become increasingly intertwined, vast amounts of unreported private wealth have been accumulated. Favoured by financial deregulation, the criminal mafias have also expanded their role in the spheres of international banking.

THE DEMISE OF CENTRAL BANKS

Moreover, the practices of central banks in many OECD countries have been modified to meet the demands of financial markets. Central banks have become increasingly independent and shielded from political influence.[5] What this means in practice is that the national treasury is increasingly at the mercy of private commercial creditors. Under article 104 of the Maastricht Treaty, for instance, "central bank credit to the government is entirely discretionary, the central bank cannot be forced to provide such credit."[6] These statutes are therefore directly conducive to the enlargement of the public debt held by private financial and banking institutions.

In practice, the central bank, which is neither accountable to the government nor to the legislature, operates as an autonomous bureaucracy under the trusteeship of private financial and banking interests. The latter, rather than the government, dictate the direction of monetary policy. In other words, monetary policy no longer exists as a means of State intervention; it largely belongs to the realm of private banking. In contrast to the marked scarcity of State funds, "the creation of money" (implying a command over real resources) occurs within the inner web of the international banking system in accordance with the sole pursuit of private wealth. In contrast to the inability of central banks to effectively intervene, powerful private financial actors not only have the ability of creating and moving money without impediment, but also of manipulating interests rates and precipitating the decline of major currencies as occurred with the spectacular tumble of the pound sterling in September 1992. What this signifies, in practice, is that central banks are no longer able to regulate the creation of money in the broad interests of society, e.g., in view of mobilizing production or generating employment. Money creation, including the command over real resources, is controlled almost exclusively by private financiers.

THE INSTABILITY OF GLOBAL FINANCIAL MARKETS

Deregulation alongside the development of large public debts have favored increasingly unstable pattern on global financial markets. Since Black Monday on October 19, 1987, considered by analysts to be very close to a total meltdown of the New York stock exchange, a highly volatile pattern has unfolded marked by frequent and increasingly serious convulsions on major bourses, the ruin of national currencies in Eastern Europe and Latin America, not to mention the plunge of the new "peripheral financial markets"—Mexico, Bangkok, Cairo, Bombay—precipitated by "profit taking" and the sudden retreat of the large institutional investors. A global financial breakdown can no longer be ruled out. Moreover, in contrast to the 1920s, major exchanges around the world are interconnected through instant computer link-up: instability on Wall Street into the European and Asian stock markets, thereby rapidly permeating the entire financial system, including foreign exchange and commodity markets.

Assessment of the Halifax Summit Communique

1. The G-7 Summit draft communique denies the existence of a global economic crisis (para 3). Despite the wave of plant closures,

mounting unemployment and the instability of global financial markets, the communique points unequivocally to an enduring recovery of the global economy: "We are encouraged by the overall performance of our economies and continued strong growth elsewhere in the world. In most of our countries, economic growth is robust and inflation is well under control" (para. 3). The data base is flawed; the most recent growth figures of the OECD indicating a significant slowdown in global growth are not acknowledged. Nor are the recent estimates of the ILO placing world unemployment at more that 800 million. The balance sheet of global poverty is not mentioned.

2. It is worth recalling that a similar aura of complacency prevailed during the frenzy of late 1920s in the United States. The possibility of a financial crash had never been seriously contemplated by the economic orthodoxy of the time. Optimistic business predictions continued even after the collapse of Wall Street in 1929.

3. The Halifax Summit Communique fails to assess the seriousness of the debt situation affecting both developing and developed countries and the destructive impact of debt collection on national economies. No concrete solutions are put forth in view of alleviating the burden of debt servicing.

4. It is essential that G-7 policymakers meeting in Halifax take cognizance of an increasingly dangerous situation. The crisis of the global economy is structural rather than cyclical. "Economic stabilization" and "structural adjustment," including the deregulation of financial markets, cannot constitute solutions to the global economic crisis. Recession used as a policy instrument cannot be a solution to the achievement of global economic growth. Similarly, poverty alleviation and job creation cannot be realized through the deregulation of the labor market (para. 8) and the compression of social sector budgets. The Summit document also calls for the curtailment of public pension programs and systems of social support (para. 9).

5. The Halifax Summit Communique unreservedly endorses the continuation of the structural adjustment program while calling for an "effective system of surveillance of national economic policies"

(para. 16). The meaning of IMF surveillance—the annual monitoring of a country's economic performance in the context of Article IV consultations—has been redefined. A new triangular division of authority between the IMF, the World Bank and the World Trade Organization (WTO) has unfolded. "Surveillance" has been redefined (countervening the substance of Art. IV) with a view to providing the IMF with more power to intervene in the internal affairs of sovereign states: "We urge the IMF . . . provide sharper policy advice to all governments and deliver franker messages to countries that appear to be avoiding necessary actions" (para. 16c).

6. The G-7 have firmly endorsed the new trade order which emerged from the completion of the Uruguay Round at Marrakesh. In this context, the relationship of the Washington-based institutions to national governments is to be redefined. Enforcement of IMF-World Bank policy prescriptions will no longer hinge upon ad hoc country-level loan agreements, which are not legally binding documents. Henceforth, many of the clauses of the structural adjustment program, such as trade liberalization and the foreign investment regime, will become permanently entrenched in the articles of agreement of the new World Trade Organization (WTO). These articles will set the foundations for "policing" countries as well as enforcing "conditionalities" according to international law.

7. On the agenda of the G-7 is the enlargement of IMF reserves (discussed at Madrid in October 1994), including a review of the SDR system. An expansion of the IMF's lending capabilities has been portrayed by the IMF as a means of securing a "durable, more broadly based sustained high-quality growth [with a view to raising] living standards worldwide."[7] Yet what these loan agreements imply in practice is something quite different: the proposed expansion of lending, rather than "helping the poor," would reinforce the IMF's control over national governments. It would provide the IMF with added political leverage to impose sweeping macro-economic reforms.

8. An enlargement of IMF lending, without redefining its mandate, will contribute to increasing rather than alleviating the burden of global debt. This proposed expansion of IMF resources would largely support the interests of international creditors: "new money"

is lent to pay back "old debt." . . . In addition to obliging governments to faithfully abide by IMF policy prescriptions, the new loans
would also require the signing of parallel agreements regarding debt
servicing with the official and commercial creditors. In a sense, the
inflow of multilateral money acts as a catalyzer which promotes a
substantially larger outflow of financial resources from indebted
developing countries.

9. The proposed expansion of IMF resources is to be instrumented
    through the establishment of a new standing procedure under the
    "Emergency Financing Mechanism" to be used by countries facing
    "Mexico-type crises" (para. 17). This procedure would require dou-
    bling the amounts currently available to the IMF under the General
    Arrangements to Borrow (GAB) provided by the G-11 countries
    (G10 plus Saudi Arabia).

10. The emergency procedure does not address the causes of the crisis.
    The funds would be granted largely to enable indebted countries to
    meet the demands of their international creditors. Rather than as-
    sisting countries in distress, the Emergency Financing Mechanism
    constitutes "a social safety net for the creditors." The proposed
    measure would have the added consequence of boosting the public
    debt of G-11 countries, that is private debts are transformed into
    public debts.

11. The G-7 fails to analyze the causes of the Mexican crisis. The fi-
    nancial sector reforms played a key role in triggering the crisis.
    "The prevention of crisis is the preferred course of action (para.
    16): the proposed solution—sound/fiscal and monetary policies—
    requires reinforcing the thrust of the macro-economic reforms, in-
    cluding the deregulation of the financial sector and the privatization
    of State assets. The prevention of crisis is to be implemented through
    the application of the same "economic medicine" which is the cause
    of crisis (para. 16 and 17). In other words, these procedures adopted
    without any revision of IMF economic policy prescriptions are likely
    to trigger the outbreak of Mexican-type crises. The proposed solu-
    tion becomes the cause of the crisis.

12. "We [the G-7] welcome the recent positive turn of events in Mexico"
    (para. 15). The Communique is referring to the "rescue package"

supported by the U.S. Treasury, the IMF and the Bank for International Settlements. The latter was largely intended to allow Mexico to meet its debt servicing obligations (in short-term dollar-denominated *tesobonos*) with international creditor banks and financial institutions. Private debts were conveniently recycled and transformed into public debts. In turn, the Mexican economy will be crippled for years to come, leading to a far deeper political and social fracturing. Under the deal, Mexican banks will be thrown open to foreign ownership and the country's entire oil export earnings are to be deposited into a bank account in New York managed by its international creditors.

13. The Halifax Summit Communique fails to acknowledge the disruptive impact of financial markets. The Communique calls for the removal of remaining capital market restrictions (para. 22b) "coupled with strengthened policy advice from international financial institutions on appropriate supervisory structures."

14. The proposal to tax speculative foreign exchange transactions (Tobin tax) is not on the agenda. The consensus at Halifax is that governments should not intervene; financial markets should establish their own patterns of regulation, with regulators appointed by the various stock market authorities. It is worth recalling in this context that the so-called "circuit-breakers" (introduced by Wall Street regulators after the 1987 crash) have proven to be totally ineffective in preventing a meltdown. The circuit breakers, which consisted of freezing computerized program trading once the Dow Jones fell by more than 50 points during an explosion of panic trading on Wall Street in October 1992, were unable to avert a near repeat of the 1987 crash.[8] Moreover, a report by the Bundesbank published in 1993 warned that trade in derivatives could potentially "trigger chain reactions and endanger the financial system as a whole."[9] The chairman of the U.S. Federal Reserve Board, Alan Greenspan, also recognized that: "Legislation is not enough to prevent a repeat of the Barings crisis in a high tech world where transactions are carried out at the push of the button."[10]

15. The Halifax Summit Communique exhibits a lack of foresight in assessing the workings of the global financial system. G-7 governments and international financial institutions fail to understand that

the macro-economic framework, including the curtailment of budget deficits, have contributed since the 1980s to exacerbating rather than alleviating the debt crisis. The accumulation of large public debts, and the pressures exercised by creditors on the State system, are at the heart of this crisis, requiring effective public regulation and intervention in financial markets—namely, a form of "financial disarmament" in view of constraining the destabilizing activities of speculators.[11]

16. Concrete financial mechanisms which secure the cancellation of the external debt of developing countries and the write-down of the public debts of the developed countries are also required alongside regulatory policies, which carefully monitor the activities of the Bretton Woods institutions and "democratize" the structures of central banks. The world community should recognize the failure of the dominant neo-liberal system. Of crucial importance, is the articulation of new rules governing world trade as well as the development of an expansionary ("demand side") macro-economic policy agenda geared toward the alleviation of poverty and the worldwide creation of employment and purchasing power.[12]

Notes

1. General government gross liabilities for all OECD countries combined was of the order of 72.9 percent of Gross Domestic Product. See OCDE, *Perspectives de l'OCDE*, No. 56, December 1994, Annex: Table 33.

2. Projection of the U.S. public debt corresponding to July-September 1995. See "The Debt's the Limit," *Investor's Business Daily*, April 13, 1995, p. B1.

3. In the U.S. the contribution of corporations to federal revenues declined from 13.8 percent in 1980 (including the taxation of windfall profits) to 8.3 percent in 1992. See *U.S. Statistical Abstract*, 1992.

4. Estimate of Jack A. Blum presented at *Jornadas: Drogas, desarrollo y estado de derecho*, Bilbao, October 1994. See also Jack Blum

and Alan Block,"Le blanchiment de l'argent dans les Antilles" in Alain Labrousse and Alain Wallon, eds., *La planète des drogues,* Paris: Le Seuil, 1993.

5.   Carlo Cottarelli, *Limiting Central Bank Credit to the Government,* Washington, D.C.: International Monetary Fund, 1993, p. 5.

6.   *Ibid.*

7.   Michel Camdessus, "Recovery Must Be Used Wisely to Secure Sustained, High-Quality Growth," *IMF Survey,* October 17, 1994, p. 307. See also "Managing Director's Closing Press Conference," *IMF Survey,* October 17, 1994, p. 316.

8.   See "Five Years On, the Crash Still Echoes," *The Financial Times,* October 19, 1992.

9.   For further details, see Martin Khor, "Barings and the Search for a Rogue Culprit," *Third World Economics,* No. 108, March 1-15, 1995, p. 10.

10. Martin Khor, "Barings Exposes High Risks of Derivative Trade, *Third World Economics,* No. 108, March 1-15, 1995, p. 11.

11. The term "financial disarmament" was coined by the Ecumenical Coalition for Social Justice, "The Power of Global Finance," *Third World Resurgence,* No. 56, March 1995, p. 21.

12. See the proposal contained in *The Copenhagen Alternative Declaration* adopted by some 620 non-governmental organizations and networks at the World Summit for Social Development, March 1995. This requires substantive modifications of the rules of international trade as defined in the Final Act of the Uruguay Round and the articles of agreement of the World Trade Organization.

"Goods for Some Are Bad for Others"

Kevin Watkins*

Does mention of the World Trade Organization make your eyelids heavy? Well, it's time to wake up. Behind that dense fog of trade jargon, the environment, your rights as a consumer and those of the world's poorest people are under attack.

In December 1996, trade ministers from more than 100 countries met in Singapore for the first WTO ministerial summit. The aim was to chart a course for trade into the 21st century and to accelerate the creation of a global market free of trade restrictions. The outcome will affect everyone's life.

Every time we buy fruit in a supermarket, or purchase a shirt or a television, we are engaging in trade and thus taking decisions which affect the environment and link us to producers in developing countries. The problem is that our ability to make informed and responsible choices about how we trade is circumscribed by WTO rules.

At the core of these rules is an apparently innocuous legal distinction between traded products and "processing and production methods." Governments are entitled to use trade restrictions against products on scientifically established health grounds, but cannot limit imports because of social or environmental concerns over the way they are produced.

---

* Kevin Watkins is a senior policy editor for OXFAM.

This approach evolved from a 1991 ruling in which a WTO panel overturned a U.S. prohibition on imports of tuna from countries whose fleets used such methods as purse seine net fishing that kill large numbers of dolphins. It was a preposterous ruling, in effect outlawing the use of any trade measures to protect the environment or to conserve species.

For a glimpse of its implications take a look at Mexico's *maquiladora* zone. Blue-chip American companies, such as General Motors, Du Pont and General Electric, have relocated some of their most pollution-intensive operations here, partly to escape U.S. environmental legislation. Heavy metals and toxic chemicals have been dumped on a massive scale, turning the region into what the American Medical Association has called a "virtual cesspool and breeding ground for infectious disease." But GM can export its gearboxes to Europe at prices which bear no relation to the human and environmental costs of the production methods.

In a global economy increasingly dominated by transnational companies that can maximize profits by locating production in sites with the weakest social and environmental standards, this is a recipe for disaster.

Even the most myopic trade junky will admit privately that international market prices do not reflect the costs of cutting down forests, polluting waterways, eroding soils and over-fishing. Yet in contrast to other areas of world trade, where the sale of goods at artificially low prices is forbidden, "ecological dumping," or the sale of commodities at prices below their real costs of production, is celebrated as a market virtue. You cannot sell a color television at prices below production cost, but you can export mahogany toilet seats from Indonesia at prices that bear no relation to the cost of lost livelihoods, soil erosion or the loss of species.

New trade rules are needed which recognize the value of the environment, and which permit import controls on goods produced in environmentally damaging circumstances. A WTO social clause to protect basic workers' rights while addressing the most exploitative forms of child labor should be another step.

Unfortunately, Third World governments at the WTO regard any social and environmental regulation of trade as a protectionist threat to their trade interests. Governments may be motivated by a concern to maximize foreign exchange earnings, but precisely what interest vulnerable communities have in being poisoned by toxic wastes, displaced from their forests or seeing their fisheries stocks depleted is unclear.

In the industrialized world, too, the WTO's rules permeate our lives to disastrous effect. If, for example, you like your milk without growth hormones, you have a problem. A WTO panel is about to rule that a European Union resolution on the use of bovine somatatropin (BST)—a hormone which raises milk yields by up to 25 percent—is a breach of international trade law. The case was brought to the WTO by the U.S. government on behalf of Monsanto, a chemicals company which holds the patent for BST and stands to make in excess of $500 million annually from access to the EU market.

According to Monsanto, there is no scientific evidence of any health risk from BST, so the EU's import ban really concerns the method used to produce milk, and is therefore a violation of WTO rules. Even though medical research has pointed to BST as a potential risk factor for breast and gastrointestinal cancers, the WTO does not recognize caution as a legitimate reason to restrain imports.

Perhaps you harbor the hope that food labeling laws will protect your right not to eat foods that you regard, rightly or wrongly, as a threat to your health. After all, consumer sovereignty is supposed to be the governing principle of the free market. Well, forget it. Under the WTO's rules, you have no right to know what is in your food. For example, the Swiss chemical conglomerate Ciba Geigy has threatened to contest at the WTO the EU's refusal to market a variety of genetically engineered corn. As the genes in question, derived from a soil bacterium, have never formed part of the human food chain, their health effects are unknown. What is known is that they confer a resistance to ampicillin, one of the most common antibiotics.

The WTO restrictions on environmental labeling schemes are equally prohibitive. For instance, the EU has developed an ecolabeling scheme for sustainably produced paper that could help to promote the greening of the industry, enabling consumers to express through the market a preference for sustainably produced goods. In practice, the scheme is unlikely to get off the ground, since the U.S. Paper Manufacturers Association has warned that it will contest at the WTO any discrimination between paper products on the basis of how they are produced.

Paper is just the tip of the iceberg. The Canadian government has asked the WTO to confirm that all ecolabeling schemes between similar products, for example, sustainably and unsustainably logged timber, are illegal. Even voluntary certification schemes drawn up by development and environment groups to indicate fairly traded tea and coffee, organically produced food and sustainably produced wood could be banned, thus crippling one of the most potent forces for change from below.

As it is, a wide range of environmental and conservation measures won through intensive campaigning are already under threat. A Dutch import ban on fur from animals caught in leg traps has been threatened with action at the WTO by the U.S. and Canada; a U.S. ban on imports of shrimps caught without measures to protect endangered sea turtles has been challenged by Thailand and Singapore (two of the worst offenders); and Indonesia, Malaysia and Brazil have threatened recourse to the WTO if the industrial countries attempt to restrict imports of unsustainably logged timber.

Against this backdrop, prospects for the WTO summit make depressing viewing. In a world so profoundly threatened by environmental problems, so scarred by poverty, we desperately need new rules and new institutions to govern international trade. People—as well as corporations—have rights.

Worse than NAFTA

Scott Nova and Michelle Sforza-Roderick*

In popular mythology, economic globalization is a natural phenomenon like continental drift: impossible to resist or control. In reality, globalization is being shaped and advanced by carefully planned legal and institutional changes embodied in a series of international agreements. Pacts like the General Agreement on Tariffs and Trade (GATT) and the North American Free Trade Agreement (NAFTA) promote the unregulated flow of money and goods across borders and strip elected governments of their regulatory authority, shifting power to unaccountable institutions like the World Trade Organization (WTO).

Virtually unreported, the latest and potentially most dangerous of these agreements is now under negotiation at the Organization for Economic Cooperation and Development (OECD). The purpose of the Multilateral Agreement on Investment (MAI), as the proposed pact is known, is to grant transnational investors the unrestricted *right* to buy, sell and move businesses and other assets, wherever they want, whenever they want. To achieve this goal, the MAI would ban a wide range of regulatory laws now in force around the globe and preempt future efforts to hold transnational corporations and investors accountable to the public. The agreement's backers (the United States and the European Union) intend to seek assent from the 29 industrial countries that comprise the OECD and then push the new accord on the developing world.

---

*The authors are, respectively, director and research associate at the Preamble Collaborative: Preamble Center for Public Policy in Washington, D.C.

Negotiations are already at an advanced stage. Yet few Americans have even heard of the agreement. Trade officials are treating MAI information like nuclear secrets; the mainstream media is oblivious. Whether the MAI is adopted (and, if so, just how far its deregulatory tentacles will extend) depends on whether opponents can force the proposal from its present obscurity into the light of public debate.

As proposed, the MAI would force countries to treat foreign investors as favorably as domestic companies; laws violating this principle would be prohibited. Under these conditions, transnational corporations would find it easier and more profitable to move investments, including production facilities, to low-wage countries. At the same time, these countries would be denied the tools necessary to wrest benefits from such investment *like laws mandating the employment of local managers.* Efforts to promote local development by earmarking subsidies for home-grown businesses and limiting foreign ownership of local resources would also be barred. If adopted, the MAI will mean foreclosure of Third World development strategies, increased job flight from industrial nations as well as new pressures on countries, rich and poor, to compete for increasingly mobile investment capital by lowering environmental and labor standards.

A key MAI provision could also threaten corporate accountability laws championed by progressives in the U.S. The MAI takes aim at statutes in any nation that link subsidies, tax breaks and other public benefits to corporate behavior. This ban could be used to challenge a host of local, state and federal measures, including laws requiring subsidized firms to meet job-creation goals, community reinvestment rules that require banks to invest in underserved areas and the *living-wage* laws that are the focus of activist campaigns across the country.

Perhaps most disturbing, the MAI would preempt strategies for restricting corporate flight to low-wage areas—a major cause of job loss and income stagnation in the industrialized world. On top of the damage done by plant closings and layoffs, corporations use the threat of flight to undermine the bargaining power of unions and scare policymakers away from the tough regulation and strong public investment necessary to raise living standards. Although remote from today's policy agenda, rules limiting the capacity of corporations to flee are essential to restoring the ability of government and labor to deal with corporations on a level playing field. The MAI would bar such rules in any country that is a party to the agreement.

In its scope and enforcement mechanisms, the MAI represents a dangerous leap over past international agreements. It grants any corporation with a regulatory gripe the right to sue a city, state or national government before an international tribunal—with a binding outcome. Governments would enjoy no reciprocal right to sue corporations on the public's behalf. And the MAI ignores most of the exceptions in previous agreements allowing governments leeway in critical areas like public health and resource conservation. The full extent of the drafters' ambitions is reflected in WTO Director General Renato Ruggerio's recent characterization of the MAI negotiations: "We are writing the constitution of a single global economy."

If the MAI is a *constitution*, its bill of rights is for investors only. The agreement contains no standards to protect workers or consumers or to shield small businesses from anti-competitive practices by transnationals.

The Clinton Administration backs the MAI for the same reason it supported NAFTA: the view that increased international commerce is inherently beneficial and that whatever is good for corporations is good for the nation. Negotiators plan to complete the agreement by June 1997, and present it to OECD countries for approval as a treaty. This could mean a vote in the U.S. Senate by next Fall.

Organizations like Citizens' Trade Campaign, Global Trade Watch and the AFL-CIO have made major strides educating congress and the public on trade and investment issues. If unions, consumer groups, environmentalists, state and local officials, and small businesses build on this work and make their voices heard, it is not too late to modify or even derail the agreement.

The outcome is critical—not just because of the destructive provisions of the MAI itself, but because it is the next battleground in an intensifying campaign to institutionalize corporate dominance. While pundits rhapsodize about the triumph of unrestrained capitalism, corporate leaders know that social democratic politics may yet make a comeback. And they aspire to tie the hands of future policymakers by using their present political clout to inscribe deregulation indelibly in international law. Frances Fukuyama may be satisfied that the current winning streak of market ideology heralds the *end of history*. The corporations, however, want to put it in writing.

On the Costs of Economic Globalization: Voices from the International Forum on Globalization*

Susan Hunt

Globalization produces both winners and losers. This is common knowledge to economists. Even if they believe everyone will be better off in the long run, prudent policymakers should acknowledge the fact that in the short run there will be losers and cushion the blow by providing adequate safety nets. With respect to trade liberalization, unforeseen losers are more common than unforeseen winners. The literature on international economics places great emphasis on the "gains from trade" but very little on the losses. The inadequacy of international economic theory with respect to the losers is reflected in the policy debates surrounding NAFTA, GATT and trade liberalization and globalization in general. Potential losses have been virtually ignored in government debates on free trade. Outraged at the extent of the harm being perpetrated on the world's poor and on the environment in the name of free trade, many environmental organizations and other NGOs have assumed responsibility for filling in the gaps in trade theory.

In 1996, a few dozen critics of free trade banded together to found the International Forum on Globalization (IFG). This new alliance is made up of leading activists, economists, researchers and philosophers

*An earlier version of this paper was published in the *Ecological Economic Bulletin,* Vol. 1, No. 1, January 1996, pp. 19ff. The author is an economist who has long played an active role in TOES.

representing 19 countries. They have joined together to respond to the threat of free trade to the environment, to communities, to human rights, to equity and to democracy. To focus attention on the major issues surrounding the rush to globalize, they conducted teach-ins on the "Social, Ecological, Cultural and Political Costs of Economic Globalization" in several cities in North America, including New York City and Washington, D.C. The size of the attendance, over 1,000 people in New York City when the organizers expected perhaps 200, attests to the importance ordinary citizens attach to free-trade issues as well as their willingness to make an effort to understand globalization and to take responsibility for the impacts of trade liberalization on their communities, and on communities throughout the world.

Extending the Scope of the Debate: A Necessary First Step

The ecological costs of present-day economics have been well articulated. Maude Barlow of Council of Canadians calls forcefully for a strong moral vision and for a "fierce protection of the environment." Lori Wallach of Public Citizen reports that the General Agreement on Tariffs and Trade (GATT) did away with the tuna-dolphin laws because they are alleged to constitute a "non-trade barrier." The Marine Mammal Protection Act is also accused of being a non-trade barrier. Article 16.4 of the GATT obliges each signatory to conform all national laws to the GATT, so laws like these must be rescinded.

The International Forum on Globalization extends the scope of the free-trade debate beyond concern for the environment by describing the highly significant social, political and cultural costs of globalization. They move beyond intellectual rhetoric to focus on the difficult challenges requiring urgent action. These are challenges we all face, no matter what country we happen to live in.

Cynthia Brown of Southerners for Economic Justice explores the issue of distributive justice. She explains that one in ten working families in southern United States are poor. But when news reaches them of companies coming in to create much-needed jobs, there is no mention of environmental impact. Consequently, there are "cancer alleys" throughout the South, the result of industrial pollution. You can be sure that those who can afford to move from polluted areas have done so long ago, leaving only the poor who have no choice but to stay and suffer the consequences of somebody else's winning the economic game.

For Ted Halstead of *Redefining Progress*, it is important that those who win from freer trade acknowledge that there are losers.

> We have an economic system built on passing the buck. Damages
> and social costs are passed farther and farther down the social lad-
> der until there isn't anywhere else to go. That's why the poorest
> minority neighborhoods suffer the most from environmental pollu-
> tion. Corporations and the rich can externalize costs, shipping their
> garbage down the social ladder or to the Third World, because this
> makes "good economic sense."

Mark Ritchie of the Institute for Agriculture and Trade Policy (IATP)
in Minnesota reiterates the emphasis on human rights. When
globalization causes hunger and homelessness, it violates human rights.
"We have to go on the offensive to assert these human rights," he says.

Globalization Is Not about Fulfilling Basic Human Needs

During her extended stay in the Tibetan community of Ladakh,
anthropologist Helena Norberg-Hodge of the International Society for
Ecology and Culture witnessed first-hand the psychological impact of
globalization on the indigenous population. She insists that globalization
is not about fulfilling the basic needs of non-Western peoples. Most
indigenous communities have been perfectly capable of satisfying their
needs on their own and in their own ways. Globalization is about the
need of corporations to create an artificial need for their products before they will sell. Corporate need-creation devalues the traditional culture and ways of doing things. The old ways are no longer good enough.
Without realizing that industrial processes have a negative impact have
on environment and community, people begin to "need" industrial products. Norberg-Hodge insists that "we must halt the uprooting of indigenous communities who already have many of the environmental, cultural and economic issues sorted out."

Norberg-Hodge also found that globalization makes people feel
threatened. They respond with self-hatred and prejudice, and are turning inward. Economic competition and the threat to people's identity
posed by corporate need-creation causes tremendous insecurity, and
this leads to increasing racism and fundamentalism. To counter these
trends, we have to rebuild local communities and re-localize the economy
to restore a sense of self, of meaning and of belonging. Growing the
local economy involves such actions as establishing local food links
that shorten the distance between producer and consumer, and creating

local currencies, commerce and trade.

Ignacio Peon Escalante of Mexico's Pacto de Grupos Ecologistas reports that what has happened to Mexico in the wake of NAFTA has been much worse than even the pessimists predicted. For years now, environmental degradation has been on a "fast track." The root of the problem is land tenure. People have been and are being driven from the best land by transnational corporations (TNCs) and their industrial model of agriculture. At present, 35 percent of the Mexican population lives on small farms. The government's goal is to reduce their number to 5 percent. In effect, they are being starved off the land. But what neither the Mexican government nor the U.S. government seem willing to acknowledge is that those rural Mexicans who cannot make a living on their own land must move into the cities, which have never supplied enough jobs, or immigrate to the U.S. Many rural people would rather stay in rural areas if they could.

No Wonder There's a Revolution in Chiapas!

Physician David Werner, founder of HealthWrights and author of *Donde Hay No Doctor (Where There Is No Doctor),* describes the continuing struggle of indigenous peasants in Piaxtla, Sinaloa, to take back their own land (Werner, 1994). In the 16th century, the Spanish Conquistadors tricked the Indians in Piaxtla and throughout Mexico into buying back their own land. In the late 19th century, President Porfirio Dias ignored their rightful ownership and, backed up by the Mexican army, gave the entire Piaxtla river valley to one of his cronies. The Mexican Revolution and the 1917 Constitution stipulated land reform, but to this day little decent land has actually been redistributed. In Piaxtla in 1965, a group of *campesinos* asserted their legal right to land by "invading" one of the large plantations which should have redistributed to them long before. They planted and harvested their crops, and posted armed guards to protect them. In response, the *latifundistas* shot their leaders to death with machine gunes in broad daylight. Machine guns are available only through the army, but there was no investigation. Although their right to the land is assured by the Mexican Constitution, pervasive government corruption effectively nullifies any law that is not in the interest of the wealthy.

Denied access to the rich soils in the river valley, the *campesinos* began to clear and cultivate the steep hillsides above. Each year a *campesino* would clear a new patch of land, and borrow money from the *latifundistas* to buy wire for fences to protect the crops from the cattle baron's cattle. Consistently unable to repay their loans, each year *campesinos* would forfeit their newly fenced and cleared plots to the cattle baron, who thus obtained fenced and cleared land, planted with cattle fodder, for the price of fencing wire.

The growth of cattle ranching in Mexico during the past few decades has been a nationwide phenomenon, and the social costs have been substantial. Rather than growing corn, beans and rice—the staple crops of the poor—large swaths of the best land in Mexico have been converted to pasture for cattle to serve a growing urban demand for meat. According to Philip Howard and Thomas Homer-Dixon, co-directors of the University of Toronto's Project on Environment, Population, and Security:

> Sixty percent of the productive territory in Mexico is pastureland, producing meat for a population, 50 percent of whom never eat meat. Ranching accounts for some 60 percent of tropical forest loss in Mexico. To support the cattle industry, a growing number of farmers have switched from foodgrains to feedgrains. During the late 1970s, this trend cost Mexico its food self-sufficiency. In 1996, Mexico imported a third of its food, primarily from the United States (Howard and Homer-Dixon, 1996).

The emergence of NAFTA and the neo-liberal agenda it symptomized was a tremendous blow to Mexican *campesinos*. The *ejido* system of land tenure, established in 1917 by the Mexican Constitution, prohibited the sale of lands held in common by Mexican peasant communities. It also placed limits on the size of any single landholding in Mexico. *Ejido* land could not be forfeited for non-payment of debt. This part of the Mexican Constitution was considered a "barrier to trade," and since the laws of NAFTA countries are required to conform to NAFTA, they had to go. Pressured by Washington, in 1992 President Salinas forced the Mexican congress to repeal Article 27 of the Mexican Constitution and of the Agrarian Code, the legislation that made land reform a central tenet of the Mexican state (Collier, 1994: 84-85). This effectively removed the possibility of land reform in Mexico, and dashed the hopes of native peoples in Mexico that land rightfully belonging to them would ever be returned, at least through legal channels. These constitutional changes put a stop to the legal invasion and redistribution of illegally large landholdings, such as those in the Piaxtla River Valley of Sinaloa. Salinas' justification for undoing all that was fought for and won by indigenous peasants during the Mexican Revolution was that Mexican agriculture had to be modernized to increase the productivity of millions of peasant-held hectares not competitive in the world market.

The distribution of agricultural lands is becoming ever more skewed as large farmers, engaged in capital-intensive cash cropping for export, buy out small farmers. In many parts of Mexico, large landholder force *campesinos* off their land at gun point, backed by the Mexican army or their own militias (Barry, 1995). The result of this agricultural squeeze is pervasive poverty. Sixty percent of *campesinos,* 47 percent of Mexico's rural population of 29 million, were considered near-landless or landless in 1988. Since the bulk of the rural population is concentrated on marginal and over-worked cropland, the carrying-capacity of this land is being reduced still further. Per-hectare wheat yields nationwide have shown no increase since 1985, and per capita food production in 1991 was only 96 percent of the 1979-1981 level. One Mexican in five is now malnourished. Most authors point to Mexico's relatively high rate of population growth as an explanation for recent food shortages (Myers, 1995: 86-88). But it is not necessary to dig too deeply to discover that there is more to the story than population growth. Eventually, when the land is used up and can no longer support them, some *campesinos* are forced to migrate. For over a century the survival strategies of Mexican *campesino* families have included sending some of their numbers to the city or to the United States to earn the money that will allow the extended family to survive (Massey, 1987, 1991, 1994). As far back as the late 1970s, 600,000 people were leaving the countryside each year, and today the total could be over one million.

When Corporations Rule the World

Mexico is not the only place where government legislation makes it easier for corporations to expropriate land belonging to indigenous people. Sia Kaxinawa of the Union of Indigenous Nations lives in Brazil on the border with Peru:

> Governments have laws that are not respected because there are corporations that don't respect the law. Corporations have become bigger than the government. So corporations come in and cut illegally from the forest with impunity. So we have to get organized or the corporations will soon rule the world. But the government sometimes makes laws against us. So we have to fight against the government and the corporations. What will happen in the next 20

years? What will we see when we look back on what the government, corporations and technology have done to us? So we talk and talk at these conferences. But we are not doing enough to protect our culture. We have to remain rooted. Sustainable development has to come from our communities. In Brazil, a new law, Decree 22, will allow ranchers and loggers to contest the demarcation of Indian land. This is what I want to tell you about. Where is the money from the exploitation of nature going? Not to us, but to the First World. This is what is called progress. This Decree 22 could bring a war, and the invasion of Indian lands in Brazil. I'm sending around a petition for you to sign. I hope we can work together on this and other problems. I hope together we can work for human rights.

Carlos Heredia of Equipo Puebla in Mexico thinks working together is a good idea. He used to work in Mexico's Ministry of Finance. The first thing he learned when he started working on NAFTA with colleagues in the U.S. and Canada is that trade agreements are not about two countries negotiating. They are about sectors and classes in both countries who share the same interests (e.g., corporations and their subsidiaries) negotiating with each other. Large sectors of the populations of both countries are left out of the negotiations. Presumably these are the people who stand to lose rather than gain from trade. Heredia urged workers, environmentalists and progressive NGOs from the countries involved to work together to develop their own vision, their own program, that will not harm the majority and benefit only the few.

Our Common Task

Sara Larrain of the Chilean Ecological Action Network describes how the Chilean military dictatorship under Pinochet laid the groundwork for the economic and trade dictatorship that followed. With the help of the CIA, Pinochet overthrew Allende and replaced his socialist system with a system that was very efficient, but very regressive. By the time Pinochet left office, Chile had anti-labor laws and no environmental laws. The rate of economic growth had been 6 percent for ten straight years, but now there are twice as many poor. Chile still has the same constitution it had under Pinochet, and the same labor laws and economic program centered on the export of natural resources that Pinochet put in place. The end result is that the richest 20 percent of the population earn 60 percent of the national income, and the lowest quintile gets 3.3 percent. Chile's reputation as a Latin American "tiger" is built on natural resource exports—mining and therefore pollution.

This is the situation as Chile is being invited to join NAFTA. But what does NAFTA mean for Chile except an intensification of all that was put in place by Pinochet? Observes Larrain: "There is not a single representative of citizen's groups, labor unions, or people's movements on the Chilean negotiating committee for an expanded NAFTA. Only corporations. The means that an expanded NAFTA is not a democratic process."

Globalization Is Nothing but a Modern Form of Colonization

According to Martin Khor of the Third World Network in Malaysia, "What is called globalization today has been called colonization in the Third World for the past 500 years, ever since the Indians discovered that Columbus had landed on their shore." What globalization means to the South is that an already bad situation will get worse.

Khor is concerned about TRIMs: trade-related investment measures. The TNCs are pushing for a new round of trade talks because they did not obtain the desirable TRIMs during the Uruguay Round of the GATT. In December 1996, they met in Singapore to discuss the possibility. What they want is the right to enter any country they want, establish operations in any country they want, buy whatever they want, repatriate as much profit as they want and demand the "harmonization" of environmental and labor laws to any extent they want. This would strip governments of their ability to regulate corporations and investment. For Third World countries, it means a return to colonialism. The same corporate need for new sources of raw materials, new markets, new land and minerals in order to expand, cut costs and remain competitive that drove colonialism is driving globalization. As a result, patterns of economy, society and culture all over the world are being displaced by the American model. "People in our countries of course resist," said Khor. The Third World has fought back through UNCTAD and the New International Economic Order, and used the WHO to protect itself from pesticide residues. But the empire struck back through the IMF, the World Bank and the World Trade Organization (WTO). During the 1980s, World Bank structural adjustment policies meant the effective impoverishment, and even genocide, of the bottom third of the population of "developing" countries. Now the same model is being imported back into the U.S. by Newt Gingrich and the Republican Party: "Killing off 1/3 of the population of each country in both the South and the North so that the remaining 2/3 can enjoy more. If the Republican Congress gets its way, the majority of Americans will become the next Third World country."

Khor articulates what is fast becoming recognized as an essential element in any solution: The people who suffer the negative impacts of globalization must be at the forefront when any strategy for change is developed.

> Our common task is to replace the laissez faire model with some kind of new economics that takes care of everybody, the poor as well as the rich. Local people have to regain control of local resources and gear local economic systems to meeting local needs rather than the needs of the international market. We should allow those parts of the South that are poor to grow, to produce clothes, food, education and health care, but in an appropriate way, not by building skyscrapers and expanding infrastructure such as the highway system. Giving everyone a car is not environmentally or culturally possible. It is not good to be so materialistic. But we also need the people of the North to set an example by rejecting materialistic values. There is a need for people who have the analytical tools and the information to build relationships with people on the ground. We are meeting in the country that is the center of the problem. If U.S. public opinion doesn't change, the world is doomed.

Grand Cru du GATT: Resistance Spreads Beyond the Third World

Agnes Bertrand of the Institut d'Étude sur la Globaliasion Économique says that the "homogenization of Europe" and "development at the point of a gun" are meeting resistance in Europe as well as in the Third World. To protest the GATT, French free-trade resistors sent bottles of wine with "Grand Cru du GATT" and a skull and crossbones on the label to every member of parliament, along with an explanation and information. In Britain, there are protests against new highway construction. In France, where 60,000 cafés closed in the past year, small shopkeepers struggle against supermarkets. Small farmers are fighting the tunnel being built under the Pyrenees. It is not a matter of right and left, but a question of economic concentration. It is about the consequences of handing over decision-making to bureaucrats in

Brussels who are very responsive to TNCs. Farmers and fishermen pitted against each other in competition by the market are now beginning to talk together and find ways to collaborate. One strategy to fight globalization is a local exchange system in the Pyrenees, where the people are turning their backs on European homogenization.

David Korten of the People-Centered Development Forum (PCDForum) argues that pressing for growth beyond what the planet can sustain accelerates competition between rich and poor. According to Korten, "The one thing at which the global economy is truly efficient is transferring wealth from the many to the few." Development projects displace both people and nature and convert them to more economically profitable purposes. Korten is calling for a new civilization based on life-affirming, rather than money-affirming, economies. "Life is about living," he says, "not consuming."

That globalization leads to increasing income inequalities is a recurrent theme among the critics of increased free trade. John Cavanagh of the Institute for Policy Studies points to the 350 billionaires in the world today whose combined income is almost as great as the combined income of the bottom half of the world's people. In other words, the richest 350 people control assets roughly equivalent to those of the poorest 50 percent of the world's population. Cavanagh's solution is to dismantle corporate rule and democratize the economy as well as forge new paths that are equitable and sustainable. He stresses the importance of educating the public so that the ability to name the problem accurately is more widely exercised. Calling the present "a teachable moment," Cavanagh believes we can learn from the anti-NAFTA campaign how to build a movement. "In the United States, there is a flowering of community fights for community rights to shape their own economic destiny." Communities fight to abolish corporate tax breaks and they struggle against the weakening of environmental standards.

Carl Pope of the Sierra Club wonders why, if the tendency toward globalization is such an irresistible and inevitable force, corporate powers and their allies in government spend so much effort squelching any opposition. Most free-trade critics emphasize that globalization is not inevitable. Movement toward a globalized economy is the result of policy choices promoted by heavily financed corporate interests. When people in the developed world fail to understand how and why globalization is pursued and what its impact is on the rest of the world, the consequences can be tragic. Pope recalls that Ken Saro-Wiwa and the other eight environmental activists were executed in November of 1996 by the Nigerian government to make it easier for Royal Dutch Shell to do business there.

Colin Hines of Greenpeace International argues for a "new protectionism." "To protect or to be protected is something we usually want for ourselves and our families," he observes. "Then why is it good to leave your economy exposed? We need to rebuild local economies and nurture local sustainability. What we want is a General Agreement on Sustainable Trade." To that end, "we have to inform ourselves about what a corporation is and how it got that way," says Richard Grossman of the Program on Corporations, Law and Democracy. "What is property? Does the community have property rights in the corporation? In the end, it is the colonization of our minds that we have to overcome. If we don't, we won't just be out of our jobs, we'll be out of our planet."

The Economic "Golden Rule"

Ralph Nader of the Center for Responsive Law touches on an issue that did not receive much attention during public discussions of NAFTA and GATT: the way corporations use the law to push for limited liability. David Morris of the Institute for Local Self-Reliance, also in a legal vein, suggests that we need to establish a set of rules that honor a sense of place, rules that favor our neighbors and discourage foreign ownership. Employee-owned firms count the negative social costs of unemployment (violence, drug addiction, alcoholism) in decisions to close plants, while foreign corporations do not.

John Mohawk, editor of *Daybreak* magazine, argues that economic globalization is the politics of impoverishment, the social construction of poor people. For the 17th century colonialists, the Golden Rule went roughly as follows: "Those who have the gold make the rules; those who make the rules get the gold." Now 350 people have 50 percent of the world's wealth. They make rules that tilt the playing field so the money rolls into their pockets. But a series of myths has deflected people's attention from the processes that create poverty. According to Mohawk, "We need to deconstruct the mythologies that got us to where we are—the myths of industrialization, of progress."

He further notes:

Indigenous people are always at the front lines. They are the ones whose timber is cut, who provide cheap labor, who are recruited into the sex trade. Out in the field today they are shooting at indigenous people who are trying to protect their resources. "Civilization" and "progress" are words that mask brutal exploitation and expropriation. And just when you figure they've taken everything, they find something else they want. Even now they're sitting offshore with their military and their lawyers.

For Tony Clarke of the Action Canada Network, the age of globalization is also an age of global tyranny. "We lost the fight against the US/Canada Free Trade Agreement, but we won an understanding of the power structure that's behind these agreements." The driving forces behind NAFTA and GATT, as well as structural adjustment in both North and South, are the same driving forces behind environmental deregulation and the Contract With America—corporate rule and corporate power. What it boils down to is a fundamental conflict between corporate rights and human rights. The latter are being hijacked by the former. Are we prepared to fight for those rights?

Clark adds that there was been a major shift in the rights of government. In contradistinction to the Keynesian notion that government enters the marketplace on behalf of the common good and the common interest, we now allow the government to intervene only on behalf of the transnational corporations and profit. This must be turned around.

Clark advocates three steps for social change: (1) Target corporate rule. The business roundtable is promoting a policy agenda; (2) Resist corporate rule. Develop capacities and tools. Get a handle on the power structure that enables the corporations to drive the agenda; and (3) Dismantle corporate rule. Seize democratic control. Put together an agenda. Decentralize corporate power. Use legal channels to revoke corporate charters and recharter corporations. Overhaul the corporate welfare system. Destabilize the mechanisms of corporate power—campaign financing and political advertising. "We have been on the defensive. Now it is time to go on the offensive," Clark urges. "We've spent a lot of time talking the talk. Now it's time to start walking the walk."

References

(Except otherwise noted, quotations in this essay are taken from the Teach-in on the Social, Ecological, Cultural and Political Cost of Economic Globalization sponsored by the International Forum on Globalization, New York City, November 10-12, 1996.)

Barry, Tom (1995), *Zapata's Revenge: Free Trade and the Farm Crisis in Mexico*, Boston: South End Press.

Collier, George A. (1994), *BASTA! Land and the Zapatista Rebellion in Chiapas*, Oakland, CA: The Institute for Food and Development Policy.

Halstead, Ted. *Redefining Progress*, 1 Kearney Street, 4th floor, San Francisco, CA 94108; tel: 415-781-1191; fax: 415-781-1198; e-mail: Ted.Halstead@rprogress.org.

Howard, Philip, and Thomas Homer-Dixon (1996), *Environmental Scarcity and Violent Conflict: The Case of Chiapas, Mexico*, Toronto: University of Toronto Project on Environment, Population and Security; reprint, Washington, D.C.: American Association for the Advancement of Science.

Institute for Agriculture and Trade Policy (IATP), 2105 First Avenue South, Minneapolis, MN 55404; Tel: 612-870-3400; Fax: 612-870-4846; http://www.iatp.org/iatp.

International Forum on Globalization (IFG). For more information and a list of the names and addresses of IFG speakers and contributors to the books that grew out of the teach-ins, contact IFG at 950 Lombard Street, San Francisco, CA 94133; tel: 415-771-1102; fax: 415-771-1221; e-mail: vmenotti@igc.apc.org. For an "Economic Globalization Book Order Form," contact The Learning Alliance, 324 Lafayette Street, 7th floor, New York, NY 10012. To order by credit card, contact tel: 212-226-7171; fax: 212-274-8712; e-mail: lalliance@blythe.org.

Lapp, Frances Moore, and Joseph Collins (1979, 1982), *Food First: Beyond the Myth of Scarcity* New York: Ballantine Books.

Massey, Douglas S. (1991), "Economic Development and International Migration in Comparative Perspective," in Sergio Daz-Briquets and Sidney Weintraub, eds., *Determinants of Emigration from Mexico, Central America and the Caribbean*, Boulder/San Francisco/Oxford: Westview Press.

Massey, Douglas S. (1987), et al., *Return to Aztlan: The Social Process of International Migration from Western Mexico* Berkeley: University of California Press.

Massey, Douglas S., and Emilio Parrado (1994), "Migradollars: The Remittances and Savings of Mexican Migrants to the USA," *Population Research and Policy Review* 13: 3-30.

Myers, Norman (1995), *Environmental Exodus: An Emergent Crisis in the Global Arena*, Washington, D.C., Climate Institute.

Public Citizen's Trade Watch. To subscribe to the Public Citizen's Global Trade Watch internet subscription list, write "subscribe TW-LIST yourfirstname yourlast name" and state that you are a member of Public Citizen, e.g., "Jane Jones, Public Citizen, CA." Send this message to Listproc@essential.org.

Renner, Michael (1997), "Chiapas: An Uprising Born of Despair," in *WorldWatch* magazine, Vol. 10, No. 1, January/February.

Third World Network, 228 Macalister Road, 10400 Penang, Malaysia; tel: 04-373713/373511; fax: 04-368106; e-mail: http://www.southside.org.sg and http://www.twnside.org.sg. Third World Network publishes books by Martin Khor, Vandana Shiva and others, as well as the magazines *Third World Economics: Trends and Analysis*, US$60 (airmail), US$40 (surface); and *Third World Resurgence*, US$45 (airmail), US$30 (surface).

Werner, David (1994). "¡Viva Zapata! How the Uprising in Chiapas Revitalized the Struggle for Health in Sinaloa," in *Newsletter from the Sierra Madre*, #29, June. Subscriptions are $15/yr. for 3 issues. Order from HealthWrights, 964 Hamilton Avenue, Palo Alto, CA 94301; tel: 415-325-7500; fax: 415-325-1080; e-mail: healthrights@igc.apc.org.

Multinational Corporations and Crimes Against Humanity

*Ward Morehouse**

Corporations and Human Rights in the Changing Global Political Economy

The global political economy has changed dramatically in the last half-century. At the end of the Second World War, the international arena was dominated by a handful of nation-states in Europe and North America, particularly the United States. Vast stretches of what we have since come to call the Third World were still under colonial rule.

Today direct political colonialism hardly exists, although many analysts of international economic and political relations regard developing countries as subject to neo-colonial rule through indirect means, both political and economic.

What is perhaps more striking, especially in more recent decades, has been the emergence of giant global corporations with gross incomes

* The author is president of the Council on international and Public Affairs and co-director of the Program on Corporations, Law and Democracy. Contact address: Suite 3C, 777 United Nations Plaza, New York, NY 10017; tel: 212-972-9877; fax: 212-972-9878; e-mail: cipany@igc.apc.org. This paper was prepared for a discussion at the International Conference on TRIPS, Multilateral Agreement on Investment and Spread of Global Dominance of MNCs, Delhi, November 1-15, 1996).

49

greater than the gross domestic products of most nation-states. General Motors is bigger than Denmark. The 100 largest corporations are larger than most member states of the United Nations. (See accompanying table on Nations vs. Corporations on the following page.) Some 70 percent of world trade is controlled by the 500 largest corporations—i.e., the Global 500.

According to Frederic Clairmont in the new edition of his classic work, *The Rise and Fall of Economic Liberalism,*[1] annual revenues of the Global 500 are $10 trillion, around twice the size of the gross domestic product of the United States, the largest economy in the world. In 1994, Global 500 revenues increased by 9 percent and its profits soared by a collosal 62 percent. But notwithstanding such huge profits, the Global 500 in the same year (1994) eliminated 262,000 jobs.

These pervasive changes in the international arena have had an equally pervasive impact throughout the world on all human rights, but especially economic, social, cultural and environmental rights in developing countries. Today the dominant engine of economic development is not aid but trade and investment. The time as come to recognize that corporations, and especially the Global 500, have become too important in their impact on human rights and the quality of life all around the world to be ignored or given only peripheral attention by those struggling to build a more just and sustainable future for humanity.

The impacts of corporations on human rights, such as those set forth in the Universal Declaration of Human Rights, the two companion Covenants—on Civil and Political Rights and on Economic, Social and Cultural Rights, and the Declaration on the Right to Development, are both direct and indirect, positive and negative. Consider some of the basic rights set forth in the Universal Declaration of Human Rights, all of which have parallel and often more explicit expression in the two Covenants:

- The right to social security (Article 22);

- The right to freedom of peaceful assembly and association (Article 20);

- The right to work and free choice of employment with equal pay for equal work, just remuneration and joining trade unions (Article 23);

NATIONS vs. CORPORATIONS
December 1996

Country/CORPORATION	GDP/REVENUES FOR 1994	Country/CORPORATION	GDP/REVENUES FOR 1994
1. United States	$6,648,013	51. NIPPON TELEGR/TELEPHO.	$70,844
2. Japan	4,590,971	52. Malaysia	70,626
3. Germany	2,045,991	53. MATSUSHITA ELE. INDUST.	69,947
4. France	1,330,381	54. TOMEN	69,902
5. Italy	1,024,634	55. Singapore	68,949
6. United Kingdom	1,017,306	56. Colombia	67,266
7. Brazil	554,587	57. GENERAL ELECTRIC	64,687
8. Canada	542,954	58. DIAMLER-BENZ	64,169
9. China	522,172	59. Philippines	64,162
10. Spain	482,841	60. IBM	64,052
11. Mexico	377,115	61. Iran	63,716
12. Russia	376,555	62. MOBIL	59,621
13. South Korea	376,505	63. NISSAN MOTOR	58,732
14. Australia	331,990	64. Venezuela	58,257
15. The Netherlands	329,768	65. NICHIMEN	56,203
16. India	293,606	66. KANEMATSU	55,856
17. Argentina	281,922	67. DAI-ICHI MUTUAL LIFE INS.	54,900
18. Switzerland	260,352	68. SEARS ROEBUCK	54,825
19. Belgium	227,550	69. PHILIP MORRIS	53,776
20. Austria	196,546	70. CHRYSLER	52,224
21. Sweden	196,441	71. Ireland	52,060
22. MITSUBISHI	175,836	72. Pakistan	52,011
23. Indonesia	174,640	73. Chile	51,957
24. MITSUI	171,490	74. SIEMENS	51,055
25. ITOCHU	167,825	75. New Zealand	50,777
26. SUMITOMO	162,476	76. BRITISH PETROLEUM	50,737
27. GENERAL MOTORS	154,951	77. TOKYO ELECTRIC POWER	50,359
28. MARUBENI	150,187	78. Peru	50,077
29. Denmark	146,076	79. VOLKSWAGEN	49,350
30. Thailand	143,209	80. SUMITOMO LIFE INSURANCE	49,063
31. Hong Kong	131,881	81. TOSHIBA	48,228
32. Turkey	131,014	82. UNILEVER	45,451
33. FORD MOTOR	128,439	83. Egypt	42,923
34. South Africa	121,888	84. Algeria	41,941
35. Saudi Arabia	117,236	85. NESTLE	41,626
36. Norway	109,568	86. Hungary	41,374
37. EXXON	101,459	87. DEUTSCHE TELEKOM	41,071
38. NISSHO IWAI	100,876	88. FIAT	40,851
39. Finland	97,961	89. ALLIANZ HOLDING	40,415
40. ROYAL DUTCH/SHELL GRP.	94,881	90. SONY	40,101
41. Poland	92,580	91. VEBA GROUP	40,072
42. Ukraine	91,307	92. HONDA MOTOR	39,927
43. TOYOTA MOTOR	88,159	93. ELF AQUITAINE	39,459
44. Portugal	87,257	94. STATE FARM GROUP	38,850
45. WAL-MART STORES	83,412	95. NEC	37,946
46. Israel	77,777	96. PRUDENTIAL INSURANCE CO.	36,946
47. Greece	77,721	97. OESTERREICHISCHE	36,766
48. HITACHI	76,431	98. MEIJI MUTUAL LIFE INS.	36,344
49. NIPPON LIFE INSURANCE	70,840	99. Czech Republic	36,024
50. AT&T	75,094	100. DAEWOO	35,707

SOURCE: Corporation data, "Fortune's Global 500: The World's Largest Corporations," *Fortune* magazine, August 7, 1995; Country information, "*The World Development Report*," The World Bank, 1996. (Figures in $US.)

- The right to a standard of living adequate for the health and well-being of everyone and his or her family, i.e., including food, clothing, housing and medical care and necessary social services (Article 25);

- The right to education (Article 26);

- Entitlement to a social and international order in which the rights and freedoms set forth in the Universal Declaration can be realized (Article 28);

- Freedom from discrimination (various Articles especially Article 7);

- And, of course, the right to life, liberty and security of person (Article 3).

These rights are further strengthened in a number of international human rights instruments that have emerged since the Universal Declaration of Human Rights was adopted by the UN General Assembly almost 50 years ago. A good example is the Declaration on the Right to Development, which was adopted by the General Assembly in December 1986. In its very first Article, the Declaration proclaims that "the right to development is an inalienable human right" and that "all peoples are entitled to participate in, contribute to, and enjoy economic, social, cultural and political development."

The fundamentally changed global political economy noted above stands in contrast to much of the rest of the Declaration on the Right to Development. That declaration gives primary responsibility for the realization of this right to nation-states, the capacity of which to deliver development is being diminished as their sovereignty is eroded and more and more political and economic power flows into the hands of major corporations. On the other hand, the final Article (number 10) in the Declaration asserts that "steps should be taken to ensure the full exercise and progressive enhancement of the right to development . . . at the national and international levels," and since this article is not limited to states, it could presumably be interpreted as encompassing non-state actors, such as corporations as well as other social, economic and political institutions.

The Human Rights Impacts of Corporations

Corporations, large and small, national and multinational, all impact human rights in varying degrees and in different ways. But because the largest corporations in the world today have become so large that they overshadow many nation-states, their impacts are likely to be much greater.

These corporations impact human rights in all countries, but especially developing countries, through their own actions as dominant players in the economies of countries and through subsidiaries, joint ventures, strategic alliances and supplier/customer relationships with domestic firms in those economies. They also make their influence felt through international associations of corporations such as the International Chamber of Commerce and through international institutions such as the newly created World Trade Organization in which they play decisive roles.

These changing roles for corporations, both multinational and national, are accompanied by a market-driven ideology through which critical economic and social choices are left to the marketplace. While proponents of this ideology argue that only through rapid economic growth, made possible by removing government restrictions on economic activity, will the fundamental economic and social rights of all persons be met, opponents insist that without the protection of these rights by the state, vulnerable segments of society will experience increasing material deprivation as productive resources on which they have relied in the past are appropriated by corporations and these segments of society are displaced through direct action by corporations or other agents or through environmental degradation.

Large corporations and their advocates will argue that corporations as institutions for the conduct of economic activity create jobs, improve livelihoods, help to strengthen economic and social structure, including education and health care facilities, produce useful products, and in general promote the common welfare.

Critics of corporations assert that whatever may be the positive contributions of corporations to the fulfillment of internationally recognized human rights, their negative impacts are much greater. These impacts are both direct and indirect and include repression of workers, adverse impact on smaller competitors, lack of transparency and anti-democratic decision-making, capital intensive modes of production that displace labor, environmental degradation and increasing polarization of income. When a major corporation establishes itself as a significant presence in the economy of a developing country, it often preempts large amounts of productive agricultural land, water and other natural resources, in the process denying the right to livelihood for thousands, or even millions, of persons who in the past have depended upon these resources for their very survival.

Corporations, their critics also argue, embrace an economic paradigm of growth through consumption which is inherently unsustainable in terms of its impact on the environment and, ultimately therefore, on human livelihoods. Furthermore, consumption-driven economic growth not linked to more equitable distribution is inherently injurious to poverty alleviation and therefore antithetical to fundamental human rights values.

Taken cumulatively, these human rights violations by the Global 500, because of their severity, their systemic character and the vast scale in which they are occurring, constitute in my view crimes against humanity, a point on which I shall elaborate further below.

According to many of these same critics, the threat to such human rights noted above is rapidly increasing in the "post-Uruguay Round" world in which laws and regulations that inhibit trade but protect worker and environmental rights are being dismantled, all too often in violation of the international treaty obligations of countries that have ratified these human rights instruments or reaffirmed their commitment and support at major international conferences. Indeed, the governments of the world in a succession of recent UN World Conferences at Vienna, Cairo, Copenhagen, Beijing and Istanbul have by consensus and with unanimity repeatedly affirmed that the right to development is a universal and inalienable right and an integral part of fundamental human rights, and have gone on record as advocating "full exercise and progressive enhancement" of the right to development.[2]

Reliance on corporations as the principal engines of economic and social change, and therefore the principal means by which basic economic and social rights will be achieved, is perhaps nowhere revealed more sharply than in the Declaration and Program of Action which emerged from the World Summit for Social Development, which was held in Copenhagen in March 1995. The stated purpose of this international conference was to alleviate poverty and social discrimination while enhancing productive employment. Notable among the instrumentalities for achieving these lofty goals is "promoting enterprise, productive investment and expanded access to open and dynamic markets" and more specifically, "implementing fully and as scheduled the Final Act of the Uruguay Round of multilateral trade negotiations."[3]

Notwithstanding the extent to which reliance on markets, the principal agents of which are corporations, has come to dominate discourse on international development and the inevitable and pervasive consequences this state of affairs has for human rights in all societies, the role of corporations has been almost universally ignored in human rights discourse and in human rights circles.

Human Rights Standards Especially Relevant to the Activities of Corporations

There are three principal sources of human rights standards especially relevant to the activities of corporations. The first of these is the International Covenant on Economic, Social and Cultural Rights which begins with two key rights that are both civil and political and economic, social and cultural—self-determination (for nations and peoples) and non-discrimination.

Within this broad frame work, the Covenant sets forth three broad economic rights clearly relevant to the activities of corporations—the right to work, the right to protection from economic insecurity and the right to an adequate standard of living. This last-named has three critical components—right to health (Article 12), right to food (Article 11) and right to education (Article 13). Also relevant is Article 10 of the Covenant which asserts that "the widest possible protection and assistance should be accorded to the family, which is the natural and fundamental group unit of society." Less immediately apparent but of fundamental importance is Article 15 which recognizes the right of everyone to "take part in cultural life" and demands respect for the "freedom indispensable for scientific research and creative activity." Today's giant corporations, especially those that market consumer products globally, are exercising a profound influence on cultural values, institutions and standards of societies throughout the world.

The second significant source of human rights standards potentially relevant to corporations is the Declaration on the Right to Development adopted by the United Nations General Assembly in December 1986.

Such a right was surely implicit in the Universal Declaration of Human Rights, as well as in the International Covenant on Eco-

nomic, Social and Cultural Rights. After reaffirming the existence
of the right to development, the General Assembly went further
and elaborated the content of that right.[4]

The right to development has been reiterated and further elaborated
at several recent UN conferences, such as human rights (Vienna, 1993),
population (Cairo, 1994), social development (Copenhagen, 1995) and
women (Beijing, 1995). It is worth noting that while the 1986 UN General Assembly decision was not obtained by consensus (the U.S. was
conspicuous as the sole dissenter apart from a few abstentions), at each
of these UN conferences the right to development was *unanimously*
reaffirmed as a "universal and inalienable right and an integral part of
fundamental human rights." Analysts of international human rights law
argue as a consequence that the right to development is not merely an
ideological slogan but a human right protected by international law.[5]

Development is defined as "a comprehensive economic, social, and
cultural and political process, which aims at the constant improvement
of the well-being of the entire population and of all individuals" and "in
which all human rights and fundamental freedoms can be fully realized." Its main component rights are the right of participation (Article
2), the right of persons to be "the central *subject* of development" (Article 20) and the right to "fair distribution" of the benefits of development (Preamble). Other component rights of the right to development
include the rights to non-discrimination, self-determination, "free and
complete fulfillment of the human being" and against trade-off (the
promotion of certain human rights cannot justify the denial of other
human rights).

The third major source of human rights standards relevant to corporations is the new "global consensus on development" which has
emerged from the UN World Conference continuum that began with the
environment in Rio in 1992 and continued through the Habitat Conference in 1996. During this time period no fewer than six UN World
Conferences or Summits have been convened, an unprecedented level
of effort in the history of the United Nations. Among the major features
of this new global consensus—drawn from the declarations and programs of action at these six World Conferences—are sustainability and
"people-centeredness." This in turn has geared fulfillment of the right
to development toward the objectives of poverty-alleviation, human
resource capacity-building, empowerment and betterment of human well-being. The Vienna Human Rights Conference also emphasized the development process must be accountable to standards of good gover-

nance. Vienna also reaffirmed that development is an inalienable human right.[6]

Critical to the task of applying human rights standards to the activities of corporations is the status in international law of these various instruments, processes and events. There exists today a body of *international law on development*, which includes the UN Charter; the Universal Declaration of Human Rights; the 1986 General Assembly Declaration on the Right to Development; the Covenants on Economic, Social and Cultural Rights and Civil and Political Rights; a variety of international human rights and environmental treaties; and the declaration and programs of action from the round of UN World Conferences from Rio to Istanbul previously mentioned.[7] The central challenge, especially when considering the impact of major global corporations on human rights, is to develop effective means of enforcement. (This body of international law has been subject to meticulous elaboration and scholarly analysis by James C. N. Paul—citing some 150 conventions and agreements.[8]

No less a figure than the current Secretary General of the United Nations has argued similarly that the major world conferences convened by the United Nations since 1992 "represent something new and different. They are linked. They are cumulative. They foster global consensus on interlocking global issues."[9] They thus articulate a present-day global consensus of development and help to define in international law a wide range of human rights, not only economic, social and environmental but also civil and political.

As corporations have come to be asserted as the principal vehicles of development (for example, at the World Summit for Social Development), their actions increasingly fall within the scope of this body of international law on development and are—or at least should be—subject to its standards and sanctions.

A central issue which needs to be addressed is whether or not corporations should be held liable for violations of human rights recognized in international law. On the one hand, corporations have submitted themselves to international scrutiny for several decades through the International Labour Office by participating in drafting various ILO Conventions applicable to the actions or non-actions of corporations. On the other hand, it is argued in some circles that more recent international human rights law does not apply to corporations, at least directly.

In this view, the responsibility for upholding international human rights standards is primarily, if not solely, the responsibility of nation-states and traditionally applies in the first instance to their own actions as states. An extension of this view argues that states are also obliged to see that these standards are not violated by entities operating within their political boundaries.

While clearly nation-states have a major obligation to observe international human rights standards, the harsh late 20th-century reality is that giant global corporations are now so large that they are beyond control by nation-states in many critical aspects of their activities. The treatment of Union Carbide Corporation, the perpetrator of the world's worst industrial disaster in Bhopal, India, is a good illustration of the inability of national governments to hold large corporations liable for their violations of internationally recognized human rights.[10]

The Ultimate Human Rights Standard: Crimes Against Humanity

The growing dominance of the global political economy by the 500 largest corporations has been accompanied by increasing inequality and rampant poverty. The human community is now confronted with a crisis of epic porportions which demands a corresponding response. Even the World Bank, one of the principal agents of corporate domination of the globe, acknowledges "that around 800 million people go hungry daily and their number is expected to soar." If current trends presist, 1.3 billion people are expected to survive on less than a dollar a day by the year 2000, 200 million more than in 1990.[11] Thus hundreds of millions of persons are being denied not only their human rights but indeed that most essential of all rights, the "right to be human."[12]

The time has come when we must devise strategies of resistance commensurate with the crisis confronting us. Denial of the "right to be human" on such a vast scale is surely a "crime against humanity," certainly as it is defined in Canadian law C-71 (An Act to Amend the Criminal Code, the Immigration Act, 1976 and the Citizenship Act) which was passed by the Canadian Parliament on August 28, 1987.

This act defines a "crime against humanity" as meaning:

> . . . murder, extermination, enslavement, deportation, persecution
> or *any other inhumane act or ommission* that is committed against
> any civilian population or any identifiable persons, whether or not
> it constitutes a contravention of the law enforced at the time and in

the place of its commission, and that, at the time and in that place, constitutes a contravention of customary international law or conventional international law or is criminal according to the general principals of law recognized by the Community of Nations (emphasis added).[13]

I have chosen Canadian Law C-71 to apply to the Global 500 because Canada is a member of the Group of Seven—i.e., the major industrialized countries. Most of the 500 largest corporations in the world are headquartered in the G-7 countries, and the G-7 governments have an obligation to protect internationally recognized human rights, certainly when they involve violations as serious as crimes against humanity. But it should be understood that the doctrine of crimes against humanity is solidly embedded in international law. The definition quoted above is drawn from the Charter of the International Military Tribunal at Nuremberg, as subsequently reaffirmed and extended to acts committed at any time (not just wartime) by the United Nations General Assembly.[14]

The International Law Commission, furthermore, has been engaged in its recent sessions in elaborating on the definition given above, making it even more applicable to the actions of giant global corporations. It makes explicit what is implicit in the Nuremberg Charter—namely, that inhumane acts become crimes against humanity when they are "committed in a systematic way or on a large scale and instigated or directed by a Government or by any organization or group." The reference to "any organization or group" clearly includes non-state actors such as global corporations bigger than most nation-states.[15]

It is clear that under the Canadian definition, the Nuremberg Charter (as reaffirmed by the UN General Assembly) and the work of the International Law Commission that the Global 500 corporations are susceptible to indictment for crimes against humanity.

However, to make this charge credible we need a deliberative process guided by basic principals of due process in gathering evidence and presenting it to appropriate judicial bodies. The first step will be the systematic collection of evidence of human rights violations by the Global 500 through citizen-created and -led "Truth Commissions" and other appropriate means. The Permanent Peoples Tribunal on Corporations and Human Rights, now being planned for the autumn of 1998, would provide a forum for framing an indictment of the Global 500, based on evidence accumulated through the preparatory process leading up to the Tribunal.

What then should follow is the trial of each of the Global 500 in appropriate forums around the world, whether they be established courts of law or people's tribunals. The results of these trials should then be aggregated into one comprehensive verdict on the Global 500. The target date might be the year 2000—the end of one century and millennium and the beginning of another.

The next task will be to devise a sentence appropriate to the severity of the crimes committed by these giant corporations. Under the Canadian Law cited above, the principal sanction applied against those indicted for "crimes against humanity" is expulsion. Dismantling the Global 500 would be an appropriate analogous penalty.

As we approach a new millennium, let us make history by agreeing that this is our goal and establishing a framework to carry forward the process to its proper conclusion.

Notes

1. Frederic Clairmont, *The Rise and Fall of Economic Liberalism: The Making of the Economic Gulag,* Penang: Southbound and Third World Network, 1996.

2. Clarence J. Dias, "The Right to Development: The Right Way to Development," unpublished paper, 1996.

3. United Nations: World Summit for Social Development: *The Copenhagen Declaration and Program of Action,* March 6-12, 1995, New York: United Nations, 1995, p. 44. For a vigorous critique of the Social Summit and its impact on human rights, see Upendra Baxi, "'Summit of Hope' in the Depths of Despair?: Social Development as Realization of Human Rights," New York: People's Decade for Human Rights Education, n.d. (?1994).

4. Clarence J. Dias, Background Paper on Human Rights for UN Conference on Habitat II, January 1966, p. 4.

5. *Ibid.,* p. 5.

6. See Ayesha K. Dias, "Corporations, Communities and Sustainable Development—Moving Ahead; From Development Agency

Prospectives," unpublished paper, June 1996.

7. Dias, Habitat II paper, *op. cit.,* pp. 1-2.

8. James C. N. Paul, "The United Nations and the Creation of an International Law on Development," *Harvard International Law Journal,* Spring 1995, pp. 307-28.

9. Boutros Boutros Ghali, *Foreign Affairs,* March/April 1996, p. 88.

10. See Ward Morehouse, "Unfinished Business: Bhopal Ten Years After," *The Ecologist,* October 1994.

11. *World Bank, Strategy for Reducing Poverty and Hunger* (Washington, 1995) and *World Development Report: Workers in an Integrating World* (Washington, 1995) as cited in Frederic Clairmont, *The Rise and Fall of Economic Liberalism: The Making of the Economic Gulag,* Penang: Southbound and Third World Network, 1996, p. 339.

12. The phrase is that of Upendra Baxi. See his essay, "From Human Rights to the Right to Be Human: Some Heresies," in Smitu Kothari and Harsh Sethi, *Rethinking Human Rights: Challenges for Theory and Action,* New York and Delhi: New Horizons Press and Lokayan, 1989.

13. Government of Canada, Parliament, "An Act to Amend the Criminal Code, the Immigration Act, 1976, and the Citizenship Act, C-71," August 28, 1987.

14. Charter of the Nuremberg Tribunal, as given in Leon Friedman, ed., *The Law of War: A Documentary History,* Vol. II, New York: Random House, 1972. Crimes against humanity as defined in the Nuremberg Charter were reaffirmed by the UN General Assembly in Resolutions 3(I) of 13 February 1946 and 95 (I) of 11 December 1946. It should be noted that crimes against humanity are crimes even if such acts do not constitute a violation of the domestic law of the country in which they were committed.

15. United Nations, International Law Commission, *Report of the 48th Session,* May 6-26, 1996, pp. 93ff.

Part Two

What Is Real Wealth?

Chapter 2: What Is Real Wealth?

Economic modernity, as well as modernizing economic development today, begins when wealth creation is idealized as a spontaneous self-organizing market process for the growth of a national economy. Concerns within traditional society for the preservation of the commons for the benefit of communities and regions are viewed as transcended in the increased "Wealth of Nations," or what today is metaphorically called " increasing the size of the pie." But this goal of wealth creation fails to acknowledge any conflict between the limits of the planet's ecology and modern societies' accumulation, or any related tendency toward self-destructive social inequality. Only Karl Marx continues the promethean project of wealth creation as fundamental to the perfection of the human species while simultaneously raising critical issues of justice. But Marx's concept of the dialectic between the "humanization of nature" and the unjust "naturalization of mankind" remains centered upon the extensions of the production process as the material preconditions for justice. Hence, both capitalism and Marxist socialism legitimates the endless pressing forward of "progress" as the material precondition for the liberation of humanity from natural "necessity"; they are different versions of the same modern project of wealth creation.

Consequently, many recent critiques have emerged that no longer center on the primacy of greater wealth creation, but concentrate on the gap between wealth creation and the greater risks, distribution of insecurity and direct human and ecological violence. The constant search for opportunities for greater techno-economic progress no longer exclusively structures everyday life in a "globalizing" economy, instead the problems of the hazards and insecurities created by this power increasingly focuses individual and organizational attention. In this way, Ulrich Beck argues that a new global social order is emerging amid the neo-liberal, wealth-creating order. A "risk society" begins new trends where the risks and hazards no longer follow class divisions and become accumulative and "equalitarian," in the ironic sense that there are no exclusions to suffering their consequences.[1] In the emerging social order, reassessments of "wealth" and human prosperity are reflexively created by the movements resisting the current neo-liberal economic integrations. Most perplexing for hyper-modernizers of right and left are culturally based rebellions and collective actions that advocate a "sufficiency limits" ethic of real wealth. These communities and individuals are deeply opposed to the economic globalization mentality that submits abstractions of economic value as the only standard of wealth. They are innovating new ways of evaluating "real wealth."

For example, a "commons" arrangement within communities or muncipalities promotes a sufficiency limit to "development" that is essentially an agreement providing self-restraining limits ("enoughness") for those who share the use of an "indigenous resource" essential for life, such as water use, forests, biodiversity, mineral or wildlife access, use of open or city spaces,indigenous seeds, etc.[2] Explicating the logic of the commons agreements , Vadana Shiva has shown how the imposition of the logic of economic value maximizes the single goal of profit realization which actually disvalues the multiple uses of the forest that are more central to the real wealth, or sustainability, for forest communities.[3] Ever changing in response to new circumstances, commons agreements are the means by which many people, especially those labeled "poor," respond to commodifications of resources and the formal legal enclosures that accompany state or market formations.

Advocating this view of real substantive wealth, Gusteva Esteva, a widely respected Mexican theorist, argues that "disvalue is the secret of economic value and it cannot be created except with violence and in the face of continuous resistance"; to enforce economic value as the only standard of wealth is to destroy and discredit real wealth:

> Establishing economic value requires the disvaluing of all other forms of social existence. Disvalue transmogrifies skills into lacks, commons into resources, men and women into commodified labor, tradition into burden, wisdom into ignorance, autonomy into dependency.[4]

This is a radically substantive viewpoint on human prosperity that defines local knowledge for self-reliance and socio-cultural institutions that provide self-restaint and shared practices of "enoughness" as the real wisdom and wealth of human existence. This is not a backward-looking defense of traditional worlds, but an affirmation of common sense wherever the violent abstractions of progress have become intolerable.

Working Alternatives to Neo-Liberal Economic Integration

Luis Lopezllera Mendez describes in his essay, "The Indigenous Rebellion in Chiapas," the assertion of the commons' interest in protecting the lands and communities of Chiapas when the North American Free Trade Agreement came into existence in Mexico. Beginning with the Indigenous Congress of Chiapas (circa 1974), this action was a final outcome of the first truly autonomous and authentic expression of regional indigenous organizations in Mexico from a base of more than 2,000 communities and four principal ethnic groups. Whereas other groups and perspectives became involved as the complex events unfolded, the rebellion remained focused on the transformation of power and institutions to enable local autonomy and democracy. These events have not come to a final outcome, but have brought attention to the depth of the impetus to restore the real wealth of rural communities, rather than have them absorbed into national and international integrations. At the same time, it has brought our attention to the reality that national economic integrations have to be reconciled with the sustainability of regional integrations.

Emerging as a theoretical reflection on these Mexican realities, David Barkin's essay on "Local Autonomy, National Development and International Integration" defends the need for local self-sufficiency, which has always made rual communities sustainable and the stewards of their places. The imperatives of food security and the local production of a diversity of essential goods and services characterize the uniqueness of the real wealth of rural communities that would otherwise be disvalued in forced economic integrations into national and international economies. In this perspective, sustaining the autonomy of rural communities is essential for regional autonomy and for a national strategy that is both ecologically and democratically sustainable. Barkin theorizes that securing the domestic and internal economy from the disvaluing distortions of a free-trade driven internationalism is essential for national and local autonomy as well as the viabililty of ecosystems.

Models of "Enoughness" as Working Alternatives

Social limits, or "enoughness," emerge from interactive practices in which internal logic cannot be formalized, only practiced and renewed in new situations. Capability to establish "enoughness" requires an intactness of socio-cultural institutions within communities and municipalities that can yield consensus about socially valid limits. If communities, municipalities and regions are misguided into facilitating growth, while their internal mechanisms for establishing consensus on limits atrophies, they have been co-opted for colonizing development. Models for the regeneration of this internal wholeness—or as Romesh Diwan reminds us, a "fullness"—are embedded in the stories from India that seem at first to be the epitomy of scarcity but in actuality are its opposite. These stories are used to introduce the ongoing project of a Gandhian economics that takes a radically different approach to real wealth.

Likewise the approaches taken to balancing needs with capacity in Africa, described by Winifred Armstrong, provide additional models of how culturally and/or community-based practices are the models that provide viable concepts for real wealth rather than the top-down imposed economic abstractions. In a provocative way, the final essay in this chapter reveals that the human encriptions on the Tuscan landscape mirror back to the community the attitudes with which they husband it. As a model of enoughness it reminds us that the expectations for more and more that accompany the modernizing wealth-creation process mirror back to us the unfulfilled unhappiness of boundless greed.

Notes

1. Ulrich Beck, *Risk Society: Toward a New Modernity,* Newbury Park, CA: Sage Publications, 1992.

2. The Ecologist, *Whose Common Future: Reclaiming the Commons,* Philadelphia: New Society Publishers, 1993, pp. 8ff.

3. Vandana Shiva, *Monocultures of the Mind,* Penang, Malaysia: Third World Network, 1993, ch. 1.

4. Gusteva Esteva in Wolfgang Sachs, ed., *The Development Dictionary,* London: Zed Books, 1992, p. 18.

The Indigenous Rebellion in Chiapas*

Luis Lopezllera Mendez

At dawn on January 1, 1994, a thousand Indians of the until then unknown Zapatista Army of National Liberation, the EZLN—men and women, well-disciplined, masked, uniformed and fairly well-armed, came out of the jungle and took over the city of San Cristobal de las Casas, a major commercial, tourist and religious center in the highlands of the state of Chiapas, Mexico. At the same time, they took Ocosingo and other small surrounding cities and attacked a well-known military base. Their military leader, Subcommandante "Marcos" (not an Indian) was their primary spokesperson and the focus of media attention.

The indigenous rebellion in Chiapas coincided with the implementation of the North America Free Trade Agreement (NAFTA), signed by the democratically elected governments of Mexico, Canada and the U.S, but supported more by corporate interests than by any real national consensus.

The EZLN published its "Lacandonian Jungle Declaration," protesting centuries of humiliation and exploitation of the Indians, and demanded authentic development for the region. The Declaration discussed issues of democracy in Mexico, the influence of foreign invest-

---

* This article originally appeared in "Popocatepetl," No. 14, as an enclosure in *La Otra Bolsa de Valores,* No. 34, Tlaloc 40-3, Col. Tlaxpana, CP 11370, Mexico, D.F., Mexico, tel: 566-4265/535-0325; fax: 592-1989; e-mail: espacios@laneta.apc.org *or* pdp-cres@geo2.poptel.org.uk. The author is director of Promoción del Dessarrolo Popular in Mexico City.

ment on the Mexican economy and the violation of human rights. Although the EZLN called for drastic solutions, they struck a chord, receiving sympathy beyond belief from a wide spectrum of Mexican society.

The government's reaction was immediate. Federal troops, well-armed and supported from the air, counterattacked. A week of armed conflict, searches and sieges followed, ending with the retreat of the rebels into the jungle. Between 200 and 500 civilian and military personnel had been killed. The government declared a unilateral cease-fire and offered amnesty and dialogue to the rebels, largely as a result of pressure from Mexican civil society. Ordinary citizens had taken to the streets of Mexico City to demand peace and justice for the Indians. About 500 journalists arrived in Chiapas, which has remained in the world news ever since. An important politician, Manuel Camacho Sols, acted ably as the government's spokesman.

The State of Chiapas is in the southeast of Mexico bordering Guatemala. It is very rich with petroleum and hydroelectric dams that produce electricity for export to the center of the country. Although cattle ranchers have destroyed a large part of the jungle, it is still abundant in fine hardwoods, medicinal plants and wildlife. Coffee, cocoa and gum are the region's typical agricultural products.

Chiapas is home to a variety of ethnic groups: the Tzeltales, Tzotziles, Choles, Tojolabales, Lacandones, Mames and Zoques. These colorful peoples and their handicrafts contribute to a thriving tourist industry, which also benefits from the region's beautiful landscapes and Mayan archeological sites. But, for the most part, the modern economy has favored only a minority of businessmen and traders with ties to the government, *caciques* (men with land and power) and the military. This minority exploits the large Indian population, which lives in extreme poverty and barely survives.

For decades, the Church, led by Bishop Samuel Ruiz, has served as an advocate for the Indians. In a way, Bishop Ruiz continues the work of Fray Bartolome de las Casas. In the 16th century, the latter denounced the atrocities the Spanish committed during the Conquest, and defended the Indians against the economic interests of the time by successfully arguing that Indians have souls and therefore cannot be enslaved. The Spanish repaid his defense of the Indians with threats and slander. The same thing is happening today to *Tatic* Bishop, as the Indians call him.

The Indigenous Congress of Chiapas was established with broad-based support in 1974. It was the first truly autonomous and authentic expression of regional indigenous organizations in Mexico—not "indigenists" manipulated by public officials—with a base of more than 2,000 communities and four principal ethnic groups. The government later tried to co-opt the idea for such a congress in other ethnic regions of Mexico, but in a weakened version that could be controlled from outside.

The Indigenous Congress of Chiapas made several proposals for dealing with major problems—land, health, education, production and commerce, and human rights. Since then, a large number of experiments in local improvement were begun, but these were greeted with repression.

The proximity to Guatemala implied large flows of refugees, mostly indigenous, escaping the army. From the 1950s onward, Guatemalan government forces waged a counter-insurgency campaign against guerrillas, employing military techniques that ranged from relocating communities to massacres. The war intensified after the Sandinista victory in Nicaragua raised the possibility that such events could take place in El Salvador and other places. During the 1980s, approximately 100,000 refugees settled in various camps along the Chiapas border with Guatemala. The diocese of San Cristobal de las Casas gave them aid.

From the beginning, the presence of Guatemalan refugees hiding in the jungle gave the organization of the indigenous communities in Chiapas a strong symbolic charge. In effect, government land was being colonized by a generation of young people migrating from the overcrowded mountains where the overexploited land held no future. Early on, attracted by this phenomenon, people from other parts of Mexico with other political orientations, particularly Maoist, began to arrive. Grassroots organizations with an interest in economics and politics emerged in the 1970s and 1980s. At the beginning of the 1980s, a military influence arrived and began to work behind the scenes with the Indians. The uprising on January 1, 1994 is the outcome.

The next 20 years saw the spread of many civil and social organizations dedicated to the economic advancement and organization of the region. Some international agencies gave priority to Chiapas when they agreed on support. President Carlos Salinas' National Solidarity Program (PRONASOL) distributed large sums of money through a corrupt system of favored *caciques* and dubious small or large businesses. The Catholic and Protestant churches as well as the government's National Indigenist Institute also played a role in Chiapas. Ecologists, anthropologists and paramedics arrived and discovered a region full of contrasts between the wealth of a few and poverty and misery of the many.

Despite local, communal, cooperative and *ejidal* efforts to overcome the almost subhuman conditions, the authorities refused to respond. *Xi 'Nich*, a protest march of a thousand indigenous people, mainly Choles, for 1,000 kilometers from Chiapas to the capital in Mexico City, was without real results. Instead, the authorities increased their control and intensified their repression. As a result of the large number of deaths they have caused, the army in Mexico has an extremely poor image. The commemoration in 1992 of the 500-year anniversary of the arrival of the Spaniards in America provided the occasion in Chiapas for multitudinous marches, in which the Indians continued to show their rage for not receiving a substantive response from the government to their misery.

But differences between the indigenous groups themselves also grew. Some were in favor of patient, progressive negotiations with the government while waiting for the government to initiate aid programs; others wanted to take a harder line. In one place, Chamula—a traditional nucleus of ethnic power—alleged 25-year-old religious differences between Catholics and Protestants came to a head, ending with the exile of 20,000 Indians.

Although the Chiapas rebellion was greeted with public approval nationwide, these differences did not go away. Even though the population of Chiapas is polarized, with Indians on the one hand and a system of landlords, cattle dealers, *caciques* and the army on the other, there are still thousands of peasant families who did not take part in the rebellion. They did not even take sides. Even so, they have become refugees and are now forced to live in camps administered by the government and the Red Cross. Not all those who sympathize with the goals of the rebellion agree that the insurgents should have taken up arms or worked underground. And they fear that violence could become more widespread if the armies of the landlords become involved. People feel insecure not only because of warring political factions, but also because they fear bandits.

The mass media at both the national and international levels has become a major protagonist in this conflict. Alongside the military conflict, there has been a war of words, images, symbols, declarations and even poems. The government may hold a better position in terms of conventional political and military power, but the capability of the EZLN is vastly superior in terms of creativity and its ability to generate widespread sympathy across a broad range of social sectors. The EZLN's ability to muster public sympathy takes the Chiapas conflict beyond the conventional Central American guerrilla warfare typical of this half-century. What we are witnessing is a new way of doing politics which originates at the local level, but is debated in the international arena. For this reason, some commentators have called the Chiapas rebellion a "post modern" conflict. The rebels themselves say that they are not trying to get into power, but instead are struggling to change the power structures and institutions of society. Their successful efforts to elicit widespread sympathy for their cause and their program for change have galvanized civil society and generated a non-belligerent army of witnesses.

In August of 1994, the EZLN convoked a Civil Society Convention. It was held in a place in the jungle named "Aguascalientes," which evoked another meeting held in a place with the same name in 1914 during the Mexican Revolution. Six thousand delegates came from every part of Mexico with their own "army" of journalists. The outcome was the National Democratic Convention, or CND, which was supposed to become a force for change in the direction of democracy and justice that goes beyond opposition political parties.

Meanwhile, one disturbing event followed another at the national level. Presidential candidate Luis Donaldo Colosio, who seemingly leaned toward real change, was murdered. The power of the drug cartels appeared to have permeated every level of government to the point where a Roman Catholic Cardinal could be murdered with impunity. Evidence of financial corruption was everywhere, including favoritism toward privileged groups at the national and international level from the presidency on down. As always, in such situations, there were rumors of CIA intervention.

Nevertheless, the PRI candidate again won the presidential election, signifying that society does not like the idea of civil unrest in the midst of economic turmoil for which no one has offered a convincing solution. At the national level, the inertia behind the words becomes more evident with each passing day.

In Chiapas and throughout Mexico, the NGOs have been working for peace. The Espacios por la Paz, or ESPAZ (Room for Peace), and CONPAZ groups emerged to find a way to prevent the army from resuming its armed persecution, and also to generate solidarity with the poorest segments of the population. Despite their efforts, in February of 1995 President Ernesto Zedillo revealed the identity of

Subcommandante Marcos and ordered the detention of several people he accused of terrorism. The army penetrated farther into the jungle and took control of a larger area. People who supported the EZLN left their communities and escaped to the mountains, but hunger, thirst and lack of shelter soon persuaded them to return. The government then resumed negotiations, which continue slowly and intermittently. In these negotiations, the role of Bishop Samuel Ruiz as middleman has been fundamental. He knows the region, he has respect for the Indians and has a markedly independent personality. His work earned him a nomination for the Nobel Peace Prize.

Chiapas has been on the minds of all Mexicans during the past 26 months. It has branded the public consciousness with the question of indigenous groups, who have been systematically mistreated despite any rhetoric to the contrary or their favorable image in museums. Because of the EZLN, Mexico is now made aware of the problems of 55 ethnic groups with a population of over 10 million in various ways, most of them non-violent. Government attempts to control the situation mainly take the form of economic support programs and propaganda. But today one hears calls even for territorial autonomy.

National and international development agencies, both private- and government-sponsored, arrived in Chiapas to offer financial support to local development projects. Their intentions were not purely philanthropic; they were also trying to dismantle the rebellion ideologically and to reduce the number of its adherents. Local reactions to their efforts were various, and ran the whole gamut from a total lack of trust to mutual taking of advantage.

The EZLN asked for a national survey regarding its future. Alianza Civica, a network of hundreds of NGOs, agreed to organize the survey and had the results ready at the end of August 1995. Now they are organizing a referendum on economic issues. Students and others aware of the misery of the Indians and desiring to activate structural changes organized caravans to deliver tons of material aid to the indigenous regions in different parts of the country.

At the end of 1995, Mexicans were suffering the worst economic depression in their country's history. It is now obvious that the Mexican economy depends largely on foreign financial capital interested not in true development but in speculation. The governing elite have lost all credibility, and even if they could manage to come up with an endogenous solution to Mexico's economic problems, they lack the autonomy to govern. Because anything that happens in Mexico is thought by the

U.S. to impact American security, the U.S. intervenes constantly, although not always overtly, in Mexico.

Some Questions without Any Order

In this context, what strategy can local groups, peasants, Indians and urban people, harassed by hunger and unemployment, propose to wider audiences? Civil society,expressed in an increasing number of NGOs, claims to have solutions but has not overcome the "protest syndrome" or "democratic representation." With each new crisis comes an increasing awareness that "the local" has become more subdued by international forces outside the sovereignty of the supposedly disappearing nation-state. Is it still possible to think in terms of "outside aid" when it is manipulated—either blatantly or with some sophistication—from centers of power, and when there is no evidence of the capacity to generate real economic autonomy at a human level? What kind of a local/global strategy has to be found to overcome our not always obvious subjugation to the transnational firms? In extreme situations, is violence acceptable and, in light of the results, are the costs admitted or not? Is the territorial autonomy demanded by ethnic groups possible when there is so much dependency on the outside and when groups of people tend to divide and subdivide themselves according to values and habits? Are the efforts to make civil society visible in politics not overlooking the economic dimension? Should the NGOs and cooperative agencies test new kinds of relationships among themselves, with other organizations, with the government or with business people toward a real "social market"? What can be the role of an effective solidarity of the people at a global level?

Local Autonomy, National Development and International Integration: Challenges for Today, Models for Tomorrow

David Barkin*

An alternative is needed to the global pressures for regional economic integration, unbridled capital flows and free trade. New models are required to defend local economies and promote development in the face of economic policies that are destroying the societies on which people depend for their existence and well-being. Such policies are being proposed throughout the Third World, and here in Mexico they are at the very top of the agenda for debate and social struggle.

In 1995, a national coalition of NGOs, spearheaded by the Civic Alliance, sparked this effort by an imaginative call for a "Freedom Referendum" to fill out the details of a 12-point program for national reconstruction. It continues a long tradition of reflection about the desirable and the possible, in Mexico and throughout the world. Unfortunately, even most economists have never read Keynes masterful essay, "On National Self-Sufficiency" (1933); today, his admonitions about the dangers of relinquishing to international markets the domestic production of goods considered essential for people's welfare seem more pertinent than ever, as does his plea for nations to maintain local capital

* Professor of Economics at the Universidad Autonoma Metropolitana, Unidad Xochimilco, Mexico D.F., Mexico, tel: 525-724-5100; fax: 525-724-5235.

76

markets independent of the moguls of international finance. The program called for a three-pronged effort to reactivate the domestic economy, recuperate the internal market and redefine the nation's international economic relations. Similarly, the Zapatista Army has proposed its own program for local autonomy for the indigenous regions of Mexico, calling for a unique blend of self-governance and national integration that would enable the reconstruction of local economies and ecosystems while strengthening local structures of governance. They have forcefully argued that this approach is the only one consistent with a national development policy to counteract the most noxious effects of globalization.

A Model for Sustainable Development

Although there are many opportunities to promote sustainability, and for implementing approaches that move us in a new direction, there are also significant obstacles to such progress. Overcoming these obstacles requires more than well-intentioned policies; it requires a new correlation of social forces, a move toward broad-based democratic participation in all aspects of life, within each country and in the concert of nations. Strategies to face these challenges must respond to the dual challenges of insulating these communities from further encroachment and assuring their viability.

In this alternative view, the world system is one of increasing duality, polarized between the rich and the poor nations, regions, communities and individuals. A small number of nations dominate the global power structure, guiding production and determining welfare levels. The other nations compete among themselves to offer lucrative conditions that will entice the corporate and financial powers to locate within their boundaries. Similarly, regions and communities within nations engage in self-destructive forms of bargaining—compromising the welfare of their workers and the building of their own infrastructure—in an attempt to outbid each other for the fruits of global growth. This dynamic is not conducive to promoting sustainable development. The regions unable to attract investment suffer the ignoble fate of losers in a permanent economic olympics, condemned to oblivion on the world stage. In their struggle for survival within the global marketplace, many of the world's rural populations are doomed to marginality and permanent poverty.

Sustainability is not possible in rural Latin America as long as the expansion of capital enlarges the ranks of the poor and impedes their access to the resources needed for mere survival. Capitalism no longer needs growing armies of unemployed to ensure low wages, nor need it control vast areas to secure regular access to the raw materials and primary products for its productive machine; these inputs are now assured by new institutional arrangements that modified social and productive structures to fit the needs of capital. At present, however, great excesses are generated, excesses that impoverish people and ravage their regions. Profound changes are required to facilitate a strategy of sustainable development: it is possible and necessary to promote new structures—structures that allow people to rebuild their rural societies and produce goods and services in a sustainable fashion while expanding the environmental stewardship services they have always provided.

Food Self-Sufficiency and the Relationship between Production and Consumption

As Keynes pointed out, the first issue that must be dealt with squarely is that of self-sufficiency versus integration into the global trading system with a tendency toward specialization based on monocropping systems. Sustainability cannot be tantamount to autarchy, although it is conducive to a much lower degree of specialization in all areas of production and social organization. Food self-sufficiency emerged as a necessity in many societies because of the precariousness of international trading systems; specific culinary traditions developed on the basis of highly localized knowledge of fruits and vegetables, herbs and spices. Although the introduction of Green Revolution technologies raised the productive potential of food producers tremendously, we soon found out how hard it was to reach this potential and the high social and environmental costs that such a program might entail.

The complexity of the task of ending hunger has been widely recognized. But recent literature has stressed the social rather than the technical (or supply-based) origins of famine and hunger. Sen (1982) is a particularly effective exponent of this point while others have gone into greater detail about the "social origins" of food strategies and crises (Barraclough, 1991). The "modernization" of urban diets in Nigeria, by substituting wheat and rice for sorghum and millet, is an egregious case of creating dependency, reducing opportunities for peasant producers and raising the social cost of feeding a nation (see Barkin, Batt and deWalt, 1990).

Food self-sufficiency is a controversial objective that cogently raises the question of autonomy. Development practitioners are virtually unanimous in rejecting calls for an extreme position, although Mexico's declaration in favor of such a program in 1980 to the World Food Council was broadly applauded by Third World representatives. Today the discussion is more complex, for there is general agreement on two contradictory factors in the debate:

- On the one hand, local production of basic commodities that can be produced equally well but more efficiently elsewhere is a luxury few societies can afford, *if and only if* the resources not dedicated to the production of these traded goods can find productive employment elsewhere; and

- On the other hand, there are probably few exceptions to the observation that greater local production of such commodities contributes to higher nutritional standards and better health indices. In the context of today's societies, in which inequality is the rule and the forces discriminating against the rural poor legion, a greater degree of autonomy in the provision of the material basis for an adequate standard of living is likely to be an important part of any program of regional sustainability. It will contribute toward creating more productive jobs and an interest in better stewardship over natural resources.

There are many parts of the world in which such a strategy would constitute a wasteful luxury. It would involve the diversion of resources from other uses which could be more productive in contributing to the availability of goods for trading. But even in circumstances in which wholesale importation of basic commodities is advisable, people concerned with sustainable development raise questions about modifying local diets so that they are more attuned to the productive possibilities of their regions; in the current scene, the tendency to substitute imported products for traditional foods is particularly troublesome with terrible consequences for human welfare in many societies.

Food self-sufficiency, however, is only part of a broader strategy of productive diversification in which tenets are very much a part of the sustainability movement. The principles of greater self-reliance are fundamental for the whole range of products and services which a society would like to assure itself. Historically, rural denizens never have been "just farmers," or anything else for that matter. Rather, rural communities were characterized by the *diversity of the productive activities in which they engaged to assure their subsistence.* It was only the aberration of transferring models of large-scale commercial agriculture to development thinking in the Third World that misled many into ignoring the multifaceted nature of traditional rural productive systems. Sustainable development strategies directly face this problem, attempting to reintroduce this diversity, as they grapple with problems of appropriate scales of operation and product mix.

Autonomous Development: A Strategy for Sustainability

Global integration is creating opportunities for some, nightmares for many. In this juxtaposition of winners and losers, a new strategy for rural development is required: a strategy that revalues the contribution of traditional production strategies. In the present world economy, the vast majority of rural producers in the Third World cannot compete on world markets. Unless insulated in some way, their traditional products only have ready markets within the narrow confines of poor communities suffering a similar fate.

But these marginal rural producers offer an important promise: they can support themselves and make important contributions to the rest of society. Present policies are driving peasants from their traditional activities and communities (Barkin, Batt and DeWalt, 1991). Peasants and indigenous communities must receive support to continue living and producing in their own regions. Even by the strictest criteria of neoclassical economics, this approach should not be dismissed as inefficient protectionism, since most of the resources involved in this process would have little or no opportunity cost for society as a whole.

Many analysts dismiss peasant producers as working on too small a scale and with too few resources to be efficient. While it is possible and even necessary to promote increased productivity consistent with a strategy of sustainable production, as defined by agroecologists, the proposal to encourage them to remain as productive members of their communities should be implemented under existing conditions.

In much of Latin America, if peasants ceased to produce basic crops, the lands and inputs are not often simply transferable to other farmers for commercial output. The low opportunity costs of primary production in peasant and indigenous regions derive from the lack of alternative productive employment for the people and the lands in this sector.

Although the people would generally have to seek income in the "informal sector," their contribution to national output would be meager. The difference between the social criteria for evaluating the cost of this style of production and the market valuation is based on the determination of the sacrifices *society* would make in undertaking one or the other option. The theoretical basis for this approach harks back to the initial essay of W. Arthur Lewis (1954) and subsequent developments that find their latest expression in the call for a "neo-structuralist" approach to development for Latin America (Sunkel, 1993).

We are proposing the creation of an separate sphere for autonomous development. By recognizing the permanence of a sharply stratified society, the country will be in a better position to design policies that recognize and take advantage of these differences to improve the welfare of people in both sectors. A strategy that offers succor to rural communities, a means to make productive diversification possible, will make the management of growth easier in those areas developing links with the international economy. But more importantly, such a strategy will offer an opportunity for the society to confront actively the challenges of environmental management and conservation in a meaningful way, with a group of people uniquely qualified for such activities.

Much of the literature on popular participation emphasizes the multifaceted contribution that the productive incorporation of marginal groups can make to society (Friedmann, 1992; Friedmann and Rangan, 1993; Stiefel and Wolfe, 1994). While very little has been done on specific strategies for sustainability in poor rural communities, it is clear that much of the experience recounted by practitioners with grassroots groups (e.g., Glade and Reilly, 1993) is consistent with the principles enunciated by theorists and analysts like Altieri (1987).

The dual structure characteristic of this new economy is not new. Unlike the present version that permeates all our societies, confronting rich and poor, the proposal calls for creating structures so that one segment of society that *chooses* to live in rural areas finds support from the rest of the nation to implement an alternative regional development program. The new variant starts from the inherited base of rural production, improving productivity by using the techniques of agroecology. It also involves incorporating new activities that build on the cultural and resource base of the community and the region for further development. It requires very specific responses to a general problem and therefore depends heavily on local involvement in design and implementation. While the broad outlines are widely discussed, the specifics require investment programs for direct producers and their partners. (For a more general discussion, see Barkin (1990, ch. 7.)

FUNDE (1994) offers a specific program for the reconversion of El Salvador based on the principles discussed in this essay. The proposals of groups like the IAF and RIAD offer specific examples of ongoing grassroots efforts to implement initiatives like those discussed in the text. The Ecology and Development Center in Mexico is pursuing a program of regional development consistent with the proposed strategy (Chapela and Barkin, 1995).

What is new is the introduction of an explicit strategy to strengthen the social and economic base for the autonomous regions. By recognizing and encouraging the marginal groups to create an alternative that would offer marginal groups better prospects for their own development, the proposal for autonomous regions might be mistaken to be the simple formalization of the "war on poverty" or "solidarity" approach to the alleviation of the worst effects of marginality. This would be erroneous. Rather than a simple transfer of resources to compensate groups for their poverty, we require an integrated set of productive projects that offer rural communities the opportunity to generate goods and services that will contribute to raising their living standards while also improving the environment in which they live.

The Limitations of Ecotourism: The Monarch Butterfly

The Monarch butterfly and its 5,000-mile trek between Canada and Mexico has come to symbolize the bridge that is bringing the three nations of North America closer together, forging a single trading bloc. The phenomenon of the overwintering of the Monarch butterfly was "discovered" some 20 years ago (1974-1976) when researchers from the University of Florida finally traced the flight path from Canada. Of course, their presence was well known to local residents and to a broader segment of the population in west-central Mexico from time immemorial, but with the publication of the details of the journey in *Scientific American* and *National Geographic* magazines, its social and economic significance altered conditions in the region.

Once announced to the world, the spectacle of the wintering lepidoptera began to attract hundreds of thousands of sightseers, who make the pilgrimage to the reserves that were created so that this winged visitor might enjoy some degree of protection from the ravages of encroachment by human activities. As a result, many of the people living in the region have come to resent the intruder; its annual visits have brought increasing government regulation of their lives, effective appropriation of their lands, intense social conflict and heightened misery.

There are serious social and economic problems in the protected area. Many of these problems are simply local manifestations of the larger crisis of Mexican society, making it difficult for poor rural producers to survive by continuing their traditional activities. In this protected area, people have been particularly affected by specific conservation measures that intensified the adjustment process. The declaration of certain important areas to be part of the nuclear and buffer zones of the reserve led to a prohibition or severe restriction on traditional forestry activities. Further, communities or their members were not offered compensation for the reclassification of their lands or alternative productiveopportunities with which they might earn a livelihood elsewhere in the region.

The region's problems and those of the communities did not begin in 1986 and cannot be attributed solely to the butterflies. Local systems of control by economic elites and political bosses were an important part of the local scene long before the visitors acquired their new-found fame. Industrial demand for sources of pulp, and local mechanisms to concentrate the wealth and opportunities, were already creating pressures on the forests and dividing individual communities as well as pitting one against another. The opportunities created by the unbridled expansion of tourism and the arbitrary distribution of the spoils among a very small group of people compounded the problems.

In this environment, a new approach to regional development is required. While there is a general recognition that ecotourism can offer more opportunities to the people, it is also clear that, without other, complementary productive activities creating jobs and income, the people in the region will continue their environmentally destructive activities that also threaten the viability of the fir forests in which the Monarch nests. We have started to implement such a strategy, establishing a local structure in which agroindustrial production will stimulate sustainable agroforestry projects. In this way, we are attempting to provide some tangible mechanisms to construct alternatives to the seemingly unstoppable advance of regional integration for one group of people who have no future in the global economy.

A local network of NGOs and confederations of communities and productive groups has begun to play an important role in creating these opportunities. There appears to be an understanding of the great cost incurred as a result of the internecine warfare that the strategies of bureaucratic imposition created. The principal limitation, I think, is the lack of a mechanism for the various groups to implement realistic productive strategies; they need information about resources and markets as well as mechanism to channel available resources more effectively. The organizations require a process of local cooperation, constructed on a firm basis of broad-based effective local participation. This is the route toward creating a "dual society," in which ecotourism would contribute to an overall strategy of sustainable development.

References

Altieri, Miguel A. (1987), *Agroecology: The Scientific Basis of Alternative Agriculture,* Boulder, CO: Westview Press.

Barkin, David (1992), "Morelia hacia finales del milennio," *Las Ciudades Medias,* Mexico, D.F.: Red Nacional de Investigación Urbana.

_____ (1990), *Distorted Development: Mexico in the World Economy,* Boulder, CO: Westview Press.

_____ R. Batt and B. DeWalt (1990), *Food Crops vs. Feed Crops: The Global Substitution of Grains in Production,* Boulder, CO: Lynne Rienner.

Barraclough, Solon (1991), *An End to Hunger? The Social Origins of Food Strategies,* London: Zed Books and UNRISD.

Chapela, Gonzalo, and David Barkin (1995), *Monarcas y Campesinos: Estrategia de Desarrollo Sustentable en el Oriente de Michoacán,* Mexico D.F.: Centro de Ecología y Desarrollo.

Friedmann, John (1992), *Empowerment: The Politics of Alternative Development,* New York: Basil Blackwell.

Friedmann, John and Haripriya Rangan (1993), *In Defense of Livelihood: Comparative Studies on Environmental Action,* West Hartford, CT: Kumarian Press.

Fundación Nacional para el Desarrollo (FUNDE) (1994), *Bases para la Construcción de un Nuevo Proyecto Económico Nacional para El Salvador,* San Salvador: FUNDE.

Glade, William, and Charles Reilley, eds. (1993), *Inquiry at the Grassroots: An Inter-American Foundation Reader,* Arlington, VA: Inter-American Foundation.

Lewis, W. Arthur (1954), "Economic Development with Unlimited Supplies of Labour," republished in A.N. Agarwala and S.P. Singh (1963), *Economics of Underdevelopment,* New York: Oxford University Press.

Sen, Amartya (1992), *Inequality Reexamined,* Cambridge, MA: Harvard University Press.

Stiefel, Matthias, and Marshall Wolfe (1994), *A Voice for the Excluded: Popular Participation in Development: Utopia or Necessity?,* London: Zed Books and UNRISD.

Sunkel, Osvaldo (1993), *Development from Within: Toward a Neostructuralist Approach for Latin America,* Boulder, CO: Lynne Rienner.

Gandhian Economics: Enoughness as Real Wealth

Romesh Diwan*

Mahtama Gandhi was very fond of *Ishopanishad,* invocation to which (in English translation) reads:**

> *This is Fullness, That is Fullness*
> *From Fullness, Fullness comes*
> *When Fullness is taken from Fullness*
> *Fullness Remains.*

Sanskrit for "Fullness" is *puranta,* which also relates to "Enoughness." Gandhi also used to say that nature is compassionate and provides enough for the needs of all, but not for the greed of even one. It is from this concept of enoughness and fullness that many propositions in Gandhian economics and policies for sustainable development are derived. Such socio-economic and sustainable development is based only on an alternative concept of wealth where ethical values take precedence on material production and consumption. Al Gore recognized its relevance when he said that the real solutions to the major ecological disasters emanate only from the spiritual realm. As the first story below informs us, Gandhian economics works. It work well even

---

* Professor of Economics, Rensselaer Polytechnic Institute, Troy, NY 12180, tel: 518-276-6386; e-mail: diwan@rpi.edu.

** There are translation problems as Sanskrit is a spiritual language while English is that of commerce and imperialism.

in a hostile social and technical infrastructure; imagine how much more effective it can be with a supportive infrastructure. It is far more productive and efficient—however productivity and efficiency are defined—because economic sufficiency and equality, the flipside of an ethical society, is a major goal of development that is sustainable.

Gandhi Is Alive in Ralegaon Siddhi: Meet Shri Anna Hazare[1]

Ralegaon Siddhi, about 85 kilometers from Pune, lies in the drought-prone area of Maharashtra, with rainfall of about 15 inches a year; for the last two years it was less than six inches. The total land of the village is about 2,200 acres. Of this about 1,700 acres is arable. The soil is of poor quality, the land undulating so that water runs off quickly. Twenty years ago only about 70 to 80 acres were irrigated through wells. The village was destitute: about a fifth of the families ate just once a day; half to two-thirds borrowed grain from other villages at a high cost. There was little work in the village. Men went outside to earn a pittance breaking stones; women suffered prostitution. Family after family was in debt. A major proportion of the land had been mortgaged to moneylenders. With no other source of income, people had taken to manufacturing liquor: there were 35 to 40 liquor stills. Drunkenness was common and with it came feuds and crime, especially against women. The village had a temple around the *samadhi* of "Yadavbaba," but it had broken down. The wood from it had been used as firewood in the liquor stills. After liquor, a good part of the meager earnings of these people went up in tobacco smoke; the sale of tobacco products amounted to around 60,000 rupees (about $US 20,000). Although a few village wells were still useable, these were major sources of disease and illnesses. Ninety percent of the families were stricken by abdominal ailments. Child mortality was high.

It was to this village that Anna Hazare returned 17 years ago. The temple was the first thing to be repaired, and today is the hub of every activity of the village. Anna Hazare himself lives in a little room to one side of this temple, and it was here that he conducted his fast. The temple, from which wood had been taken for firing the liquor stills, now houses a "Grain Bank." Any family in need can borrow grain from this bank, repaying with a little "interest," for the village has decided that things obtained free are not valued. The "bank" started with the growth of community spirit. The village resolved that every family with surplus grain should contribute, and the assessment was done by the villagers themselves. There has not been one case of a family having "defaulted" on the "loan" as they all know that they are borrowing from themselves. The village is run by an elected all-woman *panchayat* and decisions are taken by the entire village sitting together in the *Gram Sabha*.

Water is now systematically harvested by percolation tanks, check dams wells being recharged. Of the 1,700-odd acres of arable land, 1,100 to 1,200 acres are under irrigation. Today three crops are grown worth 50 to 60 lakhs (one lakh = ca 3,300). The results are what others would scarcely dream of. The village, in which a fifth of the families ate no more than one meal a day, now markets vegetables, grains, and milk. While neighboring villages await the government tanker bringing drinking water, Ralegaon has enough not only for everyone in the village, but also for the hundreds who troop into the village every day to see the wonder that has been wrought there.

Today there is not one liquor still—in fact, liquor has been banished from the village; the people took a vow not to touch the stuff. Not a single shop in the village sells cigarettes, not even the *bidi*. In 1987, the entire village resolved to rid itself of tobacco and its addiction. They purchased all the tobacco and tobacco products in the village shops, which were burnt at the Holi festival instead of wood.

These achievements are only the beginning. The very way of life and relationships within the village have been transformed beyond recognition. Twenty years ago the village was riven by disputes due to poverty and addiction, and now every family contributes voluntary labor by one adult every week. Almost everything new that one sees has been built and accomplished through community labor. Between three to four lakh trees have been planted, adopted by families and individuals who look after them as their own. Community effort has lifted the poorest, especially Harijans who were deep in debt; productivity of their lands was raised and debts paid off.

For the last 17 years, the village has been marrying its boys and girls in community marriages held every three or four months. Youth volunteers assist the parents in preparing estimates, shopping and making sure that no family is fleeced by dowry demands. Parents contribute about Rs. 1,300 to 1,400 toward marriage expenses, and the village provides needed items, such as *shamiyanas*, utensils and loudspeakers. Couples of all castes and creeds are married together—there is no distinction. Each ceremony is kept to the simplest, with the precise ritual tailored to suit the traditions of each family.

Buildings worth over 35 lakhs have been constructed, including a school of 18 rooms and a Yadavbaba hostel that accommodates 150 students.Instruction content has been overhauled. All too often, Anna Hazare says, those who get degrees leave our villages; those who acquire a specialization leave our country. And so instead of gearing up students for a "degree-factory," the school is viewed as a Jeevan Shiksha Mandir—a temple that prepares them for life. Arising at 5:30 every morning, children go for a run in the village playground. From 6 a.m. there is a physical training led by a retired ex-serviceman. The children have planted over 50,000 trees. They run a plant nursery, preparing around a lakh of saplings every year for sale. Children from all over Maharashtra who have dropped out of school are eligible. "The S.S.C. results of these students have been between 80 to 90 percent," Anna Hazare reports, "and some students have secured as high as 82 to 85 percent marks also. These students are good at school sports and bag a third of all the prizes in the *tehsil* level competitions." The village school has been top-rated in regard to small savings in Ahmednagar district, through the student work program, with a technical school also in the works.

It is not surprising that hundreds of people from all over the country come to see this development miracle. And all this has been achieved by the dedication of Shri Anna Hazare over two decades, who came from a poor family in debt and took early retirement from the army as a truck driver, inspired by Swami Vivekananda's dictum,"The purpose of life is to serve others." He is following in Mahatma Gandhi's footsteps, having learned from Gandhi-ji to never preach without practice and that to gain people's trust, one's conduct has to be beyond doubt. That is what Gita's *sholak* about *shauchi* is all about. One would think that serving others is obviously a "good" thing. Yet such social service involves helping people to rid themselves of exploitation, and so is threatening to all officialdom—of both the market and state—because both systems depend on such exploitation. After all, government and officials are powerful because they represent the very system that Hazare wants to change, even uproot. Functionaries of the exploitative system—political leaders, bureaucrats, journalists—will find every possible means to stop those fighting exploitation.

Kittiko Hachchiko: Gandhian Economics Works Again[2]

The Harihar Polyfibres (HF) owned by the Birlas—the largest commercial and industrial conglomerate in India—was started in 1972 on the banks of the Tungabhadra at Kumarapattana in the Ranebenbur Taluka of Darwad District in the State of Karnataka, India. Since its inception, the state government of Karnataka has been supplying it eucalyptus wood at Rs. 24 (about 70 cents) per ton while the market price is Rs. 700 (about $20). Thus the government has been subsidizing this private company at the rate of $19 per ton. In addition, the manufacture of polyfibres results in not only air pollution but pollution of the river affecting the lives of 100,000 poor people—mainly fishermen, shepherds, farmers and laborers who use the river as a source of fish and drinking water. The only recourse to the victims was a direct action in the form of massive *satyagrah* (truth force, a method popularized by Mahatma Gandhi) on October 2, 1984, Gandhi's birthday. People have been labeling polluted air as "Birla perfume," polluted water as "Birla *teertha* (holy water) and eucalyptus as "Birla Kalpatru."

In February 1985, the state government of Karnataka's Forest Development Corporation launched a joint sector company in partnership with Birla—namely, Karnataka Pulpwood Ltd. (KPL for short)—for growing eucalyptus trees on forest and village common lands to provide wood to HF. The partnership deed revealed that the Karnataka government owned 51 percent of the shares and was a 100-percent guarantor to all its borrowings, but received only 12.5 percent profits. Some 30,000 hectares (74,130 acres) of forest and village common lands were leased to KPL for 40 years at the rate of one rupee (less than one nickel) per year. What a gift from the so-called democratic government to a particular industry at the expense of poor and helpless voters! Lands used by the people for centuries were now bulldozed by KPL for a plantation of eucalyptus trees.

Such a huge subsidy based on the suffering and exploitation of poor people—so common in imperial days—touched the conscience of a number of caring people who formed different NGOs to help affected people fight this injustice and loss of their economic resource. One of these organizations, Samaj Parivartan Samudya, was initiated by S. R. Hiremath, who had left a well-paying job in Chicago to serve the exploited people back in his home district. These NGOs started a two-pronged strategy to undo this exploitative arrangement. They helped the affected people organize *satyagrah* (non-violent action), seeking relief through the courts. Various non-violent methods culminating in *kittiko hachchiko* (pluck and plant) by 2,000 *satyagrahis* on November 14, 1987, which attracted worldwide attention. Over 100 eucalyptus trees were uprooted and 100 conventional trees planted. World Watch Institute's *State of the World, 1989* described this as follows:

> In November 1987, 2,000 low-caste laborers and farmers from Karnataka, India, performed one of the most peculiar acts of civil disobedience in the nation's long Gandhian history. They uprooted 100 trees as a part of the government's massive reforestation campaign. That villagers should destroy trees in such a fuel-wood-starved land appears little less than self-destructive. In fact it was perfectly reasonable. The tree, eucalyptus to be used in the production of rayon, were planted by a private company on what had been common lands where poor gathered wood. The poor were defending what was theirs (p. 165).

It is instructive to note how even well-meaning scholars of an environmentally friendly institute can miss some of the essentials.

After a series of such *satyagrahs*, wide publicity and legal action, the Supreme Court rendered a stay order on March 24, 1987, bringing the KPL to a virtual halt. Still the corporation's hold on the government was so strong that the government disregarded the Supreme Court judgment and transferred another 12,000 hectares of forest land to KPL—an action that required the filing of a contempt petition in July 1988. There were many ups and downs during the next two years. At last, the Karnataka cabinet resolved unanimously on October 3, 1991 to wind up KPL. Like the Chipko movement, which has drawn a lot of world attention, this has been another successful case in which the people, by joining together and through non-violent action, have been able to regain their rights to their common lands—rights one would have thought would be safe in a democratic set-up. This long struggle has generated large amount of wealth in the form of cooperative spirit, political knowledge and self confidence among the people; they can now do anything.

Notes

1. Adapted from Indian journalist Arun Shourie's two columns: "A Living Treasure" (December 13, 1996), and "Have You Seen the Deranged Absorbed in Themselves?" (December 23, 1996).

2. Adapted from Sadanand Kanwalli, *Quest for Justice*, Dharwad, Karnataka: Samaj Parivartan Samudya, 1993.

African Contributions to Concepts of Real Wealth

*Winifred Armstrong**

Africans are doing important work at both the conceptual and grassroots levels to develop and demonstrate alternative approaches to economic organization. These approaches will help us get beyond the current concept of linear growth measured by the consumption of resources that underlies both capitalism and socialism. The world's peoples are already consuming more resources than can be regenerated, and our wastes are quantitatively and qualitatively damaging our future resouce base.

So there is an immediate need for a paradigm shift away from economic systems, which posit the goal as production and consumption of more goods, and toward systems which aim to balance the resources people use with those the earth can regenerate. By contrast, the U.S. Government halted its initial modest steps to develop natural resources accounts in response to pressure from a few congressmen. Almost no headway has been made in the past two years within the Bureau of Economic Analysis of the U.S. Department of Commerce to further develop or apply natural resource accounts in the U.S.

What do such changes in economic goals, values and measures

---

*The author is an economist with the Regional Plan Association in New York. A previous version of this article appeared under the title "African Contributions to the Sustainable Development Concept" in the April 1994 issue of the *Newsletter* of the International Society for Ecological Economics, Vol. 5, No. 2, and appears here with the permission of ISEE.

mean in relation to Africa? They mean that African countries can come much closer to balancing needs with capacity, and production with consumption, than at present. Since "more is better" has been an aim of both capitalist and socialist economic planning, so-called poorer countries have by definition been at a loss. When the aim is to balance resource use with resource consumption, then, as the people in Burkina Faso said to me, "We're in better shape than our Ivorian neighbors because we aren't used to the large houses, cars and lifestyles that our own economy can't sustain." And in Burkina, there were more buses, motorcycles, mopeds and bicycles than cars, and we all rode them. Access to transport, rather than numbers of vehicles per capita, can be a valid measure of well-being.

What might it mean to African countries to include in their national accounts the cost of using (up) renewable resources (trees) or non-renewable resources (minerals)? Companies and governments could not mine and sell all the copper or gold, count it all as profit and walk away leaving polluted water or a hole in the ground as if there were no "cost" to using up the resource or to leaving behind a damaged environment.

Some African countries are taking into account such resource use, and modifying their national accounts and investment policies. In Botswana, the newspaper headlines, referring to President Quett Masire's speech on the 25th Anniversary of Independence, read, "Diamonds Are Not Forever"— meaning Botswana was counting the mining and sale of diamonds in its latest Development Plan not just as revenue gained, but also as a resource "lost" or used up. To balance this "loss," reinvestment in other productive activity would be made. In Namibia, President Sam Nujoma in a recent State of the Union address bragged that Namibia was ahead of most nations in adopting such natural resource accounting.

In Niger, aiming to keep themselves and their resource base sustainable, a local tree-growing, wood-selling cooperative worked on a 20-year cycle with trees that take 20 years to grow: the woodcutters cut 5 percent and plant 5 percent each year.

There is another critical mssing element in our current economic formulations which, if corrected, will result in an improvement of Africa's productive capacity.

In currrent economic analysis, we often fail to include subsistence agriculture or informal trade in how we count production—that is, what people produce for their families or trade on a non-cash basis with their neighbors. In Africa, depending on the country, roughly 50 percent to 90 percent of the people gain all or part of their livelihood from such subsistence and informal activities. But often the national and international economic policies that have been adopted—whether internally or externally generated—fail to count the significance of this percentage. A policy that omits 50 to 90 percent of a people's economic activity is almost inevitably skewed. The notion that "If you don't count it, it doesn't count" obfuscates reality—and by designing policies that principally reinforce only cash or market values, people and their productive activities may be bypassed, excluded or destroyed.

In Zaria, Nigeria, a livestock officer provided a representative example of how failure to count the value of people as producers, and not just the value of the production, can destroy the producers and cause poverty and community degeneration. This livestock officer told of how a World Bank research project in which he was engaged purportedly was designing ways to improve cattle production and land use, but only through encouraging private ownership of land and cattle. Yet in Northern Nigeria, people have for generations traveled and worked with cattle and land in jointly used, communal arrangements. This Nigerian officer had urged that World Bank policy and investment be directed not only at the 20 percent he said could successfully engage in private ownership, but also include the 80 percent who would continue the more traditional pattern and who, if ignored, would be lost to the formal productive system and probably further impoverished. He did not see these policies as mutually exclusive; on the contrary, he thought it should be deliberate policy to enhance the capacity of all the people to contribute to production and maintain themselves in the process. But when I asked what had happened as a result of his recommendations, he remarked, "It is not only research that informs policy: it is also policy that informs research."

Nonetheless, in many quarters where economic policy is not working for Africans, Africans are revising theory through grassroots action. For example, "Six S" farmers' groups in Burkina Faso and other West African countries count as value the knowledge and technology they bring to the further development of their communities. When I visited a village dam and asked a young man what his contribution had been, he whipped out from under his shirt a much-used school notebook in which he had written the daily contributions made to the design, technology and labor involved in the dam project of every man, woman and child who took part from beginning to end. Everyone was expected to contribute something; everyone was expected to have something to contribute. So everyone had some role in and understanding of the process. Such outside help as might be required was rigorously defined and limited, to enable local people to retain managerial and financial control—and thus sustainability.

It is not hard to find other examples of local knowledge valued as wealth. ORAP in Zimbabwe—an organization of rural agricultural producers—similarly puts a value on local knowledge and posits as a goal the participation of everyone in the economic process, unlike the World Bank project in Nigeria mentioned above. In the Philippines, an organization called Green Forum has developed a process and measures for what they call Community Centered Capitalism, putting a value on community. We on Manhattan's Upper West Side of New York City similarly insisted on the value of community when we knocked out Donald Trump's original behemoth project that would have "gentrified" the neighborhood and successfully proposed an alternative that maintains the multi-ethnic, multiracial neighborhood we value. Such efforts to construct and apply a wider set of economic values are taking place worldwide.

The Geography of Nowhere Has a Chianti Counterpoint

*John Navone**

Environmentalists and Green parties inspire much serious thought about our landscapes. James Howard Kunstler, for example, in *The Geography of Nowhere: The Rise and Decline of America's Man-Made Landscape* (New York: Simon & Schuster Trade [Touchstone], 1994), deplores the fate of the human habitat in America, which he says has been nearly wrecked by those who occupy it. The destruction of both the natural and the man-made environments will produce "a landscape of scary places, the geography of nowhere, that has simply ceased to be a credible human habitat."

Mr. Kunstler asserts that we are happiest when we inhabit physical surroundings worth caring about. Small-town charm accomplishes this; nothing is more important to the human enterprise than the sense of community that small towns ostensibly encourage.

From atop a tower in a Tuscan village, one sees a landscape that might well realize Mr. Kunstler's ideal. One day, while driving through this magical place, a friend exclaimed to me, "Have you ever seen a landscape that looks so loved, treasured and cared for?"

Years later, I discovered a basis in history for the well-loved look of Tuscany's Chianti country. The investiture oath of the Chianti League, which was formed at the beginning of the 14th century for the adminis-

---

* The writer, a Jesuit priest, is a professor of biblical theology at the Pontifical Gregorian University in Rome. He contributed this comment to the *International Herald Tribune,* March 8, 1994, p. 7.

tration and defense of the region, begins, "I promise to keep myself close to nature, to give a religious meaning to my life, to look around me with optimism and with love." Our landscapes and townscapes often reflect inner visions and feelings. The Tuscan landscape, part natural, part husbandry, is lovely because it is loved.

Unfortunately, the devastation of our landscapes and the decay of our townscapes—the ugliness of unloved persons and places and things—often reflect the moral ugliness of our greed, indifference and exploitation. So much of loveliness and beauty is rooted in love itself. Contemplation, the loving gaze that beholds beloved persons, places and things, has much to do with their loveliness. The Creator, according to Genesis, contemplates creation to affirm its goodness; and creation is good because it is affirmed, treasured and cared for.

The possibility of our enjoying anything is based in a kind of humility that takes nothing for granted, recognizing all as a gift. An attitude of entitlement, in contrast, takes things for granted. And when we clamor for more, in continual dissatisfaction, we destroy everything, including happiness.

Our radical acceptance of and gratitude for everything, taking nothing for granted, is part of what the poet Gerard Manley Hopkins called our "inscape," our individually distinctive and fundamental beauty, the precondition for true knowledge and delight. Contemplation is the communion of inscapes.

Tuscan painters, beginning with Ambrogio Lorenzetti in the early 14th century, contemplated their landscapes and townscapes. Lorenzetti's frescoes of "Good and Bad Government" in the Sienna Town Hall depict the first townscape and landscape in the history of European painting.

Tuscan landscapes seem familiar because they were a favorite background for almost all the Italian painters of the High Renaissance. From Petrarch (1304-74) onward, Tuscan humanists expressed the joy they took in the flora and fauna of the countryside. The pleasure in the countryside expressed in Pius II's "Commentaries" was echoed in his choice of site for his palace at Pienza with its spectacular view of Monte Amiata. That entire Tuscan towns are as they were four or five centuries ago bespeaks the undying affection of a people for its townscapes.

The Chianti League has given the world some of its most beautiful landscapes and townscapes. With realistic optimism, the Tuscans assume that their deals can be only partially fulfilled. Rather than focus their attention on the area of non-fulfillment in a state of constant resentment (and the surest way to be unhappy is to make one's happiness dependent on the fulfillment of impossible conditions), they appreciate their limited Tuscan world, contemplating it with an optimism and love that has led to a strenuous desire to improve it. Their contemplation does not mean passivity. If Tuscany is good, it deserves to be improved. Such basic commitment, like appreciation, takes nothing for granted.

Chapter 3: What Works for Re-Embedding the Economy?

Economic theory tends to incorporate more and more political and social spheres until the entire "techno-economic-administrative system" is viewed as a "drive mechanism" led by the "self-regulating market." This theoretical abstraction is challenged by growing awareness of how neo-liberal economic integration undermines local-regional communities and environments. As the previous chapter has shown, more flexibility at local and regional levels is essential and indeed is being innovated by people. New approaches to community development and new experiments in self-reliance begin to emerge as viable paths—a "new people-oriented economics" is forming.

Everywhere social and ecological structures are emerging in the midst of the market system that are spontaneously generated social protections to normatively "re-embed the market" in specific contexts. By mediating pure market evaluations by community or sectorial norms, they deflect the economic disvaluing of real wealth and anticipate working altneratives for a more sustainable re-embedding of economics into socio-cultural contexts. Taken together, or woven together by conscious planning, they represent new macro-arrangments of a people's economy on new social foundations.

In an attempt to bring these experiments together, the General Agreement on a New Economy (GANE), as described by Ruth Caplan, is based on the premise that the new arrangements that people are working out can come together into a new socio-economic order, which represents the values of environmental sustainability, equity and meaningful work. Taking the best practices of many groups and communities and putting them together to create a new people's agreement would outline possible designs for a new economy. This begins by initiating community visioning processes in which diverse groups come to common ground about community ends, rights, assets and the future integration of all of these into a community development plan which can be implemented with the aid of federal, state and local partnerships. That is, decentralization requires the cooperation of wider governace structures that would be essential to form a community federalism where accountability is rooted at the local level.

Re-Embedding the Non-Commodity Spheres: Land/Ecology and Money

All of the above are resistances to extension of commodifications into spheres where community, ecology and other forms of real wealth are protected from the single goal of economic value. Karl Polanyi identified land, labor and money as fictitious commodities that could not be adequately evaluated by the purely economic evaluations of market-system exchange.[1] Opposing such economistic reductionism, social protection spontaneously emerge from different sectors and classes to secure these spheres. These movements to re-embed land (including ecological value), labor and money occur simultaneously with the extension of markets for genuine commodities; together these phases create a dynamic that Polany calls the "double movement" of social change.

This notion of the "double-movement" retains the logic of a "dialectical relation," or reciprocal causalities, that cannot be analytically separated, but must be analyzed as a holistic interrelation. Polanyi's double movement retains the Marxist insight into the human resistance to the imposition of a quasi-natural causality of commodification upon components that are essential for maintaining a human world and a productive nature. But Polanyi's post-Marxist understanding of this holistic interrelation is a historical claim that human actions to protect the real wealth of non-commodities have always emerged. Protecting the real substantive wealth, and not just the creation of more economic value, means retaining the world constructing capabilities of work, natural capital and the social practices of the social economy without permitting a reduction to the short-term evaluations of the market.

Polanyi's concept of "the double movement" is a historical description of the dynamics of the emergence, and consequent social and political responses, to the rise of market society. But it also provides a

framework for thinking about the protecting ("re-embedding") of fictitious commodities in local-regional communities today. To explicate
Polanyi's conception of the aspects of the double movement:

- Extensions of the market for genuine commodities are, under the
  regime of economic liberalism (and global neo-liberalism), also
  extended to the non-commodity spheres of labor, land and money;

- These market extensions undermine traditional use-values and
  intrinsic norms in these non-commodity spheres and release
  counter (class and sectional) struggles to protect these contexts
  against market evaluations and the accompanying socio-cultural
  reifications of real wealth into quantitative market value.

Thus Indian farmers create their own seed banks as social protections
against the unwanted commodification of hybrid seeds marketed in India by the Cargil Corporation. In Vandana Shiva's essay, "Biodiversity
and Sustainable Agriculture," she shows that protecting the local
farmer's knowledge and livelihods is, at the same time, a protection of
biodiversity too. In order to resist the systematic commodification and
intellectural property rights imposed on seeds and indeigenous medicine, these counter-movements require both an affirmation of cultural
practices and a new reaching out to wider governance structures for the
safeguarding of these local initatives.

Similarly, the split rate tax, innovated by 15 Pennsylvania cities,
protects the land by discouraging land speculation and profiteering.
John McConnell and Alanna Hartzok assess the results of
Pennsylvania's experiments in protecting the land while enabling urban
investment and housing policy that reduces urban sprawl and health
impacts of out-of-control land speculation. Reducing taxes on building
while increasing taxes on land provides a positive "user fee" context
for many innovative land uses and tax reform policies that will allow
many more goals for the sustainability of the earth and human settlements. Based on a rejection of the commodification of land, this old
idea of Henry George has come to fruition in Pennsylvania, and is being picked up all over the world—including the Russian Republics. As
the split rate tax is really an earthshare dividend for every inhabitant of
the region, so the extension of this earthshare logic to oil and mineral
wealth, the electromagnetic spectrum and satellite orbital zones is a
logical next step for citizens who have had the insight that no one can

really own what they did not make themselves.

Re-embedding money is an odd idea to those who have not understood that local curriences enable communities to retain more wealth locally, enable local livelihoods and get spending power, goods and services to people who otherwise would not have it.[2] Protecting local communities from forces that take money out of the community and impose usury costs on producers and consumers, a local currency re-embeds money by setting "boundaries" to the circulation of money and by providing credit for local people who could not get capital any other way. David Boyle describes several types of local currencies now operating in the U.S. and indicates how they can be applied to make local money more accountable to community concerns for ecology and social justice.

Re-Embedding Work

Not only would local currencies re-embed money, but they also enable the re-embedding of work opportunities. The theory of the market economy works for workers only as long as it provides enough income for consumption. Many people have called the "Fordist compromise" enticement for more and more consumption as a means of legitimating meaningless instrumental labor. This promotes withdrawal into the private sphere, the disintegration of social solidarity and mutual assistance and promotes asocial socializations of excessive individualism uninterested in community participation. But with economic globalization, we are at the end of the possibility of the system providing more and more for most of its workers. For this reason, functional market integration of workers facilitated by "Fordist" consumption incentives are no longer viable. More meaningful social integrations are emerging from the mutual aid cooperatives, alternative financial systems and community-centered intiatives.[3] Creating enough wealth to offer workers compensation for meaningless work by conditioning people to accept consumerism and the commercial advertising of luxury fantasies as possible realities is ending.

On the other end of the outdated right-left political spectrum, the orthodox socialist version of a work-centered system assumes it is possible to reconcile work and life by replacing the functional integrations of the market with the programmed regulation of the socialist society and "socialist consciousness" (or the expectation that functional societal integration can become a meaningful social and personal integration too). In this sense, socialist consciousness is equivalent to a professional ethic or calling that idealizes dedication to Party and the Socialist Plan as the heroic meaning of understanding one's self-activity as an instrument of historical justice and equality. Today it is becoming clear that the socialist utopia of functionally meaningful work becoming unified with personal autonomous meaning has not been realized.

Thus the efforts to create any functionally integrated modern system (either liberal capitalism or socialist) will progressively undermine social integrations by excluding the forming of reciprocal relations based on cooperation, group membership and solidarity. More meaningful work begins by re-embedding it in our choices for "right livelihoods" and social participations—these will become more central to our perferences on how we would like to spend our time. This would mean limiting the amount of time we spend at earning a living both individually and societally, such as shortening the work week, as many European countries have done, and resisting the lure of high-end consumption lifestyles.

But the power of corporations continues to dominate both societies and a "globalizing" world as well. A world of "working alternatives" will not be possible if the corporations buy out the democratic process and make political support for re-embedding the economy impossible. Using a plebiscitary democracy strategy, the corporations justify their control by equating the collective interest of government to personal liberties by depicting voters as consumers or customers and using electoral propaganda (akin to commercial advertising) to offer workers/consumers compensations for the loss of autonomy. An example is Ronald Reagan's promise to "get government off the backs of people" by turning more and more functions over to the private sector. This creates a greater decline of democratic participation in policy formation and, in this way, widens the gap between a "public" world and the networks of solidarity and social regulation in local/private spheres. Thus corporate-supported neo-liberalism compensates for this withering away of job opportunities and political process by attempting to legitimate a restriction of democracy in the interest of the more "productive" private sphere. Without transforming the corporation and changing the economic management mentality that dominates all major institutions, efforts to re-embed the economy and create sustainable communities based in real wealth will not be possible.

But, as Sumner Rosen argues persuasively, workers have begun to regroup in order to challenge the juggernaut of global capitalism. In the United States, the trade union movement has started to reassert itself in the political arena with new leadership after a long period of decline. And in Europe, notably the Scandanavian countries, efforts are underway to redefine the workplace in the emerging-late 20th-century computer-driven environment so as to protect the health and nurture the democratic rights of workers.

Institutionalizing Ecological Decision-Making

One of the most significant discourses today is the debate about how to redefine the corporation by altering the way it makes decisions and how to make it more accountable to environmental and community interests. Don Stone argues that environmental sustainability is a profitable road for corporations and outlines 10 steps that can turn good intentions into good results. Countering the received wisdom that environmental excellence is not profitable, Stone argues that a new approach is necessary—one that asserts that proper accounting of the real costs will transform the production activities by making pollution prevention and design for the environment essential. Beginning with an environmental footprint analysis, the material and energy flows of corporate practice can result in reduced waste and resource productivity as well as energy cost savings. The comprehensiveness of this carefully crafted decision-making chart for increasing ecological decision-making cannot be summarized here because the logical sequences are very technical and precise. Stone has acheived an impressive synthesis of all of the techniques now being advanced to improve efficiency and ecological sustainability, such as lifecycle analysis, value chain analysis, public environmental reporting and commitments to sustainable development.

Widening the scope of ecological decision-making, Larry Martin develops an ecological concept of the resource economics of waste which applies not only to corporate behavior but to institutions in society. Treating waste within the market model of increased competition to remove waste and lower the price and the amount of waste only goes so far—the finite limits of the earth's ecosystems are a barrier that does not show up in the neo-classical model. Without redesigning production processes and products in ways that can be recycled and made consistent with the regenerative capacities of ecosystems, we do not have a sustainable world. Interestingly enough, this involves technical innovations that would replace petrochemical products with more organically derived replacements, such as the carbohydrate economy in which renewable plant matter products would be created and which would reduce the emmisions that foster global warming.[4]

Redefining the Corporation

Much debate has occurred over the last decade about how to make corporations more accountable. Jeff Barber has facilitated a Non-Governmental Organization (NGO) report about the meaning of corporate accountability. Beginning at the Earth Summit, NGOs have been debating the excesses of corporate power and how they must be made accountable if "sustainable development" is going to be realized. This report is addressed to the United Nations Commission on Sustainable Development (CSD) in the hope that it would become recognized by governments that corporate accountability is necessary, and that they must monitor, assess and hold liable corporations that ignore the social and environmental consequences of their practices.This will require greater public access to information about corporate practices, elimination of unsustainable subsidies to corporate wrongdoers, and clean production. But local communities must be empowered against corporate blackmail, and to do this it is essential to reduce the political influence of corporations on governance structures.

Even when it is understood that this statement is aimed primarily at the governments coming to the CSD, many commentors on this statement find it inadequate. For example, Ward Morehouse argues:

> Basically, my concern with your statement stems from my conviction that the regulatory regime, which has been the central arena of struggle against corporate power, has failed, and that the main issue in a democracy where the people are sovereign is not greater "accountability" but more effective democratic control. For too long, in my view, we have allowed corporations define us and our relationship to them rather than, as it should be in a democracy, we the people defining corporations.

> To put the matter in a form of a question: How can we hope to achieve true democracy as long as so much power and wealth are concentrated in so few hands? It is this concentration of wealth and power that we need to attack as we struggle to create a society characterized by the institutions that disperse rather than concentrate, wealth and power.

This position is argued by Richard Grossman in "Only the People Can Be Socially Responsible," where he reflects critically that as we get further in time from the American revolution, the less the majority act like a sovereign people. Earlier corporations were defined as artifical entities with no inherent rights of their own and constructed by law to serve the common good. But a great step in the opposite direction occured in 1886 when the Supreme Court ruled in *Santa Clara County v. Southern Pacific Railroad* that a private corporation was a natural person before the law and therefore entitled to the protection of the Bill of Rights. Only the Populists understood that this was a concession of people's sovereignty to corporations, a taking of rights and powers away from the people.

Therefore the assumption that the corporations can become socially responsible continues the legal fiction of them being a "person"—only the people can be socially responsible. We have to re-embed them in a framework of responsive law that permits sovereign citizens to take action—to redefine the corporation, whenever and whereever essential.

Notes

1. Karl Polanyi, *The Great Transformation,* Boston: Beacon Press, 1957.

2. See Lewis Solomon's book on *Rethinking Our Centralized Monetary System: The Case for a System of Local Currencies,* Westport, CT: Praeger Publishers, 1996.

3. Andre Gorz, author of *Critique of Economic Reason* (New York: Verso, 1988) is one of the most persuasive advocates for limiting the work week and re-orienting lifestyles to "enoughness," on the one hand, and the expansion of autonomous activities, on the other.

4. See Faye Duchin et al., *The Future of the Environment: Ecolgical Economics and Technological Change* (Cary, NC: Oxford University Press, 1995) for a comprehensive treatment of these issues.

A General Agreement on a New Economy (GANE): Work in a Sustainable Society*

Ruth Caplan

Roughly a trillion dollars are exchanged daily in a speculative frenzy which has little to do with the production of goods and services. The stock market beckons all comers with the promise of income without work. Robots are programmed to replace workers on the assembly line. The end of work is proclaimed. Yet children are starving, bridges are crumbling, unemployed inner-city youth are dying from drug wars fought over sales territories, and a general malaise descends on working families who once could look forward to secure jobs.

The global economy, rife with such internal contradictions, is presented by political leaders and their economic mentors as the inevitable culmination of economic progress. Free trade agreements such as NAFTA and the General Agreement on Tariffs and Trade or GATT are considered to be prerequisites to such progress. Reformers argue that if we just get rid of sweatshops and stop advertising cigarettes to children, we will be able to continue on the global road to progress.

By contrast, the General Agreement on a New Economy (GANE), not GATT, is premised on the idea that people have the right to ask about the purpose of the economy and to imagine together how an

---

* Readers can share their own ideas by visiting the GANE website at (http://www.greenecon.org/gane) and sending e-mail from the site or by writing to the Economics Working Group at 3407 34th Place, NW, Washington, D.C. 20016.

107

economy could be structured to meet the needs of families and communities. It has evolved as a result of the ideas and feedback from people across the country. It will continue to evolve, weaving together the vibrant colors and wonderful textures of people's experiences and insights into a new vision for our economy.

GANE begins with three fundamental values: environmental sustainability, equity and meaningful work. Each value causes fundamental questions to be raised about the economy. For instance, if environmental sustainability includes the goal of goods being durable, reusable, repairable and ultimately recyclable, then how will the unneeded manufacturing jobs be replaced? If some communities have more resources than others, will only the rich become sustainable? When investment decisions are based on achieving the highest rate of return, how can the needed resources be directed toward meaningful work in our communities?

Several true stories have helped to shape GANE. The first goes back to the Great Society program under President Lyndon Johnson which created neighborhood health centers. One center was located in Mound Bayou, Mississippi, a very poor region where the cotton sharecropping jobs had been lost due to introduction of the four-row cotton picker. Dr. Jack Geiger of Tufts University and his team began their work by holding meetings throughout the area to learn about local health needs. As a result of these meetings, when the clinic pharmacy opened it dispensed food in response to local needs. When challenged by Washington bureaucrats who thought pharmacies should just dispense drugs, Geiger responded, "The last time we looked in the book, the specific therapy for malnutrition was food." To the credit of Washington's much maligned bureaucrats, that is just what the Delta Health Center continued to dispense.

Then the sharecroppers got organized, pooled their meager resources and, with financial assistance from Washington, obtained land. Within nine months they had more than enough food to feed everyone in the region. Local sustainability in a very poor region was made possible by federal funds provided in response to local initiative and need.

This story informed the drafting of the Health Service Act in the late 1970s by Leonard Rodberg working with health advocacy organizations. The act, introduced each session by Representative Ron Dellums, envisions the provision of community-based health services through a bottom-up process of community federalism where regional and federal functions are rooted in the level below. The concept of community federalism, applied more broadly to sustainability, has now become a core part of GANE's conceptualization of how to build a locally rooted, sustainable economy.

GANE also builds on the Chattanooga experience in the early 1980s. At that time, Chattanooga was the most polluted city in the nation and the polluting industries had departed, leaving high levels of unemployment and despair in their wake. When a few citizens refused to give up hope and formed Chattanooga Venture, they initiated a visioning process that drew people together across race and class to talk about what kind of future they wanted for their city. This resulted in Chattanooga mobilizing on many fronts—building a fresh water aquarium with local venture capital, starting a battered women's shelter with volunteer labor and rehabilitating housing in an historic African-American neighborhood threatened by expansion of a major hospital. The transformative nature of the visioning experience is reflected in the fact that the local banks, which had been redlining, joined with the U.S. Department of Housing and Urban Development in financing the housing rehabilitation. Again, a local/federal partnership was formed to respond to local initiative and need.

Together these stories point to a new paradigm for the economy that is resonant with Karl Polanyi's concept of embedding the economy in the society.

In GANE, the economy begins at the local level with a visioning process to establish community needs linked to an environmentally and socially sustainable future, not just individual needs so readily manipulated by the marketeers. As in Chattanooga, it is essential that this visioning process involve all segments of the community.

Once community needs have been democratically identified, there is the potential for creating work that responds to these needs and that derives its meaning within the community context. But if the work is to provide liveable incomes, there must be a way to pay the workers. A process for accumulating and employing local capital is needed. This can be internally generated from shared savings and local pension funds invested in a community bank which is available for local capital needs. It can also come from local philanthropy and venture capital being invested locally where the return is partly measured by the increased social and environmental health of the community rather than just the highest dollar return. Some of the work can be supported by local currency as is done in Ithaca, New York, with Ithaca Dollars, a form of Time Dollars.

But if there is to be equity in such a system, federal funds are needed to supplement available local capital. Both Mound Bayou and Chattanooga demonstrate how such funding can be part of a successful partnership. GANE generalizes this approach by assuming that federal funds will be provided to communities on a per capita basis, once a democratic community visioning process has been completed and plans for implementation are in place.

This then is the essence of embedding the economy in the society at the community level; however, unless the need for larger scale investments is taken into account, most of the economy will remain unrooted in society. It is also essential that local communities' efforts to become sustainable be supported by the overall structure of the economy. This is where the concept of community federalism comes into play, pointing to the need for regional and federal functions, with accountability back to the local level.

At the regional level, GANE suggests the following functions:

- *Assessing regional sustainability.* Equity demands that sustainable communities are not created by externalizing social and environmental costs onto other communities. A community could recycle, reuse, repair; use solar, wind and biogas; have composting toilets and bike paths—the whole nine yards—and be enclosed with a wall and a guard at the gate, bringing in low-paid nannies, housekeepers and gardeners who live in communities that could not afford such sustainable luxuries. To avoid such scenarios, regional assessment of sustainability, mutual assistance and federal funding are needed.

- *Regional economic activities.* Even in an environmentally sustainable economy, there is a need for developing specialized, capital-intensive economic activities beyond the local level. One can envision regional training schools in sustainability techniques, where communities can learn from each other—specialized health centers, manufacturing centers for windmills and photovoltaic cells, re-manufacturing centers for appliances and computers, to name just a few possibilities.

As implied by the use of the term community federalism, GANE also envisions a federal role which could include:

- *Remediation of ecological and social problems arising from past and ongoing unsustainable activities.* This includes continuation and expansion of present federal environmental functions, such as ensuring the clean-up of privately and publicly generated pollution and preventing ongoing pollution. It also includes setting appropriate minimum standards for protecting workers, communities and natural resources and providing appropriate assistance to those for whom the present economic system does not yet generate sufficient work at liveable wages or who are unable to work.

- *Support for conversion to sustainable economic activities.* This includes federal funding for community and regional functions.

- *Assessment of national progress.* GANE suggests an Index of Sustainable Well-Being to measure progress toward sustainability, equity and full employment, with an annual report from the President to assess national progress on these dimensions.

- *Corporate accountability.* Transnational corporations, powered by ready access to global investment funds, can readily undermine efforts at building sustainable communities and regions. Further, all corporations should be held publicly accountable for contributing to the country's sustainable well-being. Corporate charters have the potential to be an important tool for ensuring this accountability. Charters were originally granted by states under strict control of state legislatures with limited duration and clear public purpose. Today the public purpose of contributing to a sustainable economy should be included in all corporate charters.

Finally, GANE raises issues related to sustainable trade. No community or even region can manufacture or remanufacture what it needs or grow all its food, cotton and wool. Climate, raw resources, specialized expertise give some locations absolute advantage in production over others. How can trade be encouraged that will meet these needs as close to home as possible so that an integrated regional economy can emerge? Should communities and regions have a right to determine what goods and services they want to exchange locally, thus preventing their commodification in the global marketplace? Is it possible for people to retain their own cultural and spiritual expressions without being tarnished by such commodification?

The elements of GANE described here have emerged from dialogue taking place across the country. GANE is not the answer; it is a process of exploration to find a path to a sustainable economy.

Biodiversity and Sustainable Agriculture

Vandana Shiva*

I am especially attracted to biodiversity as a central focus of my work because it brings together the larger philosophical issues of, on the one hand, the democracy of life and the intrinsic value of species and, on the other, very practical activities, such as the creation of living seed banks. It also brings in important questions of individual property rights. The biodiversity issue connects all these concerns in a way that is less obvious for, say, climate change. It also connects directly to the equity issues relating to the right of all people for access to a means of livelihood and a place on the earth.

Some environmentalists believe that to protect biodiversity you must exclude people. In their view, you either have production or you have protection. I have seen farms as beautiful as a native forest. I feel it important to bring ecology and biodiversity into the heart of production rather than keeping it outside. The real issue for both people and nature is the extent to which control over seeds and other genetic materials is becoming increasingly concentrated in the hands of those whose only interest is profits.

---

* Vandana Shiva, writer and science policy advocate, is a contributing editor of the PCDForum, a member of the Third World Network and director of the Research Foundation for Science, Technology and Natural Resource Policy, A-60 Hauz Khas, New Delhi 110 016, tel: 91-11-696-8077/685-6795; fax: 91-11-685-6795/462-6699; e-mail: twn@unv.ernet.in.

In India, agriculture provides livelihoods for more people than any other sector. It also has been the cutting edge of global corporate penetration of the Indian economy. The General Agreement on Tariffs and Trade (GATT) has been one of the main instruments of monopoly penetration. Specifically, the intellectual property rights regimes being put into place through GATT, set the stage for foreign corporations to gain a total monopoly control of our food production by displacing traditional seed varieties with patented hybrids. My work on this issue has been a great education, leading me to an understanding of crops and varieties of which I previously had no idea.

This work is making me more optimistic that, if you create the right conditions, people will come to see the whole economic system in a different light and will choose the sustainability option. It has, in fact, taken the corporate sector many years and millions of dollars of propaganda to make people dependent on the unsustainable agricultural practices that generate enormous profits for global agribusiness.

Let me explain more specifically what this means in India. Typical, traditional small farms feature richly diverse intercropping methods. Through generations, the farmers have developed sophisticated systems for selecting and improving the seed varieties they plant. The methods are integrated into their rituals and are usually the responsibility of the women. It is also a well-established cultural tradition that families share and exchange seeds so that a farmer whose seeds have not done well will have his seed stock replenished from the stocks of a farmer whose seeds have proven more vigorous. For example, it is a widespread ritual practice for each family to plant nine seeds in a pot on New Years day. Nine days later the women carry all their seed pots to the river bank where they compare results to see whose seeds have done well and whose have not. Exchanges are arranged based on these results, so that when it is time to plant, all families are planting the best available seeds and thus optimizing the overall village food supply.

The Green Revolution brought a dependence on chemicals and credit. However, it was a public program that gave farmers some recourse. For example, when unfavorable weather or prices meant many farmers could not repay their loans, they were able to pressure politicians to gain forgiveness of their debts. So they rarely risked losing their land. Furthermore, while the hybrid seeds of the Green Revolution tended to lose their germination potency over four or five generation, the seeds were publicly available and farmers were able to reproduce much of their own seed.

Then in 1992, the global agribusiness firm, Cargil, came in with a program to convert farmers to hybrid seeds that have both an intensive dependence on chemicals and irrigation and that do not reproduce themselves. Farmers who use these seeds must come back to replenish their seed each year from a company that has no accountability to them. The credit is also arranged by the company, with no possibility of forgiveness in the case of crop failures or low prices. The farmer bears all the risk, while most of profits go to the corporation. There is thus a significant power shift from the community to the corporation. To draw the farmers into its system, Cargil introduced its seeds through massive promotions that involved providing farmers with free seeds and inputs over two or three seasons. They also helped farmers arrange credit for irrigation or other farming infrastructure needs as part of the package.

By the time the promotional period is over and the farmers are expected to start buying seeds and other inputs, their traditional seeds have either been lost or have degenerated. Since Cargil introduces its promotion to all the farmers in adjacent villages, the traditional seed stocks of entire regions are wiped out, leaving the farmers dependent on the seeds to which Cargil holds the intellectual property rights. Thus, in a period of only two to three years, Cargil is able both to destroy the biodiversity maintained by the living seed banks of the farmers and convert once independent farmers to dependence on Cargil-supplied seeds, chemicals, and credit. This highlights the extent to which biodiversity is a political as well as a biological necessity.

Even worse, many small farmers find that in the two or three years the company has been providing free inputs; the debts acquired in improving their farming infrastructure have added up. Many eventually lose their land to the financiers, who sell it to the large corporations that are consolidating small farm plots into agricultural estates producing for export with the aid of government subsidies provided under the economic globalization regimes. Corporate export agriculture is actually quite new in India, but is expanding rapidly under the encouragement of policies introduced though the World Bank and the GATT.

I am helping farmers counter this destructive intrusion through three practical actions: establishing living seed banks, training farmers in chemical-free sustainable agriculture methods, and engaging in policy advocacy with the Indian government to oppose legislation aimed at implementing various of the GATT provisions harmful to our small farmers.

More conventional approaches to seed banks separate the conservation of genetic material from food production. Our approach builds on traditional practice, merging conservation with alternative production methods—thus the term "living seed banks." We have seed banks in about six states. These are basically *in situ* seed banks that exist on farmers fields and in their exchange networks. They are maintained by farmers who identify themselves as "seed keepers" for the community.

The participating farmers continually regenerate the seeds through their diversified cropping practices and participate in seed exchange networks. Biodiversity, food security and farmer independence are simultaneously maintained. Our program has saved roughly 400 rice varieties, 200 millet varieties and 200 or more varieties of pulses and legumes. We did a national exhibition of all of these last winter. I asked the farmers to cook all their local dishes. The farmers have always been made to feel that their diets are inferior to city diets. Their local dishes were almost completely sold out in the first hour because people found them so attractive and tasty. This is also helping to create a new pride in local cultural and biological diversity.

In some areas, we have whole generations of farmers who know nothing other than chemical agriculture. They have lost confidence in the non-chemical methods. Our goal is to get them completely off chemicals by encouraging them to make a transition to sustainable organic agriculture over a period of four years. They start by converting a quarter of their farm to sustainable methods in the first year and add an additional quarter each following year.

The advocates of chemical agriculture try to scare us into believing that chemical agriculture is the only way we can feed the world's population. Their data, however, do not take into account the full output of biodiverse farming methods. Once the diversity is taken into account there is no loss of output. Most of the time chemical agriculture means monocropping of, say, tomatoes or rice. Successful organic agriculture almost always involves diverse agroforestry farming systems featuring significant diversity. You need to do an across-the-board output analysis to assess the productivity of such systems—looking at total production of usable biomass.

It is also necessary to take input costs into account. I have created a special matrix form for the farmers to use in assessing their results in relation to the replenishment of soil fertility, the contributions to household food security and consumption, and earnings from the marketed surplus. We find consistently that a diversified organic farm can enjoy an increased monetary income, an improved diet and better biological maintenance of the land.

We still have many regions in India where the farmers have not been hooked on chemical agriculture and much of our attention is focused here. As, obviously, there are advantages to getting to the farmers before the corporations do, I supply them with information from other farmers, other regions and other countries. This helps them to appreciate their own knowledge and the benefits of controlling their technology and to understand the implications of responding to the corporate promotions.

We also work with them to improve their traditional diversified, non-chemical methods. Last year we formed a national alliance on sustainable agriculture to do much of the sustainable agriculture training. The movement is now spreading to other regions, and we are encouraging the farmers to go out and recruit others.

Our policy work simultaneously addresses biodiversity, intellectual property rights and globalization. I am now working with the ministries of environment and agriculture to write a section on biodiversity for India's Ninth Five Year Development Plan. We have also been successful in blocking proposed intellectual property rights legislation that would have created the greatest problems. We are in fact moving to counter the push for intellectual property with our own efforts to build concepts of community and collective rights into the Indian legal system. We are trying to undo the model of agricultural development that makes it appear we can afford to get rid of most of our small farmers. The setting up of the living seed banks is one example of our efforts to articulate a different model.

The politics of knowledge has long been important to me. It is in many respects a question of whose knowledge is recognized as having value and whose is not. The monopolization of knowledge through intellectual property rights systematically devalues traditional knowledge. Yet, I am fascinated by how much there is to study in regard to small farmers and peasants and the knowledge they have created through systematic observation and traditional practice over hundreds and thousands of years. They have so much to teach us.

I also believe the food issue lends itself to local activism in our time, in part because it involves such a strong mutuality of interest between producer and consumer. The small producers want to survive and urban consumers want healthful, tasty and uncontaminated food.

There are parallel issues with regard to the health care system. I put the patenting of indigenous medicines alongside the patenting of seeds. Some 70 percent of Indians are still dependent on the non-Western health care systems. The practitioners of our traditional ayurvedic system of medicine have no concept of intellectual property rights. They do not know anything about the intellectual implications of patent rights. Indeed, they have a view of health care that is very different from the commercialized Western concept and points to alternative, non-commercial ways of thinking about health system organization. Here you have a whole tradition where the healer does not charge a fee. They wait for a gift. Furthermore, society is organized in a way that assures the healers are honored and supported by the community. It stems from a different way of valuing knowledge and its use in the service of society.

[Vandana offered the following comments on the state of the movement]:

I think the movement is stronger than it realizes and that corporate rule is weaker and more vulnerable than we imagine. The real weakness of our movement is that we have not organized strategically on a long-term basis. We tend to be primarily reactive, choosing and planning our campaigns from year to year. Many of us need to sit together to develop a strategic plan for the next 20 years. Such a plan should strive to protect the diverse and sustainable systems of production wherever they exist while at the same time addressing related concerns coming out of the heart of industrial society. We have not seriously worked on this kind of convergence yet.

Occasionally, a tribal group will get the help of an environmental group in stemming the erosion of cultural and ecological diversity. There is also a growing ecological consciousness of the people from the industrial world, who feel a need to create new alternatives within their own societies. However, we have not yet really linked the efforts of those who are trying to save themselves and those who want to move into another alternative such that the two efforts become mutually supportive.

There are opportunities to make such links in nearly every sector. One example is a Third World network meeting on the threat of genetic engineering that I organized. We linked the concerns of traditional societies whose heritage is being threatened with warnings about the dangers of genetic engineering being raised by the modern biologists. The results were far more powerful than we had imagined. We even managed to get a provision in the biodiversity treaty.

There is potential in such linkages to help people more clearly see and act on the possibilities that exist to reclaim space from corporate monopolies. Health care is an example. Last summer I was teaching a course at York University in Toronto, Canada, where I had a student who was a volunteer in the local health center in the immigrant part of the city. The center had lost all of its paid doctors as a result of budget cuts. So they went out and found women from the immigrant communities who knew traditional health practices. They then developed new health care programs around these women. This is just one example of the possibilities for transferring skills and approaches from traditional sectors.

Realizing that we have the possibility of existing outside of the corporate-ruled system is one of the most important steps toward weakening the hold corporate rule has on us. While there is need for flexible adaptation, I think most of the ingredients of a more sustainable and humane existence are already available to us. The main task is to recognize them and bring them together into the right mix.

Pennsylvania's Success with Local Tax Reform:
An Earth Trustee Policy Approach

John McConnell and Alanna Hartzok *

The earth as the birthright of all people is the paramount human right that we must now affirm. Earth's vast lands and natural resources must not only be carefully stewarded but also fairly shared. It is time to replace welfare with "earthshare." The value of our land and natural resources is the appropriate source of funding for community needs to educate children and provide for a safe and secure environment. The earth should not be a source of private profit, as it was the creation of no human effort.

The good news is that the "Liberty State" of Pennsylvania and specifically 15 cities in Pennsylvania, have been leading the country and indeed the world in pioneering a fair, efficient and effective local tax reform based on earthshare principles.

Rarely understood is the fact that the property tax is actually of two types—one upon building values, and the other upon land values. This distinction is an important one, as these two types of taxes have significantly different impacts on incentive motives and development results.

Pennsylvania's innovative approach to property tax reform makes this important distinction between land and buildings. The tax is de-

---

* John McConnell is founder of Earth Day and Alanna Hartzok, the United Nations NGO representative for the International Union for Land Value Taxation. For contact addresses, see end of this paper.

creased on buildings, thereby giving the incentive to maintain, restore and improve properties, and the levy on land values is increased, thus discouraging land speculation and profiteering in land. This "split-rate" or "two-tier" tax approach thus frees labor and productive capital while collecting the "earthshares" of the land and resource base to the benefit of the community as a whole. The policy is a practical mechanism whereby earth resources can be fairly shared by all.

There are now 15 Pennsylvania cities using the two-rate approach. Pittsburgh and Scranton were the first to implement this policy, which dates as far back as 1913. Since that time, enabling legislation was passed that gave this option to third-class cities as well.

Among the cities that have adopted the two-rate system, there is a wide spread in the land-to-building value tax ratio. For instance, the small city of Aliquippa, which led the way toward the two-rate option for school districts, taxes land 16 times more heavily than buildings. Pittsburgh taxes land at nearly six times the rate of buildings, the Titusville ratio is nearly 9 to 1, while Harrisburg's rate has been 3 to 1 (although it will soon change to 4 to 1).

The Pittsburgh and Harrisburg Stories

Let us now consider how this has worked in Pittsburgh and Harrisburg. Pittsburgh has the longest history of this approach, dating back to 1913. This city has extended its land value tax since that time, so that now land values are taxed six times more heavily than building values.

Pittsburgh has a more compact development pattern than many cities, with the big buildings concentrated in the downtown area, not sprawled across the landscape, as is the case in so many cities where land speculation forces "leapfrog" development. Pittsburgh is a high quality-of-life city on several indicators, and an average priced home is still affordable to the average income household. The city was highlighted in a *Fortune* magazine story (8/8/83) entitled "Higher Taxes that Promote Development." Research, conducted by *Fortune's* real estate editor on the first four cities to go to the two-rate system, independently verified that this approach does indeed encourage economic regeneration in the urban centers.

A recent study by University of Maryland economists, Wallace Oates and Robert Schwab, compared average annual building permit values in Pittsburgh to 14 other eastern cities during the decade before and the decade after Pittsburgh greatly expanded its two-rate tax. The results showed that Pittsburgh had a 70.4 percent increase in building permits while the 15-city average showed a decrease of 14.4 percent of building permits issued. These findings about Pittsburgh's far-superior showing are especially remarkable when it is recalled that this city's traditional basic industry—steel—was undergoing a severe crisis throughout the latter decade.

Harrisburg since 1982 has sustained an economic resurgence that has garnered national acclaim. Harrisburg has twice won the top U.S. community honor as "All-American City," along with the top state recognition from the state Chamber of Business and Industry as "Outstanding Community in Pennsylvania," all because of Harrisburg's development initiatives and progress.

Twelve years ago, under the Federal distress criteria, the city of Harrisburg was considered the second most distressed in the United States. Since then, over $1.2 billion in new investment has occurred, reversing nearly three decades of very serious decline. The two-rate system has been and continues to be one of the key local policies that has been factored into this initial economic success here. The following represent a few of the improvements that have occurred in Harrisburg since 1982:

- The number of vacant structures, over 4,200 in 1982, is today less than 500.

- With a resident population of 53,000, there are 4,700 more city residents today employed than in 1982.

- The crime rate has dropped 22.5 percent since 1981.

- The fire rate has dropped 51 percent since 1982.

These results are especially noteworthy when one considers the fact that 41 percent of the land of Harrisburg cannot be taxed by the city because it is state or non-profit real estate.

Two-Rate Tax Fights Sprawl, Encourages Housing

Low-density, discontinuous land-use development, known as "sprawl," contributes to many of the ills that plague our society. Property tax reform can create economic incentives to reverse this trend, thereby encouraging the use of transit while conserving energy and open space.

The Clean Air Act mandates the achievement of ambient air quality standards. Recent scientific studies show that merely reducing the number of vehicle miles traveled does not provide a commensurate reduction in pollution due to the preponderance of emissions that occur when vehicles are started up and those which occur even when vehicles are idle. Perhaps the most effective way to accomplish this objective is to encourage the development of housing in close proximity to jobs, schools, recreation and shopping. Compact, mixed-use development not only allows people to walk or bike to their destinations, but it also enhances the efficiency of mass transit.

All too often, land near public infrastructure at "Point A" (like a subway station or major road intersection) remains vacant or grossly underutilized because a land owner is waiting for a price in excess of what space users will pay today. This drives developers to seek cheaper sites, farther away from public infrastructure at "Point B." Once this cheaper land is developed and inhabited, the occupants of this area create political pressure to extend the infrastructure from "A" to "B." Once this occurs, land prices at "B" rise, choking off development there (even though additional capacity exists) and driving developers and users farther away to "Point C."

Property tax reform can help create economic incentives to develop land adjacent to public infrastructure and amenities while reducing development pressures at sites farther away. This reform recognizes that the property tax is really two different taxes, with very different economic consequences.

One part of the property tax is a tax on the value of buildings. Because buildings must be produced and maintained in order to have value, a tax on building values is a cost of production. All taxes on production result in lower production and higher prices. The other part of the property tax is a tax on the value of land. Land is not a product of human labor. Because a tax on land cannot be avoided by producing less land, or by moving land from one jurisdiction to another, a tax on land values is not a cost of production but functions as a fee for land use.

Landowners who underutilize valuable land sites with speculative intent contribute to sprawl and the costly, inefficient use of infrastructure. But a land value-based property tax reverses the incentive for land speculation. This type of user fee system curbs speculation and result-ant sprawl by lowering land prices and thus encouraging better utiliza-tion of sites, infrastructure and public transit. To counteract sprawl, the property tax can be reformed by reducing the tax rate applied to build-ing values while increasing the tax rate applied to land values.

Compact development, by utilizing existing infrastructure, conserves natural and financial resources and encourages walking, cycling and public transit. Of course, zoning and other community land-use con-trols should be coordinated to insure appropriate development and the establishment of public open space within the urban area.

Land derives its value from the desirability of its surroundings (lo-cation). Increasing taxes on land discourages speculation and returns to the public economic values that are largely created by public expen-ditures in the first place. A building, on the other hand, derives its value from the owner's work in constructing and maintaining it. Reducing taxes on buildings reduces the cost of housing and home maintenance.

Together, these tax changes promote the clustering of development adjacent to existing infrastructure, reducing development pressure on outlying areas and discouraging urban sprawl. A split-rate tax helps harmonize economic incentives with public policy objectives for af-fordable housing, urban economic development and environmental pro-tection.

A land value tax policy, based on the principle of earth trusteeship, harmonizes the needs for both social equity and environmental safe-guards. Most other policy approaches do little or nothing to combat poor utilization of already-developed land sites, and thus encourage urban sprawl and its many unattractive disadvantages of air pollution due to excessive automobile use, development on scenic rural areas and farmlands and the need for the expansion of costly infrastructure.

Time is of the essence. More citizens of the world need to awaken to the importance of this fair and effective tax reform. Indeed, without an involved citizenry this policy is likely to suffer setbacks rather than movements forward. Despite progress in this direction in Pennsylvania, many members of the state's legislature are nevertheless pushing tax reform options that would further impoverish the middle and lower classes while playing havoc with the environment.

Note: An expanded version of this story of Pennsylvania's tax reform is available from Alanna Hartzok, Pennsylvania Fair Tax Collector, at the below address.

Alanna Hartzok, State Coordinator
Pennsylvania Fair Tax Coalition and
    United Nations NGO Representative
123 South Second Street
Chambersburg, PA 17201
tel/fax: 717-263-2820
e-mail: earthrts@pa.net

For further information regarding Earth Trustee principles and the Earth Magna Charta (http://www.earthsite.org/index.html) contact:

John McConnell, Earth Day Founder
1933 Woodbine Street
Ridgewood, NY 11385
fax: 718-366-7028

Credit for portions of this paper dealing with issues of urban sprawl goes to: Rick Rybeck, c/o Honorable Hilda Mason, Council of the District of Columbia, Washington, D.C. 20004, tel: 202-724-8064.

Local Currency Systems

David Boyle*

It is lunchtime in Ithaca in upstate New York, and the local currency—with special photocopy-proof ink that changes color in the heat —is rolling off the presses.

Printer David St. George has not been arrested, because as long as these notes are not purporting to be dollars, the currency is legal. And they are legal: they are Ithaca Hours, and each Hour is worth $10. From the press, the notes go in the safe until Hours organizer Paul Glover can print the index numbers, turn them into money, and issue them into the community to keep the local economy moving.

Ithaca Hours is one of the most spectacular successes in the increasingly energetic field of local currencies in the United States. But it is not the only model.

For some reason, the idea of computerised LETS systems—500 of which are now thriving around the U.K. and Ireland—has not caught the U.S. imagination, although there are active LETS systems in California and Colorado.

American pioneers have been charting a range of different courses. And, thanks to a grant from the Winston Churchill Trust, I have been watching them, meeting the people behind them and seeing how they work.

---

* David Boyle is editor of *New Economics,* journal of the New Economics Foundation, Universal House, 1st Floor, Vine Court, 112-116 White Chapel Road, London E1-3JE, tel: 44-171-3775696; fax: 44-171-3775720.

I came back across the Atlantic excited at the prospects for local money under the dead hand of the threatened single European currency, after which we may urgently need local solutions and local economic levers like these. The U.S., of course, has its own single currency, and has had it since the Civil War. Some places thrive on it; some patently do not.

And in Ithaca, like many smaller cities in the U.K. as well, one of the key problems is how to make sure local earnings keep circulating locally. They are increasingly siphoned away by distant utilities and big corporations, making the local economy increasingly dependent: the massive chain Wal-mart, for example, sends all their takings from all their stores to Arkansas overnight.

This is an environmental problem too. A dependent local economy with too little cash is unable to produce and grow local goods, and it is replaced by food trucked in from what may be thousands of miles away. People living on the economic margins are even more marginalized.

Ithaca Hours were introduced to keep local money circulating locally, to encourage local farmers and businesses and to provide an income for these people. And it seems to be working. Hours are accepted in 300 local businesses, and have the enthusiastic backing of the chamber of commerce and the mayor, who accepts them for meals in his town center restaurant. One local bank pays staff partly in Hours, and you can pay your bank charges with them too.

The notes include the radical slogan "In Ithaca We Trust," and caused a stir when they recently graced the *Wall Street Journal* and the front of the *New York Times* magazine. "We wouldn't eat out if it weren't for Ithaca Hours," the divorced mother of two told Wall Street's financiers. "It feels terribly good. You see the money's value coming around again and again."

Glover calls this the "community magic act": they print their own currency and somehow it makes everybody better off. "Hours is money with a boundary around it, so it stays in our community. It doesn't come to town, shake a few hands and then wander out across the globe. It reinforces trading locally." He estimates that the 5,700 Hours in circulation have changed hands, with local transactions valued so far at about $1.5 million.

This is how it works. Every two months, Glover publishes his *Ithaca Money* newspaper, and issues new currency to the advertisers in return for their support. More is issued to local community groups, and some in interest-free loans—which are published in the paper to encourage repayment.

A recent issue, No. 29, includes everything from accounting to zipper repair, and a great deal of the basic necessities like food. "We regard U.S. money as funny money, underpinned no longer by gold and silver but by less than nothing—by the trillion dollar national debt," says Glover. "Ithaca Hours, by contrast, are backed by the skills and time of real people."

And following closely in his footsteps are at least 30 other local currencies—from Valley Dollars in Massachusetts to Ka'u Hours in Hawaii.

At the other end of spectrum of U.S. money pioneers is a law professor, who—in contrast to Glover—openly describes his new currency as "funny money." Edgar Cahn worked for Bobby Kennedy as attorney general in the early 1960s. He came up with the idea of a new "social currency"—Time Dollars—when he was in hospital after a heart attack in 1980.

How do you pay for the growing needs of a rapidly growing population, and shrinking budgets? Answer: you invent a new kind of money based on the kind of services neighbors used to do for each other for free.

Time dollars have spread to about 38 of the 50 U.S. states, operated mainly by centers for old people, hospitals, day care centres—matching the needs of old people with the time of neighbors, volunteers or anybody else who are prepared to give it. For this, the volunteers are paid in Time Dollars, and statements are sent out every month.

What they do with these Time Dollars depends on the system. Often they do nothing, or donate them to an elderly relative who needs them more. Sometimes they hang onto them until they are frail enough to need them—a kind of insurance policy. Sometimes they use Time Dollars to pay for services themselves.

In places like Miami and Washington, these "time banks" have developed as community currencies along the lines of LETS in the U.K. In others, like Brooklyn, they have been integrated into the health care system, and used to drive phone services, advice services and other systems which keep older people healthy, independent and in their homes.

But the key difference with Time Dollars is that Professor Cahn has persuaded the tax authorities that—as services from one neighbor to another—they are not taxable. There is a moral dimension to Time Dollars: they are supposed to reward altruism in a way that "real" money fails to. In Time Dollar-thinking, old-fashioned market money has what

Cahn calls a "toxic effect" on communities. "Market economics values what is scarce—not the real work of society, which is caring, loving, being a citizen, a neighbor and a human being," he said. "That work will, I hope, never be so scarce that the market value goes high. So we have to find a way of rewarding contributions to it."

Now Time Dollar projects range from the Cooperative Caring Network—covering 33 organizations and 1,600 people in Washington—to local "time banks" in cities from Honolulu to Maine. Time Dollars fuel security patrols in Ohio and food banks in Washington.

And over the past year, Edgar Cahn has been extending the concept to inner-city youth, another group facing serious neglect from the dollar economy. In five Chicago inner-city state schools, 16-year-olds are being paid to tutor 13-year-olds and younger. In Washington, he has organized youth courts under license from the struggling District of Columbia, where teenage jurors are paid in Time Dollars for trying their peers, who in turn are sentenced to community service for which they are also paid in Time Dollars.

But both projects give rise to a problem: while old people might want lifts to the shops or house painting, inner-city youths have more sophisticated needs that are not necessarily available in the Time Dollar market. The solution is computers—15 million of which are thrown out by American businesses every year. Dr. Cahn and a network of voluntary sector cronies are in the process of setting up a network of workshops to refurbish them to sell for Time Dollars. It is pump-priming the social economy.

Will it be enough to fuel Time Dollars with computers, so that they, in turn, fuel this social revolution? Time will tell. But if it is not a new project in Minneapolis might show a way forward.

Commonweal is the brainchild of Joel Hodroff, a former political activist who has devoted much of the past five years to getting the backing of some of Minnesota's most influential business people. There are two problems, he says, which might provide a solution for each other. We need to fuel the new social economy and to give local currencies real purchasing power. But at the same time, mainstream business is struggling to deal with the problem of waste and overcapacity.

Commonweal has patented a dual-track credit card that carries both social money like Time Dollars and old-fashioned dollars. Cardholders will be able to use a mixture of cash and local money or Time Dollars to buy goods, meals, entertainment. The purpose is quite different to LETS or Hours. Commonweal wants to tackle poverty head-on.

The idea was inspired by a remark by the Canadian inventor of LETS, Michael Linton, about money's measuring function. Why do we run out of money—which measures economic activity—when we never run out of inches and meters to measure distance? A strange and rather abstract thought:

> "On the one hand, our money is a unit of measure that promotes co-operation—like inches, gallons or pounds measure the value of goods and services for exchange in the marketplace," Joel Hodroff told me. Unlike inches, gallons and pounds, you never heard anybody say I can't find enough pounds to weigh this fish, but they do say I can't find enough money to do this or that. You can even have work to be done, people could be doing the work, there could even be adequate raw materials and energy and the money could just not be available.
>
> That's because the other nature of money—the other half of this duality is that our money is a scarce unit of exchange that promotes competition.

So why don't we separate the two functions of money, he asked himself? We can have another currency not based on being scarce, and use that to unlock all that over-production by companies and services.

So here we have it: a solution for those restaurant owners who spend their nights worrying about how to attract people in to eat on a Sunday morning, or airlines who hate flying empty planes across the Atlantic. They do not need the income, but they spend large quantities advertising special offers to take this surplus off their hands. If they could exchange it for a different kind of money altogether, everybody might be happy. We will soon find out: a pilot Commonweal project was launched in Minnesota in September: *New Economics* will report back on progress.

There are other models in the United States, such as the New York-based WomanShare, a scheme through which a group of 80 women trade with each other, an hour for an hour, along the lines of LETS in the U.K., as they share in a revolutionary agenda of personal empowerment and a new project by the author of *Healthy Money for Healthy Communities,* Tom Greco, in Tucson, Arizona.

All go together to make up an experimental spectrum which has yet to emerge in the U.K., however well-developed the U.K. LETS movement has become.

There are those, like Edgar Cahn, whose prime interest is to provide the outcast with more wealth. There are also those—perhaps because the idea grabbed them during 1970s hyper-infation—whose main concern is to provide a new store of value, a currency not subject to the vagueries of international finance.

It is a very American debate, as you would expect from a nation which, apart from the Scots, is the world's greatest economic innovator. As far back as William Jennings Bryan, who famously refused to let mankind be "crucified upon a cross of gold," Americans have argued the merits of free money versus real money. Some element of both are required in any new currency if it is to be of any use to anybody.

But Bob Swann and Susan Witt of the E. F. Schumacher Society, the pioneers of new money in the U.S. and publishers of the newsletter called *Local Currency News,* are particularly concerned that new currencies should base their value on something real.

It was their idea of Deli Dollars in 1989 which began much of the recent interest. When owner Frank Torterelli was refused a bank loan to move the local deli in the Society's home town of Great Barrington, Massachusetts, he sold "Deli Dollars" at $8, to be recouped the following year for $10 worth of deli food. The experiment was an enormous success. Within a month he had raised the $5,000 he needed, and the Deli Dollars were re-appearing as money in the local economy—even in the collection plate of the local church.

Bob and Susan have taken the experiment further in recent years, with Farm Notes and Berk-Shares, and are gearing up for a permanent local currency backed by the Great Barrington banks.

These are experiments with different ideas and they all have, at heart, moral sub-texts that are different. LETS is interested in self-esteem, Hours in local self-determination, Time Dollars on building communities and on what you might call moral regeneration. Commonweal is interested in finding a solution to poverty. They all emphasize different aspects of the experiment. And we may need all of them and more to keep the movement dynamic, community-driven and exciting.

If it has the increasing influence, which seems likely, local money will alter the way we all perceive the other kind of money—what Harold Wilson called the pounds in our pockets—and the role which our collective belief in any currency underpins its value. Conventional money derives its changing value from the psychology of the international market: our hopes, fears, weather patterns and mood swings all affect its value. And if value is a psychological construct, then there must be ways in which collective belief—and collective psychology—could create more of it. Local currencies are showing us how. They have provided a tool for manifesting that non-monetary wealth which we have within ourselves: our neighborliness, our wasted skills, our communities.

But they are demonstrating something else too. Somehow this is something more natural thanWall Street or City of London money: local currencies are providing a self-generating wealth. In the natural world, when a baby sucks at its mother's breast, that act of needing produces more milk. We are moving toward a kind of money that does not depend on scarcity for its value but is generated by need.

This does not mean that local money should be expected to do everything that dollars and pounds can do. But there are many areas where dollars and pounds are simply not effective: they do not build communities, they do not respond to needs, they do not build families and they do not tackle poverty.

Local money does, and we need it because of that.

Contacts

Time Dollars, Inc., P.O. Box 19405, Washington, D.C. 20015-5500, e-mail: timedollar@aol.com.

Commonweal, Inc., P.O. Box 16299, St. Louis Park, MN 55416-0299, fax: 1-612-729-1085.

Ithaca Money, Box 6578, Ithaca, NY 14851, e-mail: hours@lightlink.com.

E. F. Schumacher Society, 140 Jug End Road, Great Barrington, MA 01230, e-mail: efssociety@aol.com.

WomanShare, 680 West End Avenue, New York, NY 10025, e-mail: wshare@aol.com.

Renewing Labor's Power and Vision

Sumner M. Rosen *

New Leaders, New Energies

The first contested election in the four decades since the merger of the AFL (American Federation of Labor) and CIO (Congress of Industrial Organizations) was a wake-up call, especially to those who had consigned American labor to permanent impotence. Events since John Sweeney replaced Lane Kirkland as president of the AFL-CIO in 1995 provide evidence of new energies and a determination to restore labor as a force in economic and political life.

The AFL-CIO committed $35 million to unseat congressional members with clear anti-labor records in the 1996 election. Although not fully successful, this effort demonstrated that labor is again a force of consequence in national politics. The participation of more than 1,000 college students in "Union Summer" helped to focus attention on labor efforts to organize long-forgotten, low-wage workers in many areas and sectors. The media have begun to pay attention to these and other demonstrations of new energy and purpose.

* The author, Emeritus Professor of Social Work at Columbia University, is one of the founders of the National Jobs for All Coalition.

The "Teach-Ins and Their Meaning

A few months after the AFL-CIO election, a distinguished group of 41 artists, writers and academics published an open letter in the *New York Review of Books*, welcoming the new leaders and expressing hope for "rebuilding the labor-intellectual alliance" after decades of separation and mutual distrust. The new leadership responded positively; from these discussions came the first of 20 "teach-ins" at Columbia University in October 1996. Before the first evening plenary, and throughout the next day, long lines had formed, predominantly of young people. Sessions were full; the level of discussion engaged and open. The organizers and the union leaders were impressed and gratified. In the months thereafter, serious discussions addressed how best to restore the issues of economic and social justice in our universities, artistic and cultural life.

Labor's Promise and Problems

LOW UNION DENSITY

The percentage of unionized workers in the wage and salaried labor force in the U.S. has steadily fallen over the past 40 years and is at levels not experienced since before the organizing drives of the 1930s and 1940s. This is true in many other industrial economies as well. Low density means that the great majority of workers are unprotected and unrepresented in their workplaces, in the face of systematic downsizing, stagnant earnings, eroded benefits and reduced job security. In political life, low density weakens labor's ability to defend long-won gains or to speak effectively on behalf of working people as a whole.

LOOSE STRUCTURE

The AFL has long dominated the merged federation. Its tradition of autonomous affiliated national unions prevailed over the more tightly controlled CIO unions in steel, auto and other mass production industries. While corporations were steadily centralizing power through mergers and acquisitions, some of the affiliated unions also tried to increase their size and strength through mergers, but the AFL-CIO remained decentralized. In the era of international economic regimes like the World

Trade Organization (WTO) and the North American Free Trade Agreement (NAFTA), effective national and global strategies will need a greater degree of coordination and strategic direction at the top that many affiliated unions will be reluctant to grant.

SWEENEY'S HISTORY

John Sweeney's career was in the Service Employees International Union (SEIU), representing workers in building service, health care and other sectors where the local economy and political situation is key. His appeal as a candidate for president of the AFL-CIO came in part from his success in building the SEIU into one of the largest national unions. The SEIU is a confederation of semi-autonomous local unions and councils that require diplomatic and negotiating skills in governance and policy. In view of that history, the process of knitting together an effective national voice and presence is bound to be slow.

CORPORATE AND FINANCIAL POWER

Seldom has organized business wielded more power, with greater freedom from constraints imposed by government or labor. Massive business contributions dominate national elections. Top executives are paid far more than their counterparts in other countries in salaries, bonuses and capital distribution. The strong support by the Clinton administration of the WTO and NAFTA agreements serves primarily the purposes of large multinational corporations.

SLACK LABOR MARKETS

During the unsuccessful effort in the mid-1970s to strengthen the 1946 Employment Act, the president of the AFL-CIO, George Meany, observed that "the length of the list of demands in the plant is directly related to the length of the line outside." Efforts to restore power to workers and to achieve the AFL-CIO slogan, "America Needs a Raise," cannot succeed without a labor-led movement to restore full employment to the national policy agenda. Loose labor markets weaken the ability of workers, in or out of unions, to resist downsizing, unfair treatment and other forms of exploitation. As yet, the AFL-CIO has not given this issue the priority it requires.

Signs of Hope and Progress

Recent struggles have helped to highlight widespread abuse and mistreatment of workers and to demonstrate the role of unions in addressing them. With a minimal budget and small staff, the National Labor Committee exposed sweatshop conditions, in the United States and in Central America, for workers who produce garments sold by the Gap, Kathy Lee Gifford, Eddie Bauer, Disney and other high-profile retailers. Reinforcement from religious institutions and the media helped to secure enforceable agreements to end these abuses.

Strikes against excessive overtime and contracting out in the auto industry have won concessions from some giant corporations. Skilled and imaginative international labor cooperation reversed decertification of unions in West Virginia and nationally by Firestone-Bridgestone, now a Japanese-owned multinational corporation.

By contrast, long and bitter efforts to protect union standards in firms in Decatur, Illinois—Staley, Caterpillar and for a time Firestone—were defeated by multinational firms. Overall, the ability of unions to conserve, much less advance, hard-won gains remains limited.

Renewing International Labor Ties

International labor solidarity and cooperation, long a goal of unionists, becomes more important as the global economy pits workers in different countries and economies against one another in scenarios orchestrated by large multinational firms. For decades, the ability of the AFL-CIO to build effective relationships with counterparts in the world was weakened by the rigid anti-communism that dominated the international programs of the federation. Their close collaboration with official U.S. agencies, notably the CIA and the AID, frustrated counterpart unions in other countries, especially the Third World. Even when union effectiveness was declining, the AFL-CIO leadership paid more attention to the prospects of Solidarity in Poland and their other international client unions than to restoring their national effectiveness at home. Even the end of the Cold War failed to change these goals and activities.

The Sweeney administration has begun to reverse this pattern. In 1997, the AFL-CIO hosted for the first time ever representatives of all 15 of the international trade secretariats, representing unions of related sectors—metal, garments, journalism, telecommunications, construction and so forth—in Washington, a clear message of a new direction and focus.

Assessing Prospects

On balance, there are good reasons to be hopeful about labor's ability to stem, if not reverse, its losses and remedy the imbalance in the majority of workplaces. The AFL-CIO has put new energy into the political process and to building bridges with the academic, religious and cultural communities. Business and conservative spokespersons have responded in ways that confirm the view that they sense a challenge to their dominance of political and media discourse.

Deeper Roots of Justice and Renewal

SONG AND STORY

When workers sang "Solidarity Forever" at union meetings, they anticipated the role that "We Shall Overcome" played in the civil rights movement. Songs, plays, films, posters and other forms of expression echo and elevate struggles for justice. Andre Gortz was only partly right when he wrote: ". . . in so-called normal periods no one knows how deeply the working class feels oppressed, exploited, frustrated and dominated . . . ."

CATHOLIC SOCIAL DOCTRINE

Rerum Novarum, Pope John XIII's 1891 encyclical, began more than a century of Catholic analysis and prescription for the problems posed by urbanization and industrialization. The 1986 pastoral letter of the U.S. Conference of Catholic Bishops, "Economic Justice For All," addressed cogently the moral dimension of poverty, discrimination and inequality in the distribution of wealth and income and other features of our modern economy. Their statement, "Full employment is the foundation of a just society," spoke directly to a central problem that remains to be engaged. John Sweeney, like some of his predecessors, is a product of this tradition.

HUMAN RIGHTS

Since its founding in 1919 as part of the Versailles Treaty, the International Labour Organization (ILO) has promulgated more than 175 conventions that specify the conditions of justice and fair treatment for workers and unions. They assume the status of treaties in domestic law when states ratify them. They were important building blocks, when, after World War II, the United Nations took up the question of human rights in the Charter, the 1948 Universal Declaration of Human Rights, and in human rights covenants that have been adopted since then.

The rights of workers to full employment at "just and favourable remuneration ensuring . . . an existence worthy of human dignity" (Charter) has been elaborated on extensively. Human rights advocates, whose primary emphasis has been on the rights of persons to be free of oppressive government action—torture, slavery, unjust imprisonment, unfair trials, etc.—have begun to address the area of economic and social rights, such as employment, social security, health care, family support and the like. These pose new challenges that merit attention:

- They impose positive obligations on governments to meet the material needs of people.

- They apply not only to individuals but to collectivities, including unions.

- They require governments to impose obligations on private institutions, notably employers, both domestic and multinational.

For these reasons, this arena will remain controversial and fiercely contested.

More than "Straws in the Wind": New Developments at the Frontiers

From the early years of the study of worker morale and motivation in the 1920s by Elton Mayo, through the post-war research of Kurt Lewin in the U.S., Eric Trist and the Tavistock Institute in London, the questions around the organization, pace, governance and rewards of work have been extensively studied. This work began to achieve practical importance in Scandinavia under Bertil Gardell and his associates; they were able to test and develop ideas with support from strong unions and social democratic governments in Sweden and Norway.

Robert Karasek and his colleagues helped to disseminate the outcomes and lessons in the U.S.[1]

Sweden's co-determination law links the health of workers to democratic rights and roles in the workplace. Recent work in Sweden, reported below, has extended and deepened the foundations for further reform of work and the workplace.

The building blocks include:

- the preservation, updating and enhancement of workers' skills and knowledge;

- participation in workplace and enterprise decision-making;

- minimal hierarchies in management and oversight; and

- sharing of all relevant information.

Some of these components have been adopted in the U.S., although the firms are few in number. One extensive study by Applebaum and Batt[2] cites three firms: the General Motors Saturn plant, two plants operated by Corning and the Xerox facilities in Webster, New York.

Some union-employer efforts have addressed the needs and prospects of the sector as a whole. The ILGWU—now part of UNITE—for many years provided technological advice and help to garment manufacturers and negotiated how the fruits of the progress that ensued would be shared. More recently UNITE and the employers have developed the Garment Industry Development Corporation, a joint venture to modernize and equip the U.S. industry to cope effectively with the global expansion of garment-making.

In 1994, the Communications Workers of America (CWA) and NYNEX, which serves the New York metropolitan region, negotiated an agreement designed to minimize the burdens on workers from the adaptation to rapid changes in telecommunications. Key features of the agreement included extensive retraining and preference for retrained workers to fill jobs created by new technology. The agreement guaranteed no involuntary layoffs, a flexible spectrum of jobs that displaced workers could fill, and a commitment by the employer to link the design of new jobs the skills and background of workers at risk.[3]

The most comprehensive examination of the new frontiers of work and its control took place in Sweden between 1990 and 1995. It involved 25,000 individual projects, the expenditure of ten billion Swedish crowns (equivalent to US$1.3 billion), and touched in some way more than half of the entire four million Swedish labor force in enterprises of all sizes and sectors, including ABB which employs 30,000 in Sweden and 200,000 worldwide. It examined and tested extensively a wide range of approaches and schools of thought, from co-determination to the Japanese "lean production" model. A special institution—the Swedish Working Life Fund—was created to carry out the work, and was terminated at its conclusion.

Precedents like the Volvo Uddevalla plant, the most ambitious effort to develop an alternative to the assembly line in automobile manufacture, helped to set the stage. Two major concerns shaped this effort:

- Sweden's ability to survive and prosper as a member of the European Economic Community and in the new global economy; and

- the need to reverse the effects of half a century of highly centralized management of economic affairs under social democracy, which had left unattended the workplace dynamics that are at the heart of the economy's ability to produce and compete.

Evaluation is still in an early stage but some conclusions have begun to emerge, summarized in one report: "The most successful changes as far as productivity is concerned emanate from a development organization characterized by active involvement by all major levels and groups within the organization." The more inclusive and extensive the participation, the stronger and more positive are the results. Changes of this scope have shown a positive effect on workers' health.

Controlling Computer-Based Technology

We have no shortage of doomsday scenarios that foretell a jobless future for most, computer bondage for the rest. When Taylorist-Fordist systems are displaced in one phase of work, they find new settings in others. Nor can one doubt that in many workplaces those who manipulate computer keyboards are closely monitored, subject to health risks and reduced to serving as extensions of the machine in ways made familiar in *City Lights*, a Chaplin masterpiece.

There is much more to this story. Swedish firms and unions developed modes of computer-based design and production that preserved and enhanced workers' skills and diminished significantly the hierarchic structure of oversight that is a familiar feature of traditional enterprise management. Unions in Sweden and Germany employ highly skilled computer experts to test and validate alternatives to this model of use and have shown that it is both possible and profitable to use computers in ways that empower workers. The Metalworkers Union in the Bologna area in Italy have applied these concepts in the small enterprise manufacturing networks that have achieved world-class levels of competition.

The TCO—Sweden's federation of white collar unions—has established and enforced standards of safety from radiation with many of the world's computer manufacturers. The TCO label is like that of the Underwriters Laboratories, the assurance that safety standards have been met, an impressive accomplishment for a union representing less than 1 percent of the 70 million computer users in the world.

Conclusions: Hope and Caution in Roughly Equal Measure

Every danger, hazard and difficulty has its counterpart in our ability to understand and respond. The problem lies in the preconditions that are necessary to empower these responses. Labor's renewal will help to improve the odds that these preconditions can be met.

We have experienced a long period of shrinking hope and opportunity as power was consolidated in the hands of those who preside over a new gilded age. Nevertheless, truth can speak its message, now as always. We have no alternative to the work we do and the values we treasure.

Notes

1. Robert Karaset et al., *Health Work,* New York: Basic Books, 1990.

2. E. Applebaum and R. Batt, *The New American Workplace,* Ithaca: Cornell University Press, 1994.

3. W. Armstrong, "New Organization of Work: A Human Strategy," unpublished ms.

Moving from Good Intentions to Good Results: Ten Steps to Profitable Environmental Excellence through Environmental Accounting

*Don Stone**

There is a widespread belief that profitability and environmental excellence are in conflict, that to hold strictly to the high standards in the mission and policy statements would be excessively costly and place the firm at a competitive disadvantage to less principled competitors. It is naive to deny power of this argument, especially to owner-managers of small businesses struggling with the demands of rapid growth and intensifying competition. But often the apparent conflict is magnified by the failure to recognize and understand the full environmental cost (which includes the costs of *failing* to be environmentally excellent) that the firm is already incurring or creating. These costs are *real* but traditional accounting has made them invisible. Traditional accounting can even subvert well-designed environmental improvement initiatives by reinforcing pressures to ignore them.

Environmental accounting makes environmental costs visible and promotes understanding of their magnitude, cause and what drives them. This, in turn, facilitates environmental cost management and cost reduction by linking the costs and cost savings with the activities that cause them. It supports the pollution prevention, design-for-the-envi-

* The author is Emeritus Professor of Accounting at University of Massachusetts-Amherst, e-mail: donald.stone@acctg.umass.edu.

ronment approach which has been proven vastly superior to the end-of-the-pipe clean-up and adversarial confrontation mentality of the previous decade.

What follows are ten steps toward *profitable* environmental excellence using environmental accounting. These steps are presented in a logical, developmental order; the first steps generally must precede the later steps to produce effective results. The first few steps do not require well-developed accounting systems or expertise and could benefit even the smallest firms. The more advanced steps do require more sophisticated accounting technology. They require the skill of a business that has recognized the strategic value of management accounting and has begun developing the in-house capability to use emerging new technologies like activity-based costing and management (ABC/ABM) and Cost of Quality accounting (COQA). But whatever the stage of development, all companies can improve their environmental performance through environmental accounting.

Prerequisites: An organization committed to a level of environmental excellence that goes beyond compliance:

- Top management / owner support of environmental excellence;

- Environmental mission statement, policies and objectives in place;

- Bottom-up, buy-in to environmental mission by employees; and

- Resources specifically committed to the environmental agenda.

Environmental accounting will be of little interest or help to a business unless owners and top management have a positive and supportive attitude toward improving environmental performance for strategic and /or ethical reasons. Fortunately this attitude is becoming more prevalent among business owners and managers as "beyond-compliance," environmental excellence is proving to be profitable and to contribute to strategic competitive advantage in many different industries, by firms both large and small. Employees will buy into the environmental mission when top management's supportive attitude is backed up with specific commitment of financial and human resources.

The Ten Steps

1. *Get familiar with your "environmental footprint":* The "environmental footprint" is the material and energy flows into, through and out of your business, and the environmental impacts of these flows.

   • Develop a conceptual model of your business that shows all material and energy inputs and traces of these inputs through the firm into either value-creating products or services, or into non-value-adding leakage and waste. This model can be represented as a diagram in which the business is depicted as a "box" into which flow energy and material inputs (ingredients, packaging materials, water, paper and office supplies, etc.) and out of which flow products, services and waste (any resource use not embodied in value-adding product or service).

   • Refine the overall input-output model into more detailed process flow diagrams that show in higher resolution where product flows, leakage and waste take place at each stage of the design, production, storage, distribution and administrative processes.

   • Review and understand your legal environmental compliance responsibilities with respect to your identified environmental impacts.

   • Quantify the major physical and energy flows shown on the conceptual flow diagrams developed above. Try to get appropriate and reliable physical measures for all the input, product output and waste flows identified in the conceptual model. Since matter is never destroyed, input quantities not traceable into value-adding product *must* be waste, unless it is still sitting on the shop floor waiting to be used.

2. *Identify and understand your environmental costs.* Get a preliminary appreciation of their diversity, dispersion, magnitude and cause. Most companies seriously underestimate their environmental costs. This is due in part to using too narrow a definition of environmental cost that focuses only on the direct costs of environmental compliance activities. Underestimation is made even more likely by the

wide dispersion and indirect nature of many environmental costs. Traditional accounting systems and accountants have not focused on "environmental" as a meaningful category of cost analysis.

- Develop a broad and effective definition of environmental costs: "Environmental costs include *all waste* plus resources used or 'driven' by efforts (activity) to (i) prevent or reduce waste and pollution, (ii) comply with environmental regulations and company environmental policy, and (iii) costs of failing to comply with these environmental regulations and policies."

- Review your existing chart of accounts to identify environmental costs, but recognize that many environmental costs are buried and obscured by traditional accounting systems. Environmental costs can occur in all stages of a company's value chain, from research and design through production, distribution and customer usage, and even beyond to final reuse, recycling or disposal. Use the knowledge gained from the investigation of your firm's material and energy flows ("environmental footprint," Step 1) to identify the more hidden environmental costs. Environmental costs will be related to *activities* connected to these flows and impacts.

- Focus on employees and what they are doing in their routine business activities. Who, and what proportion of their time is devoted to these environmental activities?

- Estimate the approximate magnitude of these environmental costs. Precision is not essential at this point.

3. *Begin tracking and reporting non-financial data on the primary material and energy flows throughout the organization.* Many companies, especially smaller ones, tend to link accounting exclusively with financial measures of performance. However, non-financial measures are often far more relevant, timely and understandable, especially at the operating level where action and corrective action take place. An input-output analysis (Step 1) gets measures of physical flow, but is the result of a special study or audit, and does not collect such measures routinely and systematically. *Systematic* collection and *routine* reporting of non-financial measures provide

the feedback that can support workforce involvement and empowerment essential in achieving environmental excellence.

- Develop systems and procedures to measure and record physical quantities of the key material and energy flows identified in the input-output analysis.

- Relate physical flows to relevant measures of output (e.g., kilowatt hours per pound of product produced) and to organizational unit (department, team).

- Develop baseline measures and benchmarks that support prompt feedback on efficiency and control of waste at the appropriate operational levels. Such measurement provides the basis for effective management and achieving continuous improvement.

- Report promptly and regularly on operating performance with respect to key elements of environmental performance. Reporting should be appropriately related to individual and organizational unit activity so an effective feedback loop is established.

- Develop environmental goals and objectives in quantified terms of measurable environmental performance. Give prominence and publicity to results.

- Recognize and reward success.

4. *Begin tracking and reporting the environmental costs.* The costs identified in Step 2 can be recorded and tracked within the formal accounting system. It is the function of accounting to "make visible." Without meaningful and systematic recording of environmental costs, they will continue to remain, as they have in the past, largely invisible and understated. This applies to *internal* environmental costs, those already being incurred by the firm. All firms also have *external* environmental costs (and benefits) which are caused by firm activity but borne by other entities or society in general. But for most firms, *internal* environmental costs are already sufficiently large and growing to justify the accounting treatment suggested here.

- Tracking and reporting environmental costs will require some modification of the accounting system to create the appropriate categories and accounts. Such formal identification and tracking of environmental costs in the accounts promote greater awareness of the pervasiveness and magnitude of these costs, and is a prerequisite step to effective cost management and cost reduction.

- Begin analyzing environmental costs in terms of *cause* (the *activity* that makes the cost happen, referred to as the *cost driver*), *controllability* (at what level within the organization and by whom is the cost influenced or controlled) and *behavior* (what activity, and over what time frame, makes the cost increase or decrease.)

- Periodically report totals and trends of environmental costs and relate to levels of activity (e.g., production, miles traveled, unit sales, etc.).

- Consider developing a "Cost of Environmental Excellence" reporting system. This is patterned after "Cost of Quality Accounting" (COQA), in which costs of quality failures, detecting failure and preventing failure from happening are recorded and tracked. This seemingly simple step first revealed the magnitude of cost of quality (often as high as 25 percent of sales). Over time, COQA has documented the value of spending to prevent quality defects from happening.

- Consider tracking significant "external" environmental costs and impacts outside the formal accounting system. There is a clear and necessary trend in our society toward "internalizing" these costs through environmental legislation. The strategic-minded firm will want to stay steps ahead of this process by determining where, in the firm's "environmental footprint" there are significant "external" environmental costs being created.

5. *Review decision models and approaches used within the firm with respect to their sensitivity and comprehensiveness relative to environmental costs and environmental impacts.* Most firms use decision models and approaches that were developed before awareness of the magnitude and pervasiveness of environmental costs

and before the need for environmental sensitivity became widespread. "Environmental" decisions were seen mostly in terms of compliance with regulations or coping with threats or penalties for past environmental impacts. Environmental cost and sensitivity dimensions need to be included in all major business decisions.

- Capital budgeting models, especially those related to environmental projects, often ignore "hidden" and "secondary" environmental costs and impacts. New decision protocols have been developed and are continually being refined to mitigate the short-run and direct cost biases that have constrained environmental projects.

- Environmental costs and impacts need to be considered in decisions not generally regarded as "environmental," including sourcing decisions (make or buy), facility retirements, product and process design decisions, and product pricing decisions.

- Ultimately, environmental costs and impacts can only be significantly influenced and controlled at the design stage.

6. *Incorporate environmental objectives, costs and non-financial measures of performance into the formal budgeting and performance measurement system.* Only when the environment is given an equal footing with the other strategic and financial goals and measures of the management control system will environmental excellence emerge as a genuine commitment of organizational effort. Internal accounting and performance measurement and reward systems that ignore environmental costs and goals will subvert well-intentioned environmental policies and strategic initiatives.

- Environmental objectives and cost allowances should be specifically identified and included in managerial budgets for all organizational units.

- Managerial performance reports should include focus on environmental measures, objectives and costs as well as financial and other strategic and operational measures.

- Managerial reward and punishment should also be tied to environmental performance as well as financial performance.

7. *Develop improved methods for assigning environmental costs to products, processes and organizational units.* Use of activity-based costing (ABC) and activity-based management (ABM) holds considerable promise for reducing environmental cost and improving environmental performance. ABC and ABM enhance efforts to consider and control environmental cost at the design stage. ABC and ABM are tools and concepts, which have revolutionized management accounting, and spawned a new, more powerful role and relevance for accounting in sophisticated, globally competitive organizations. These techniques permit linking costs with the activities that create or cause them, and through that link to the products and processes that require those activities. This linking and tracing of costs (ABC) allows a far more accurate assignment of costs to products and processes than traditional accounting methods which spread environmental costs indiscriminately over all products and processes. ABM is based on the recognition that one cannot effectively manage costs directly, but rather must manage the *activities* that cause these costs. ABM determines what activities cost and what drives those activities.

8. *Extend the range of your environmental accounting and analysis beyond the boundaries of your firm through lifecycle analysis (LCA) and value chain analysis.* LCA traces environmental impacts and costs from materials and energy entering your firm back through your suppliers, their suppliers and ultimately to the biosphere from which they are drawn. It also follows your outputs of material and energy (products, services and waste flows) forward through customers and subsequent consumers to final recapture, reuse, recycling or disposal back into the biosphere. Becoming aware and informed of these "upstream" and "downstream" environmental costs and impacts is a key to finding and gaining strategic competitive advantage. Value chain analysis seeks out this strategic competitive advantage by determining where in this path from cradle to grave value is being added (or lost).

LCA begins with the accurate identification of inputs and outputs identified in a comprehensive input-output analysis (Step 1). LCA can be a very complicated and sometimes will produce confusing or contradictory results. But even when undertaken in a piecemeal and ad-hoc fashion, LCA can produce valuable benefits:

- Identify opportunity to add value to your product by product design that reduces -downstream+ environmental costs and impacts to customers and users of your product.

- Identify externalities both upstream and downstream and develop strategies for reducing these costs *before* they become internalized through regulations and fines.

- Provide a foundation for explaining your firm's "environmental footprint" to workers, management and external stakeholders.

9. *Inform your stakeholders of your commitment to and progress toward environmental excellence through external environmental reporting.* Over the past ten years, there has been a steady increase in the amount of environmental disclosure in the published corporate annual reports of U.S. businesses, especially large multinational-national firms. Many companies are also publishing separate "environmental reports," often combined with health and safety concerns. So far, almost all of this reporting is voluntary, and there are no standards or principles that guide methods of measurement or disclosure. Some of this reporting can be dismissed as public relations and promotional effort, but there are also many firms, both large and small, who have significantly extended the emerging concept of environmental accountability to stakeholders. Sun Company, Inc., a large ($10 billion annual sales) oil company began environmental reporting as a CERES signatory, and has evolved this reporting into a state-of-the-art report that includes the active involvement of their independent auditors. Real Goods Trading Company ($16 million annual sales) devotes 20 of the 32 pages in their 1995-96 corporate annual report to a detailed and comprehensive environmental and social report. This company does more than just a good job of being accountable and transparent to its stakeholders; it teaches as well as informs, and would serve as a useful guide to other companies wishing to improve their environmental performance.

Most smaller companies are either not incorporated or closely held, and thus not obligated to provide public disclosure of information on financial performance, let alone environmental performance. Even so, firms that are seriously committed to environmental excellence may find that environmental reporting to external stakeholders will "complete the loop" in their effort to be environmentally proactive and responsible. Smaller firms could use environmental reporting to promote understanding and trust within the local community. Such reporting not only validates their environmental commitment and accomplishment; it also initiates dialogue with external stakeholders and invites their participation in defining environmental excellence.

10. *Commit your organization to the challenging goal of "sustainable development."* This step has been included to affirm the contemporary societal imperative to live and act today in ways that support the continuity (sustainability) and the qualitative improvement (development) of life on the planet into the future, and to remind the reader that this challenge requires more than environmental excellence.

Environmental excellence focuses primarily on increasing resource efficiency and eliminating or reducing waste and pollution. Sustainable development adds to this concern for "eco-efficiency," the additional dimensions of scale (keeping economic activity within the carrying capacity of the biosphere) and distribution (how costs and benefits are distributed among people at the present time (intragenerational equity) and between this generation and future generations (intergenerational equity.) These are societal- and global-level concerns which are difficult to translate and define operationally at the level of the individual firm. Yet, it is clear that individual firm decisions and actions will have significant collective impact on these scale and distribution issues as well as on "eco-efficiency."

Ultimately—and according to many knowledgeable commentators—within the current generation, our global society, including all business organizations, will have to come to terms with the challenge of sustainability. This will most likely alter patterns of production and consumption in dramatic and still unimagined ways. Environmental excellence in the operation of business organizations will certainly be a key component in a sustainable society. Environmental accounting will certainly be a key element in the achievement and maintenance of environmental excellence.

Note: A fuller exposition of these ten steps is available from the author via e-mail: donald.stone@acctg.umass.edu.

References

For an excellent short introduction to environmental accounting, see: U.S. Environmental Protection Agency, *An Introduction to Environmental Accounting as a Business Management Tool: Key Concepts and Terms,* Washington, D.C.: USEPA 742-b-95-002, June 1995.

Also consult the several excellent WEB pages maintained by the USEPA, including: http://es.inel.gov/partners/acctg/acctg.html. *Environmental Accounting Resource Listing* provides a regularly updated, annotated bibliography of books, articles, bibliographies and case studies on all aspects of environmental accounting. It also allows review and downloading of several useful EPA-sponsored reports and studies on environmental accounting, including the *Introduction to Environmental Accounting,* listed above.

http://es.inel.gov/index.html. *Enviroene* provides a single repository for pollution prevention, compliance assurance, and enforcement information and data bases. Included are pollution prevention case studies , technologies, points of contact, environmental statutes, executive orders, regulations and compliance and enforcement policies and guidelines.

For a more comprehensive and in-depth coverage of environmental accounting, see Gray, Bebbington and Walters, *Accounting for the Environment,* New York: Marcus Weiner Publishing, 1993. Lead author Rob Gray is also the founder and head of the Center for Social and Environmental Accounting Research (CSEAR), which covers developments in environmental accounting worldwide and especially in the U.K. and Europe. CSEAR's WEB page address: http://www.dundee.ac.uk/accountancy/csear.htm.

Ditz, Ranganathan and Banks, *Green Ledgers: Case Studies in Corporate Environmental Accounting* (Washington, D.C.: World Resources Institute, 1995) provides a look at environmental accounting "in action" in a variety of business settings. It covers both technical and organizational aspects of conducting studies and implementing environmental accounting procedures.

Marc Epstein's *Measuring Corporate Environmental Performance: Best Practices for Costing and Managing an Effective Environmental Strategy* (Montvale, NJ: Institute of Management Accountants, 1995) surveys and summarizes both theory and practice of environmental accounting in American corporations.

Paul Hawken, *The Ecology of Commerce: a Declaration of Sustainability,* (New York: Harper Business, 1993) provides an excellent discussion of the challenge to and potential role for business in achieving the planetary imperative of sustainable development.

The Natural Step's U.S.-based operations are centered at The Natural Step, 4000 Bridgeway, #102, Sausilito, CA 94965, tel: 415-332-9394; e-mail: TNS@NaturalStep.org.

The Report of The President's Council on Sustainable Development can be found at http://www1.whitehouse.gov/WH/EOP/pcsd/index-plain.html. This report also contains useful guidelines and principles of sustainability.

The Gross National Waste Product

Larry Martin *

Comfortable consumerism has its consequences. Its maintenance leads to a increasingly large flow of natural resources into our economy as products, and out as waste. Pollution, from resource extraction and processing to product use and disposal, leads to multiple costs. The loss of old growth forests, air pollution, visual blight—perhaps even the curious rise in asthma and other chronic diseases—are another consequence. We can all think of costs owed to waste that are not included in the price of disposal.

Yet, in recent years, the price we pay for waste disposal has been dropping. Market forces have led to increased competition for the waste product, thus lowering the price for its disposal. Not a bad deal for Homo economus. As long as we were all maximizing our respective utility, who wants to shed cash to throw things away? Are the consequences also diminished, along with the price of disposal? We know they are not, and that is because, economically speaking, waste and the cost of its consequences does not count for much in the analysis. And unfortunately, the "analysis" does not extend very far past economics.

Examining waste, one begins with resource economics—the supply end of the "optimal use and distribution of goods and services." It is a theory of wealth largely concerned with scarcity. It is traditionally

---

* Larry Martin is an environmental activist, long concerned with the problem of waste in industrialized societies.

discussed from an "open-frontier" perspective of resources, limited only by a society's ability to access them, and a faith in the technological fix and the substitutability of capital (i.e., a suitable substitution will be found when existing supplies are depleted). As incredible as it may seem, by convention, economic growth is not viewed as constrained by the material limits of the natural environment.

"Waste," a by-product of resource consumption, it seems has never quite moved out of the shadow of the garbage man. It is still largely dismissed as an unaccounted cost (externality), and thus does not receive the same respect as "resources" in economic theory. When the cost of waste is addressed at all, it is typically treated as a category of production costs, or may be viewed as an additional cost of consumption. It is either presumed that the costs of waste are assumed by the producer and passed along to the consumer, or they are assumed by the consumer upon disposal of consumption by-products. An example of the latter would be the garbage hauler's fee for residential waste pick-up. In many instances, this cost is shouldered by local governments as an unfunded mandate from the business sector and borne by taxpayers.

Although the *price* of disposal represents dollar amounts traceable on balance sheets, rarely do they reflect consequences, such as health effects from pollution or opportunity costs of increased stress on ecosystems used as waste sinks. An ecosystem may operate as a functional waste receptacle for a long period of time, gradually losing some assimilative capacity, and then quite suddenly collapse from cumulative toxicity, with consequent species die-off and disruption of the natural systems that provided the ecosystem's absorptive qualities. This has been dramatically illustrated off the coast of France, where the once teeming undersea world of Jacques Cousteau has been annihilated by the dumping of toxic and radioactive wastes, for which the price of disposal was limited only to collection and transport to the ocean dumping zone.

Similarly, balance sheets do not include social costs. Economists avoid such social costs as the resentment felt by racial minorities or economically disadvantaged communities toward those they perceive as more fortunate and less impacted by pollution. Do such conditions contribute to racial tensions and debits to the community quality of life? Do they contribute to violence? Since these questions are not tidy to address in economics, they are not considered. That difficult-to-quantify costs are mostly avoided by neo-classical economics is well documented in Herman Daly and John Cobb's 1990 book, *For the Com-*

mon Good (New York: Beacon Press, 1989).

Now consider the following technological fix scenario: the invention of an industrial garbage disposal that zips wastes off into a black hole, never to be a bother to Earth's denizens again. No more pollution? Sound promising?

Would we rather this technological marvel be an expensive device or a cheap one? Economists would have an easy answer. The cheaper one would reduce disposal and management costs associated with waste, and therefore reduce production costs for industry and consumption costs for consumers. Make it cheap so everyone can have one. Make it disposable too, so you can manufacture many of them, achieve an economy of scale and further reduce costs. When it wears out just make it disappear. The price of waste management would approach zero.

Most people, and certainly economists, could only view this as a positive development. But there is still a serious problem remaining even if the waste has disappeared. While folks may be relieved that local environmental conditions and public health may improve in the absence of waste, the integrity of ecological systems, poorly understood and mostly invisible would be severely challenged.

The essential question is how long would it take to export Earth's entire biosphere into a black hole as trash? We can say that the cheaper this magical garbage disposal were to operate, the greater incentive there would be to use it, since we know from experience that costs are a disincentive. There would be a inverse correlation between cost and the export of our planet into the void. The *market solution* for cheap black hole disposal would promote and quicken the export of Earth into a cosmic debris heap.

Our "waste" is part of the various elemental and energy cycles of Earth, and if we could dispose of waste into a black hole, it would constitute a loss of the very elements that make up the Earth's geo-biosphere. We would soon destroy enough of the nutrients, carbon and organic complexes in the biosphere that we severely diminsh nature's, the very dynamic capacity for regeneration.

In this scenario, black hole disposal would result in a faster flow of resources through the economy. Because disposability has been sold to the consumer as convenience, meaning brisker sales for the producer, cheap disposal would unleash the wasteful power of industry and the consuming public. The economy would grow quicker, economists argue, without the brakes of environmental protection. More materials would flow faster from Earth into the void.

When we have an economic theory that only respects costs that can be tallied on balance sheets, without recognition of how social and ecological costs are experienced by living systems, then we have an incomplete concept of the costs of "waste," and thus a dysfunctional resource economics. Until such time as this fact is fully recognized and an alternative is adopted, we will suffer under the delusions of an anachronistic and increasingly destructive theory of wealth. Although we dislike focussing on waste, clearly the absence of an anal perspective has had deleterious consequences. We must put aside our puritanical bias and recognize that the anus is as essential a design as the consumption end.

Elements of an Alternative Resource Economics Model

An essential element is a closed-loop perspective on resource use and management rather than a linear one. We must conclude that waste is not just unwanted pollution, but includes essential resources that are required for a sustainable society. But to call waste resources is an oxymoron. We can only conclude that production by-products (PBPs) must be as carefully designed as products themselves, so that they can cycle through the economy and back into the systems of the biosphere. The same must be true of consumer products, discards must be designed so that they can be managed within closed-loop resource streams. It is not waste until it is wasted.

This design would follow a hierarchy:

- By-product is designed as input to another production process (or more generally a process grade resource). "Discards" would be retrofitted with newer technology or remanufactured.

- By-products would be feasibly processible to recover material value. Discards would be easily dissembled into component pieces for re-use or recycling.

- By-products would be designed or feasibly processible into benign materials that can be reintroduced into natural systems without exceeding their assimilative capacity. Discards would likewise be manageable for reintroduction into natural systems. Energy recovery can be evaluated for application in this phase, but only following maximum recovery of material value. The introduction of biocidal materials into natural systems would not be permitted.

Just as we design products for the client (consumers), we must design our by-product streams as either inputs to other production processes or as inputs back into ecosystems via natural cycles. This requires both a knowledge of when and where compounds and elements can be introduced into natural systems as well as natural assimilation rates. An area where substantial progress is being made is the replacement of petrochemicals with organically derived substitutes. Early auto designs were fueled with alcohol and built of cellulose-based plastics. They were compostable and based on materials more easily assimilated by ecosystems. Today the regulations on petrochemical solvent toxicity have opened a large market for such products as dimethyl sulfoxide derived from wood lignin and far less toxic and more easily assimilated by ecosystems as by-product or discard.

Apologists for "a better life through chemicals" expound on the second law of thermodynamics, cleaving to the conclusion that everything done results in some waste. We need only look to the billion years of life's evolution on Earth to see that while by-products most certainly do issue from billions of anuses, there is no "waste" except that which the Earth radiates into space as long-wave heat energy—and, as far as we know, even that is not waste in the sense of its being unwanted or polluting. The mystery of life forms a web of "resource" flows, or natural systems, where only human perspectives or actions result in "waste." Waste, in essence, is a distinctively anthropomorphic state of mind or activity. We are rather like Gods (or devils, more accurately) in this respect, creating waste from abundance and pollution from paradise.

Our "resources," similarly, are the very stuff of life and only become inanimate materials or stocks of some species or another under the supervision and guidance of our modern economic system. Early societies, dependent on their *local* resources, viewed them with reverence and as a part of their being. As for the second law, it does not mean waste is the product of every action. Although entropy exists as the straight arrow of time within the "life-system" of Earth, very long-term maintenance of low-entropy and "reverse entropy" conditions can be satisfied by the Earth's relationship with the heavens. Earth as a complete living system releases degraded energy received from Sol back to the rest of the universe. Within the open system of energy flowing though Earth, life "reverses" entropy in the biosphere by creating greater complexity and higher entropic states. Natural systems can function as closed-loops without waste because the material flows are constantly nourished by the energy of Sol. Functioning *within* the framework of natural systems and the *constraints* of the solar energy flow, entropy is not a serious concern for Earthlings, but it must be a design consideration.

Our resource economics must be guided by a hierarchy that recognizes that the Earth functions internally as an interlocking series of natural materialand energy cycles driven by energy from the sun that insures recycling of materials as integral elements of life in the biosphere. The fall from grace and banishment from the Garden of Eden can be interpreted as humankind's break with the harmony of the world, and consequent rampage over the Earth reducing life to resources and wealth to waste. Reintegrating our use of materials into the natural systems may not restore us to grace, but it is essential to building a sustainable society.

What we are describing is the nesting of resource economics into the science and art of ecology and the associated natural and physical sciences. The *a priori* is: "thou shalt not compromise life-sustaining systems." One consequence of nesting economics in ecology is that problem-solving becomes more multidisciplinary. In fulfilling an economic objective, we must fulfill the ecological and social objectives simultaneously. This would seem common sense, yet it is the absence of this common sense that sets objectives of different projects at cross-purposes in our society. Economics should not be allowed to profess solutions to the fair distribution of societies' goods and services if the theories that define these actions fail to address the full range of social and ecological consequences.

The Role of Corporate Accountability in Sustainable Development*

Jeffrey Barber

This statement reflects a deepening concern shared by a growing number of people and organizations around the world. Their concern focuses on the need for government to make greater efforts to ensure accountability of corporations to society. In assessing progress since the 1992 UN Conference on Environment and Development, the undersigned NGOs agree on two important points: (1) that corporate responsibility and accountability are essential elements of sustainable development, and (2) the issue of corporate accountability has been seriously neglected by the UN and member states in their follow-up to the Earth Summit.

Responsibility and Accountability Are Both Necessary

A great deal of discussion has taken place on the topic of corporate responsibility, on companies recognizing their own interests within the framework of sustainable development. A significant number of com-

---

* An NGO Statement to the UN Commission on Sustainable Development from the NGO Taskforce on Business and Industry, January 29, 1997. Contact the Integrative Strategies Forum, 1612 K Street, NW, Suite 600, Washington, D.C. 20006, tel: 202-872-5339; fax: 202-331-8166.

panies have indeed made impressive efforts to operate and develop products according to ethical and environmental principles, a fact deserving widespread recognition and appreciation.

Whether this trend toward corporate responsibility is due to enlightened management, customer demand or public pressure, the basic idea is for a company to voluntarily "do the right thing." The aim of the concept is to convince companies—from small, family businesses to transnational corporations—that sustainability and ethical conduct are in the interests of business.

The concept of corporate accountability, on the other hand, refers to the obligation of a company to do the right thing. The aim of corporate accountability is to be sure a company's products and operations are in the interests of society and not harmful. This concept addresses the problem of those companies that refuse to act responsibly; it also addresses those situations in which companies and employees are held prisoner by the competitive demands of the economic system and forced to choose the bottom line. Corporate accountability is especially relevant to the current situation of increasing economic globalization and the unique position of transnational corporations, which in many cases are legally accountable to no one.

Just as individuals in society require both morals and laws to guide their behavior, responsibility and accountability are both necessary to guide corporate conduct. While corporate responsibility is behavior that is encouraged, corporate accountability is behavior that is required. Thus corporate responsibility is a choice of business; corporate accountability is an obligation of government and civil society.

Who Pays for Unsustainable Development?

One ongoing question about implementing Agenda 21 highlights the costs of sustainable development and who will pay. Stubbornly chanting "no new resources," many governments, the G-7 in particular, have shifted responsibility for the costs of sustainable development to corporate investors and financial institutions. In today's world, however, corporate investment activities are too frequently subsidized by non-monetary "external" costs paid by the environment, the poor, children and the elderly, women, indigenous peoples, workers and the unemployed, local communities and the Earth at large.

Despite intentions to adopt full-cost accounting practices, whereby social and environmental costs and assets are integrated, the bottom line of public corporations continues to be its financial return to shareholders. Whereas government is accountable to its citizens, corporations are too often only accountable to their shareholders. While government and industry negotiate the financial price of sustainable development, the world is forced to pay the full costs of environmental devastation, poverty and illness.

The Limits to Self-Regulation

Some businesses, recognizing they are members of a global community, are indeed moving toward greater social and environmental responsibility and sincerely attempting to follow voluntary codes of conduct; however, this is only part of what is needed. There remains a critical need for governments and communities to monitor, assess and, when necessary, hold liable those companies neglecting or ignoring the social and environmental consequences of their behavior. Such liability is not only important to society and environment, but to those companies sincerely trying to be responsible.

Even among companies embracing voluntary social and environmental codes, transparent public reporting is minimal, with best practices publicized and bad practices shrouded in silence. One important issue is double standards, whereby companies act responsible in countries where this is required, behaving quite differently elsewhere. Without full transparent reporting on company practices, the public cannot easily distinguish between responsible practices and manipulative public relations. Communities deserve full information as well as the means to respond to the impacts of business activities affecting their health, safety and environment.

Corporate Accountability Is Essential

Unless corporations are accountable to governments and citizens, answerable for social and environmental costs and benefits beyond the monetary balance sheet, we will not make much progress overcoming the crises which Agenda 21 and similar efforts attempt to address.

We NGOs urge our government representatives and the CSD Secretariat to acknowledge the essential role of corporate accountability in sustainable development, and to address the challenge of ensuring this accountability. In the spirit of partnership, we offer the following recommendations for meeting this challenge.

SEVEN STEPS TOWARD CORPORATE ACCOUNTABILITY

1. *Acknowledge the Importance of Corporate Accountability.* We urge the United Nations and member states to acknowledge:

   (a) that corporate accountability is an element of sustainable development, that business and industry, including transnational corporations, must be accountable to the society which they should ultimately serve; and

   (b) the need to develop or improve governmental and citizen-based mechanisms designed to ensure greater accountability of business and industry, especially transnational corporations.

2. *Establish Mechanisms to Monitor and Assess Corporate Practices.* No central body yet exists to review the various claims of best and worst practices by business and industry, especially transnational corporations. Because of the tremendous impact of investment and business activities, such a body is needed to review and evaluate these impacts and to enable the voice of those affected by these impacts. We recommend that the UN and member states:

   (a) review, assess and report on current national and international legislation, treaties and other mechanisms which address corporate accountability;

   (b) (i) organize national public hearings on the issue of corporate accountability; (ii) establish national and international panels of experts, intergovernmental and non-governmental bodies; and (iii) convene an ongoing international task force of governmental, non-governmental and industry representatives to examine the issue of corporate accountability and international corporate governance, and develop a process for identifying and instituting appropriate international instruments and bodies to ensure greater accountability by business and industry, including TNCs;

(c) develop a central body within the United Nations to evaluate and report on the outcomes of the above hearings, panels and task force; develop appropriate criteria and indicators for tracking trends and identifying needs for response; and provide national and local channels to obtain and review reports by NGOs, local communities and community-based organizations on their experience and concerns about the impacts of transnational corporate practices and plans; and

(d) authorize that UNCTAD play a key role in a revived process of clarifying the obligations of TNCs to host countries as well as to social, economic and environmental sustainability; this role might involve reinstating the Center for Transnational Corporations to its former status and activity.

3. *Strengthen Public Access to Information.* In order for government and civil society to effectively evaluate the positive and negative impacts of different corporate decisions and practices on society and environment, the public as well as government needs to have access to information about such impacts. A serious vacuum continues to exist regarding information available to local communities and the general public about corporate decisions and practices that could, or do, negatively affect their health, well-being and environment. For civil society and government to ensure that specific business decisions and practices are indeed in the interests of society, we recommend that each national government:

(a) develop public education programs to enable citizens and employees with knowledge of the kinds and sources of information available about corporate decisions and practices which may affect them and their communities and to which they have a legal right to know. Such programs should teach citizens how they can access and interpret this information, including how they can pinpoint potential or actual impacts in and on their communities. Part of this education should include skills in developing community-based indicators for community assessments;

(b) enact and enforce Community Right-to-Know legislation and programs whereby citizens are legally empowered with the right to know about the toxic chemicals transported, stored, used and released by industries and individual companies within their communities, and about other potential or actual impacts on their environment, health and safety. Information on toxic substances within a company's products should be made available. Community right to know should also include education for company employees exposed to such chemicals in regard to the implications of and proper treatment for such exposure;

(c) establish and enforce laws requiring regular company reports on their toxic releases, use and storage and to make this information available to citizens. Examples of such laws include the OECD's Pollutant Release and Transfer Registers (PRTRs) and the USA's Toxic Release Inventory (TRI). This information must also be made available to citizens and company employees in an easily understandable format. Countries which do not have the resources to establish such comprehensive systems should receive help from UN organizations and development aid donors;

(d) enact full product labeling as one type of consumer education, in which all materials and their energy intensity is identified for each product, with particular attention to inclusion of toxic substances;

(e) require TNCs and financial institutions to make public the same information as required in their home country to those countries in which they are operating or investing, particularly in countries with lower environmental, health and safety standards and working conditions requirements;

(f) make available to the public lists of direct and indirect subsides, tax breaks and other government incentives to corporations and industries, particularly where there is a question about possible negative environmental or social impacts;

(g) obtain and provide to the public information on financial and other contributions made by companies to political campaigns, parties and lobbying groups; and

(h) require that the UN and member states collect and help disseminate relevant information from and about TNCs on their operations in each country, with inputs from NGOs and community organizations, making this information available internationally, especially to citizen-based organizations and representatives concerned with the impacts of such operations on the health and welfare of people and the environment.

4. *Send the Right Message: Reform Unsustainable Subsidies and Tax-Breaks; Make Wrongdoers Liable.* In discussions about financing sustainable development, the trend has been for the governments of developed countries to reject the need for "new resources," passing on this responsibility to the corporate sector. Furthermore, many countries have been reducing both foreign aid and individual aid (public welfare). On the other hand, insufficient attention and reform efforts are directed to the system of national and local governments' financial aid to corporations through subsidies and tax breaks, sometimes known as "corporate welfare." In far too many cases, this form of state assistance contributes to unsustainable development. Recommended actions are for each government to:

(a) identify those subsidies, tax breaks and other forms of government incentives to corporations which are undeserved, ineffective or encourage practices or products having negative environmental or social impacts;

(b) eliminate such negative subsidies and tax breaks and institute reforms preventing their reoccurrence;

(c) enact ecological tax reform, implementing the most appropriate program for shifting taxes away from environmentally and socially sustainable behavior (which should be encouraged) toward those practices that are unsustainable, unjust and inefficient (which should be discouraged). Suggested examples include: (i) implementing charges on unsustainable practices; (ii) tax differentiation or shifting; (iii) fees on commercial broadcast advertising (i.e., use of public airwaves) to be spent on consumer education; and (iv) creating markets to encourage sustainable consumption and production. The UN should host an international forum in which all countries can address the issue of enacting ecotax reform and moving toward full-cost accounting; and

(d) develop and enforce appropriate liability laws. Deregulation should end where human rights abuses and environmental destruction begin. Appropriate regulations are necessary for corporations to successfully operate. In turn, citizens and public interest groups depend upon the instrument of liability laws to hold specific corporations legally accountable for their actions—particularly companies abusing society's trust and engaging in irresponsible conduct or double standards. Furthermore, evidence shows that companies are more likely to solve environmental and other problems where liability claims are high. It is recommended that governments impose on investors and executive officers strict liability—extending to every country in which they invest or operate—for personal injury or loss of life, property damage and damage to the environment in order to hold them accountable for their decisions. Corporate polluters should be held liable for environmental damage and transboundary pollution, whether or not this damage or pollution results from negligence.Corporations guilty of past damage, even going back one or two decades, should also be held liable for their actions. Citizens and communities should be provided the legal resources where this is needed.

5. *Empower Local Communities.* One NGO criticism of the current emphasis on free trade (e.g., in the WTO and Multilateral Agreement on Investment) is that the economic playing field is being unfairly stacked against small local businesses and farmers and the economies of local communities in favor of greater power and advantages to large transnational corporations. Parallel to the growth of world trade and the size and influence of TNCs is the public perception of governments held hostage by corporate power. To maintain legitimacy as stewards of the public interest, governments need to demonstrate that the health and well-being of local communities has a higher priority than corporate profits. Recommended actions are for national governments to:

(a) promote international agreements and mechanisms that protect local communities from what might be called "corporate blackmail." These include situations in which communities or nations are forced to bid against each other in a downward spiral of give-away incentives to foreign businesses or chains in order to win jobs, undercutting the ability to acquire appropriate tax revenue or to protect the environment and workers' safety. WTO, NAFTA and other such multilateral agreements need to be modified to prevent and not encourage such abuse;

(b) encourage "good neighbor" practices, in which companies, especially foreign companies or national chains: (i) establish meaningful dialogues with the communities in which they locate; (ii) make adequate information available on those processes and practices which may have negative environmental or social impacts; and (iii) provide mechanisms for meaningful public input and participation in company decisions that could impact the community's health and well-being;

(c) support and help create mechanisms by which the public can more actively participate in decision-making processes that may affect them and their communities; one set of recommendations is in the UNECE Convention on Public Participation;

(d) promote national dialogues with local authorities and citizen organizations on economic strategies to promote sustainable community development and local self-reliance. Special attention should be given to the value of local consumption of locally produced goods and services; and

(e) support provided by the UN and member states to local authorities and citizen organizations in developing community-based criteria and indicators for sustainable community development, including full-cost measures of local consumption, production and investment.

6. *Make Clean Production the Standard.* One of the ways in which businesses should be accountable to society is how they produce their products and services. "Clean production" is a concept sometimes reduced to mean only eco-efficiency; however, efficiency is just one aspect of clean production. A major question is whether or not a company's production process results in harm to society or

environment. Since society should expect companies to engage in clean production processes, government and civil society need mechanisms to resolve questions as to what degree production is actually "clean" or possibly harmful, and where to place the burden of proof. Recommended actions are for governments to:

(a) adopt and implement the Precautionary Principle as part of industrial policy, putting the burden of proof on potential polluters to prove that a substance or activity will do no harm, instead of communities having to prove otherwise;

(b) adopt and implement the Preventative Approach in regulating and evaluating production processes, choosing to avoid rather than risk potential harm;

(c) adopt and implement the principle of Extended Producer Responsibility (EPR), in which producers, recognized as accountable for all the environmental and health impacts of their products, are obligated to prevent pollution and reduce resource and energy use in each stage of the product lifecycle through changes in product design and process technology. Product takeback programs, promoting reduction of waste and use of fewer and safer materials, should be implemented. The UN should host an international forum in which all countries address the issue of adopting EPR;

(d) establish and enforce legislation instituting industry- and company-wide toxic and pollution reduction targets;

(e) provide sufficient funding and support to government agencies and community-based monitoring efforts to properly check and enforce progress in meeting pollution reduction targets; and

(f) require annual, independently verified reports from all companies involved in production processes regarding their progress toward clean production goals; these reports should include community impact statements or environmental and social audits for each location in which they have factories or production operations.

7. *Reduce Political Influence of Corporations on Government.* Reform the mechanisms by which corporations, including TNCs, possess and exercise undue political influence over government policy and decision-making, especially in cases where corporate sovereignty and well-being is given higher priority than the health and well-being of local communities and their environment. Recommended actions are:

    (a) for governments to review and implement appropriate reforms to end financial contributions by corporations to political campaigns and lobbying of public representatives; and

    (b) for the UN to convene an international panel to examine and recommend reforms of the global political influence of TNCs on government policy-making. Examples of such influence include financial contributions to political parties and candidates, and investments by corporations in advertising and public relations campaigns to influence government decisions.

Only the People Can Be Socially Responsible

Richard L. Grossman*

I was stimulated to write on this theme after reading "The Role of Corporate Accountability in Sustainable Development," by Jeffrey Barber of the Integrative Strategies Forum.

In 1628, King Charles I granted a charter to the Massachusetts Bay Company. In 1664, the King sent his commissioners to see whether this company had been complying with the terms of the charter. The governors of the company objected, declaring that this investigation infringed upon their rights. On behalf of the King, his commissioners responded:

> The King did not grant away his sovereignty over you when he made you a corporation. When His Majesty gave you power to make wholesome laws, and to administer justice by them, he parted not with his right of judging whether justice was administered accordingly or not. When His Majesty gave you authority over such subjects as live within your jurisdiction, he made them not *your* subjects, nor *you* their supreme authority.[1]

From childhood, this King had been trained to act as a sovereign should. What about us?

By means of the American Revolution, colonists took sovereignty

---

* The author is co-director of the Program on Corporations, Law and Democracy (POCLAD).

from the English monarchy and invested it in themselves. Emerging triumphant from their struggle with King George and Parliament, they decided they would figure out how to govern themselves. Alas, a minority of colonists were united and wealthy enough to define *most* of the human beings in the 13 colonies as property or as non-persons before the law and within the society, with no rights any legal person was bound to respect.

Ours was a terribly screwed-up sovereignty from the beginning. Because of this immoral, atrocious structural mess, whole classes of people had to organize and struggle over centuries to gain recognition as part of the sovereign people—that is, they had to get strong enough as a class to define themselves and not let other people or institutions define them: African Americans, Native Americans, women, debtors, indentured servants and immigrants. To this day, many still must struggle to exercise the rights of persons, to be recognized as persons by law and by society.

Throughout this nation's history, there has always been plenty of genuflecting to democracy and self-governance—check out politicians' Fourth of July orations and corporations' advertisements. But the further each generation gets from the Revolution, the less the majority act like sovereign people. And when it comes to establishing the proper relationship between sovereign people and the corporations we create, recent generations seem to be at a total loss.

Yet, earlier generations were quite clear that a corporation was an artificial, subordinate entity with no inherent rights of its own, and that incorporation was a privilege bestowed by the sovereign. In 1834, for example, the Pennsylvania Legislature declared:

> A corporation in law is just what the incorporation act makes it. It is the creature of the law and may be moulded to any shape or for any purpose that the Legislature may deem most conducive for the common good.[2]

During the 19th century, both law and culture reflected this relationship between sovereign people and their institutions. People understood that they had a civic responsibility not to create artificial entities that could harm the body politic, interfere with the mechanisms of self-governance, assault their sovereignty.

They also understood that they did not elect their agents to positions in government to sell off the sovereignty of the people. In other words, there were human beings who tried to act as sovereign people. One thing they did was to define the *nature* of the corporate bodies they created. If we look at mechanisms of chartering—and at the language in corporate charters, state general incorporation laws and even state constitutions prior to the 20th century—we find precise, defining language that was often mandatory and prohibatory and self-executory in nature. These mechanisms *defined* corporations by denying corporations political and civil rights, by limiting their size, capitalization and duration, by specifying their tasks, and by declaring the people's right to remove from the body politic any corporations which dared to rebel.

Here is an example of language which sovereign people, responding to the rise of corporations after the Civil War, placed in the California Constitution of 1879, and which appears in other state constitutions at about that time:

Article I, section 2: All power is inherent in the people . . . .

Article I, section 10: The people shall have the right freely to assemble together to consult for the common good, to instruct their representatives . . . .

Article XII, section 8: The exercise of the right of eminent domain shall never be so abridged or construed as to prevent the Legislature from taking the property and franchises of incorporated companies and subjecting them to public use the same as the property of individuals, and the exercise of the police power of the State shall never be so abridged or construed as to permit corporations to conduct their business in such manner as to infringe the rights of individuals or the general well-being of the State.[3]

The principal mechanism which sovereign people used during the 19th century to assess whether their corporate creations were of a suitably subordinate nature was called *quo warranto*. The *quo warranto* form of action, as attorney Thomas Linzey has noted,[4] is one of the most ancient of the prerogative writs. In the words of the Delaware Court of Chancery, the remedy of *quo warranto* extends back to time whereof the memory of man runneth not to the contrary.

Quo warranto is simply Latin for "by what authority." All monarchs understood how to use this tool in self-defense. They realized that when a subordinate entity they had created acted "beyond its authority," it was guilty of rebellion and must be terminated.

Sovereignty is in our hands now, but the logic is the same: when the people running a corporation assume rights and powers which the sovereign had not bestowed, or when they assault the sovereign people, this entity becomes an affront to body politic. And like a cancer ravaging a human body, such a rebellious corporation must be cut out of our body politic.

During the first hundred years of these United States, people mobilized so that legislatures, attorneys general and judges would summon corporations to appear and answer to *quo warranto*. In 1890, the highest court in New York State revoked the charter of the North River Sugar Refining Corporation in a unanimous decision:

> The judgment sought against the defendant is one of corporate death. The state which created, asks us to destroy, and the penalty invoked represents the extreme rigor of the law. The life of a corporation is, indeed, less than that of the humblest citizen, and yet it envelopes great accumulations of property, moves and carries in large volume the business and enterprise of the people, and may not be destroyed without clear and abundant reason . . . . Corporations may, and often do, exceed their authority only where private rights are affected. When these are adjusted, all mischief ends and all harm is averted. But where the transgression has a wider scope, and threatens the welfare of the people, they may summon the offender to answer for the abuse of its franchise and the violation of its corporate duty . . . . The abstract idea of a corporation, the legal entity, the impalpable and intangible creation of human thought, is itself a fiction, and has been appropriately described as a figure of speech . . . . The state permits in many ways an aggregation of capital, but, mindful of the possible dangers to the people, overbalancing the benefits, keeps upon it a restraining hand, and maintains over it a prudent supervision, where such aggregation depends upon its permission and grows out of its corporate grants . . . the state, by the creation of the artificial persons constituting the elements of the combination and failing to limit and restrain their powers, becomes itself the responsible creator, the voluntary cause, of an aggregation of capital . . . the defendant corporation has violated its charter, and failed in the performance of its corporate duties, and that in respects so material and important as to justify a judgment of dissolution.[5]

Such a judgment should not be regarded as punishment of the corporation, but rather a vindication of the sovereign people. When our sovereignty has been harmed, we are the ones who must be made whole.

The concept is similar to what Hannah Arendt described in her book *Eichmann in Jerusalem.*

> The wrongdoer is brought to justice because his act has disturbed and gravely endangered the community as a whole, and not because, as in civil suits, damage has been done to individuals who are entitled to reparation. The reparation effected in criminal cases is of an altogether different nature; it is the body politic itself that stands in need of being "repaired," and it is the general public order that has been thrown out of gear and must be restored, as it were. It is, in other words, the law, not the plaintiff, that must prevail.[6]

There is no shortage of court decisions affirming the sovereignty of the American people over corporate fictions, the need to restore the general public order. In *Richardson v. Buhl,* the Nebraska Supreme Court in the late 19th century declared:

> Indeed, it is doubtful if free government can long exist in a country where such enormous amounts of money are . . . accumulated in the vaults of corporations, to be used at discretion in controlling the property and business of the country against the interest of the public and that of the people, for the personal gain and aggrandizement of a few individuals.[7]

The Illinois Supreme Court, in *People ex. rel. Peabody v. Chicago Gas Trust Co.* (1889):

> When a corporation is formed under the general incorporation act, for the purpose of carrying on a lawful business, the law, and not the statement or the license of the certificate must determine what powers can be exercised as incidents of such business . . . To create one corporation that it may destroy the energies of all other corporations of a given kind, and suck their life blood out of them, is not a "lawful purpose."[8]

The Supreme Court of Georgia, in *Railroad Co. v. Collins,* at about the same time:

> All experience has shown that large accumulations of property in hands likely to keep it intact for a long period are dangerous to the public weal. Having perpetual succession, any kind of corporation

has peculiar facilities for such accumulation, and most governments have found it necessary to exercise great caution in their grants of corporate charters. Even religious corporations, professing and in the main, truly, nothing but the general good, have proven obnoxious to this objection, so that in England it was long ago found necessary to restrict them in their powers of acquiring real estate. Freed, as such bodies are, from the sure bounds to the schemes of individuals—the grave—they are able to add field to field, and power to power, until they become entirely too strong for that society which is made of up those whose plans are limited by a single life.[9]

Justices White, Brennan and Marshall, dissenting in a 1976 case, *Bucklely v. Valeo:*

It has long been recognized, however, that the special status of corporations has placed them in a position to control vast amount of economic power which may, if not regulated, dominate not only the economy but also the very heart of our democracy, the electoral process. . . . The State need not permit its own creation to consume it.[10]

Chief Justice Rehnquist, dissenting in the same case:

. . . the blessing of potentially perpetual life and limited liability...so beneficial in the economic sphere [*sic*—RG], poses special dangers in the political sphere.[11]

A great achievement of corporations, as they set out toward the end of the 19th century to transform the law and recreate themselves, was to replace basic tools of sovereign people—chartering, defining incorporation laws, by what authority proceedings and charter revocation—with regulatory and administrative law, new legal doctrines and fines as corporate punishment. The populists understood that these changes amounted to a counter-revolution, and so they resisted with great passion and energy.

Populist farmers and workers were not willing to concede that the corporate form would define work and money, progress and efficiency, productivity and unions, justice and ethical conduct, sustainability and food, harmful and reasonable behaviour. They were not willing to concede that corporations should have the rights and privileges of persons.

So they organized, educated, resisted. They were crushed by the ability of giant corporations to use state and federal government to take rights away from people and bestow them upon corporations.

Along came the Progressives. *They* were willing to let the corporate form become dominant, to shape our culture, to define work and our communities. They, their followers and descendants conceded to the corporation the rights and privileges it had taken from the sovereign people through violence and the decisions of federal judges: personhood and a long list of civil and political rights, such as free speech and property rights, control of investment, production and organization of work. By the beginning of the 20th century, corporations had become sovereign, and they had turned people into consumers, or workers, or whatever the corporation of the moment chose to define humans as.

Public memory of the populists' analysis and their efforts was rapidly wiped clean while the Progressives were fulsomely legitimated and praised. Corporations did such a good job of rewriting history that when the Supreme Court finally began to hold New Deal legislation constitutional in the late 1930s, few understood that it was not the populist agenda of sovereignty over corporations that was being affirmed, but rather the Progressive agenda of conceding power and privilege to corporations as a form of property, of tinkering with corporate behavior at the margins, curbing corporate excess and perfecting the market.

As a result, most people do not acknowledge the massive corporate rebellion which took place. So most citizen efforts against corporations in this century have been struggles against the symptoms of corporate domination in regulatory and administrative law arenas.

But these are *not* arenas of sovereignty. These are stacked-deck proceedings, where people, communities and nature are fundamentally disadvantaged to the constitutional rights of corporations. Here, we cannot demand "by what authority" has corporation X engaged in a pattern of behavior which constitutes an assault upon the sovereign people? Here, we cannot declare a corporation *ultra vires,* or "beyond its authority." To the contrary: regulatory and administrative law only enables us to question specific corporate behaviors, one at a time, usually after the harm has been done—over and over and over again.

In these regulatory and administrative proceedings, both the law and the culture concede to the corporation rights, privileges and powers, which earlier generations knew were illegitimate for corporations to possess. In addition, in these proceedings, the corporation has the rights of natural persons: a human and a corporation meet head on, in a fair fight.

Today our law and culture concede our sovereignty to corporations. So do most of our own citizen organizations dedicated to justice and environmental protection and worker rights and human rights. Consequently, our organizations use their energy and resources to study each corporation as if it were unique, and to contest corporate acts one at a time, as if that could change the nature of corporations.

Folks relentlessly tally corporate assaults, study the regulatory agencies and try to strengthen them. We try to make corporate toxic chemicals and radiation, corporate energy and corporate banking, corporate agriculture and corporate transportation, corporate buying of elections and corporate writing of legislation, and corporate educating our judges and corporate distorting of our schools, a little less bad.

But we do not study who We the People are; how sovereign people should regard ourselves, how sovereign people should act. We need to realize what power and authority we possess, and how we can use it *to define the nature of corporations,* so that we do not have to mobilize around each and every corporate decision that affects our communities, our lives, the planet. We need to grasp that power and authority in order not to have to wage a revolution every time, we must remove a corporate cancer from our midst.

Consider now Jeffrey Barber's paper, which addresses corporate behavior. Three paragraphs on the last page are on the need to "Reduce Political Influence of Corporations on Government." This is backwards. The reason corporations are so dominant and so destructive today is that a century ago corporations took rights and powers away from the people. For example, corporations made themselves into persons under the law *before* most human beings had won their civil and political rights. Corporations' "right to manage" and "free speech" are currently safeguarded by the U.S. Constitution, thanks to legal doctrines concocted by the appointed judges of the federal judiciary.

Is not this an old story? People create what looks to be a nifty machine, a robot, called the corporation. Over time the robots get together and overpower the people. They redesign themselves and reconstruct law and culture so that people fail to remember they created the robots in the first place, that the robots are machines and not alive. For a century, the robots propagandize and indoctrinate each generation of people so they grow up believing that robots are people too, gifts of God and Mother Nature; that they are inevitable and the source of all that is good. How odd that we have been so gullible, so docile, so obedient?

But in the face of what we experience about corporations, of what we know to be true, why are so many people so obedient? Why do we hang on to the hope that the corporation can be made socially responsible? Isn't this an absurd notion? After all, organizations cannot be responsible. This is just not a relevant concept, because a principal purpose of corporations is to protect the managers and directors who run them from responsibility for their decisions.

But people can declare organizations criminal or vile—take a look at the Nuremberg Trials. And people can define organizations, business or government. Again, see the Nuremberg Trials. But only people can be responsible. How? By exercising our sovereign authority over *all* the institutions we create.

We the People are the ones who must be accountable. We are not accountable when we create monster robots which run rampant in our communities and which, in our names, sally forth across the world to wreak havoc upon other places and upon other people's self-governance.

We are not being socially responsible or civically accountable when we do not act like sovereign people.

We are not being socially responsible or civically accountable when we play in corporate arenas by corporate rules.

We are not being socially responsible or civically accountable when we permit our agents in government to bestow our sovereignty upon machines.

We are not being socially responsible or civically accountable when we organize our communities and then go to corporate executives and to the hacks who run corporate front groups and ask them please to cause a little less harm; or when we offer them even more rewards for being a little less dominating.

Sovereign people do not beg of, or negotiate with, subordinate entities which we created. Sovereign people *instruct* subordinate entities. Sovereign people *define* all entities we create. And when a subordinate entity violates the terms of its creation, and undermines our ability to govern ourselves, we are required to move in swiftly and accountably to cut this cancer out of the body politic.

With such deeds do we honor the millions of people who struggled before us to wrest power from tyrants, to define themselves in the face of terror and violence. And we make all struggles for justice and democracy easier by weakening the ability of corporations to make the rules, and to rule over us.

Some might say this is not a practical way to think and act. Why? Because corporations will take away our jobs? Our food? Our toilet paper? Our hospitals? Because we do not know how to run our towns and cities and nation without global corporations? Because they will run away to another state, to another country? Because the Supreme Court has spoken? Because philanthropic corporations will not give us money? Because it's scary? Because it's too late to learn to act as sovereign people?

Because in 1997 it is not realistic for people across the nation and around the world to take away the civil and political rights of all corporations, to take the property rights and real property corporations have seized from human beings and from the Earth?

Yes, and it *is* realistic to keep conceding sovereign powers to corporations, to keep fighting industrial corporations and banking corporations and telemedia corporations and resource extraction corporations and public relations corporations and transportation corporations and educational corporations and insurance corporations and agribusiness corporations and energy corporations and stock market corporations, one at a time forever and ever?

Our president is realistic and practical. On January 10, 1997, President William Jefferson Clinton sent a letter to the mayor of Toledo, Ohio. The mayor had asked the president for help in getting the Chrysler Corporation to build a new Jeep factory within Toledo city limits to replace the ancient one which Chrysler Corporation was closing. The President of the United States, leader of the most powerful nation the world has ever known, elected head of a government always eager to celebrate the uniqueness of its democracy to the point of forcing it upon other nations, wrote:

> ... As I am sure you know, my Administration cannot endorse any potential location for the new production site. My Intergovernmental Affairs staff will be happy to work with you once the Chrysler Board of Directors has made its decision. . . . [12]

Our president may not have a clue, but We the People did not grant away our sovereignty when we made Chrysler into a corporation. When we gave the Chrysler Corporation authority to manufacture automobiles, we did not make the people of Toledo its subjects, nor Chrysler Corporation their supreme authority.

How long shall we the people, the sovereign people, stand hat in hand outside corporate boardrooms waiting to be told our fate? How long until we instruct our representatives to do their constitutional duty? How long until *we* become responsible . . . until *we* become accountable, to our forebears, to ourselves, to our children, to other peoples and species and to the Earth?

Notes

1. Neil Berman, "A Short History of Corporations in Massachusetts," written for POCLAD, October 1995, p. 2.

2. Carter Goodrich, ed., *The Government and the Economy, 1783-1861*, Indianapolis: Bobbs-Merrill, 1967, p. 44 (Report of the Packer Committee of the Pennsylvania Legislature).

3. Excerpts from the "California Constitution of 1879," selected by the author, March 1996 (POCLAD memo).

4. Thomas Linzey, et al., "Brief in Support of Motion for Peremptory Judgment," *Community Environmental Legal Defense Fund v. Thomas Corbett, Attorney General of PA et al.*, Civ. No. 1074 M. D. 1996, p. 4, citing *Wilmington City Railway Co. v. People's Railway Co.*, 47A, 245, 248 (Del. Ch. 1900).

5. *People v. North River Sugar Refining Corp.*, 24 N. E. 834 (1890).

6. Hannah Arendt, *Eichmann in Jerusalem*, New York: Viking Penguin, 1977.

7. *Richardson v. Buhl*, 43 N. W. Rep. 1102.

8. *People ex rel. Peabody v. Chicago Gas Trust Co.*, 130 III. 230, 1889.

9. *Railroad Co. v. Collins*, 40 GA 582.

10. *Buckley v. Valeo*, 424 US 1 (1976).

11. *Ibid.*

12. Letter from Bill Clinton to the Honorable Carleton S. Finkbiner, January 10, 1997, printed in the *Toledo Blade*, 25 January 1997.

Part Three

What Is Real Sustainability?

Chapter 4: Linking Sustainability with Justice

There is a systemic ambiguity of the concept of "sustainable development" that is central to agreements of the United Nations Conference on Environment and Development (UNCED), or the Earth Summit. Many critics have asserted that sorting out the promises of the Earth Summit from its distortions and internal ambiguities is the task of the post-UNCED process. While the UNCED promises greater accountability for climate control, biodiversty, pollution prevention, and the like, the agreements are presented as if this were consistent with expanded economic growth, market commodifications and the implementations of greater "free trade." This chapter documents these discussions and assessments, beginning with an overall analysis of the injustices of the international economy.

Kishor Thanawala's, "Markets and Government in the International Economy," points out that international economic efficiency and value cannot be separated from the fairness and justice essential for equal access to markets and rewards. The power of wealthy countries distorts world trade systems and dominates international agencies like the World Bank and the International Monetary Fund. The existing rules of the game of international trade, "aid" and technology transfers are not consistent with the theories of the national free market systems, and those who see them as continuous have ignored the great inequalities and injustices of the "global economy."

Failures to Implement Sustainable Development

Daphne Wysham, in an analysis "Destroying Orissa, Fueling Climate Change: A Joint Project of the World Bank, Transnational Corporations and G-7 Governments dramatically demonstrates that the Climate Change Convention signed at the Earth Summit by world goverments has been systematically undermined by the actions of the G-7 countries working with the World Bank and transnational corporations. Instead of promoting cheap, clean energy systems, the World Bank has been instrumental in constructing polluting, environmentally and socially destructive development in Orissa. Rather than enabling sustainability and allievating poverty, the Bank and the G-7 countries have aided privatization and deregulation that downgrade their own operating standards while increasing the levels of planetary pollution. Daphne Wysham concludes that "their real priority is not to address climate change, but to circumvent the Climate Convention for their own short-sighted ends, while supporting transnationals from their own countries."

Continuing the assessment of the results of the United Nations Conferences from the Earth Summit to the Beijing Women's conference, the Women's Environment and Development Organization (WEDO) reflects on the failures to relieve global poverty, social deprivation and environmental degradations. Despite the breadth and specificity of international agreements, the globalized market economy has deepened economic polarization between developed and developing nations. Attempts to assign economic value to natural resources have resulted in a distorted notion of private property that justify patents on products, which could not be made without existing local knowledge, and add up to a new form of bio-piracy. Viewing these failures from the perspective of women's participation in creating these agreements, the evaluation continues by presenting what women are doing all over the world to provide leadership for the implementing sustainability.

New Strategies for Sustainabililty with Justice

Ignacio Peon asserts in the essay "Biodiversity, Cultural Diversity and Sustainability" that we need a new sustainable model of development that has a qualitative, post-economic, holistic point of view in which biodiversity and cultural diversity are the cornerstones of a new sustainable model of development. Diverse cultures in every corner of the world can contribute unique solutions for every geoclimatic region of the planet, while the actions of international grassroots development and environment networks become the leaders for designing and implementing a new global institutional framework with the participation of all the social actors.

Peter Montague describes the new project of a "Sustainable America" initiated at a recent conference in Atlanta. Beginning with a hard-headed assessment based on the "ecological footprint analysis," the essay questions the amount of land surface required to produce the flows of materials and energy that sustain us. One conclusion is that the lifestyle of Americans (or Europeans) would require roughly three additional planets the size of planet Earth if it were "globalized." Sustainable America has begun a campaign to organize locally and facilitate coming together nationally to promote policy alternatives that offer a greater degree of citizen control, economic stability and prudent use of ecological resources, together with a greater degree of economic equity.

Markets and Government in the
International Economy

Kishor Thanawala*

*Certain concepts have somehow arisen . . . and insinuated them-
selves into the fabric of human society. These concepts present
profit as the chief spur to economic progress, free competition as
the guiding norm of economics, and private ownership of the means
of production as an absolute right, having no limits nor concomitant social obligations.*

*This unbridled liberalism paves the way for a particular type of
tyranny . . . it results in the "international imperialism of money."*

—Paul VI[1]

This essay examines the role of market forces in promoting economic well-being in the international economy. The role of free markets
in international economics has not come under as much scrutiny as has
the role of free, unregulated economic activity within national borders.
But nations do not exist in a vacuum. Technological progress has penetrated—and, in some cases, completely demolished—the walls sepa-

---

* The author is Professor of Economics at Villanova University, tel: 610-
519-4385; fax: 610-519-6054; e-mail: kthanawa@email.vill.edu. This
abridged version of a paper "Markets and Governments in the International
Economy," presented at the annual meetings of the Allied Social Science
Associations in January 1997, was edited and prepared by Susan Hunt. Responsibility for any errors due to editing and abridging are hers alone.

rating communications and markets in various countries. It is therefore important to discuss some of the limitations of market forces in the global economy.

The View from Mars

To frame the discussion, let us imagine[2] for a moment that during the course of space exploration we stumble upon a civilization in outer space. Upon closer examination, suppose we determine that this civilization has the following characteristics:

- There are approximately 200 households that vary considerably in terms of size.

- There is a very high degree of inequality in the distribution of income among the households.

- The distribution of wealth is also very uneven.

- Trade among these approximately 200 households results in persistent deficits for a large number of poor households, offset by large surpluses for a small number of wealthy households. These trade imbalances have the consequence that the poor households keep on borrowing from the wealthy households, so the indebtedness of the poor households keeps increasing.

- The government is dominated by the minority of wealthy households. The poor households, the majority, are members of one or two governing bodies which do not have any significant authority or power.

How would we label such a society? Would we choose to be a member of one of the households without knowing beforehand whether we would belong to one of the very few wealthy and powerful households or to one of the many poor and dominated households? Would we like to be one of the households in that society without knowing *a priori* what our income level our wealth level would be?

It is perhaps clear that if creatures from Mars were to land on Earth, a civilization like this is what they would find right now, during the last decade of the 20th century. The Martian creatures (assuming they had analytical skills) might first wonder whether the global economy on this planet is efficient. The question, "Is the global economy efficient?" could be posed in two ways:

- Could the global economy generate a higher level of aggregate real income with the level of inputs currently being used? or

- Could the global economy generate the current level of aggregate real income using a level of inputs that is "smaller" than the one currently being used?

We use the word "efficiency" to mean both these things, but the Martians may not.

The Martians might also wonder if our global economy is just, equitable or fair. This second puzzlement could also mean two different things:

- Is the distribution of real incomes or economic awards equitable?

- Is the process by which real incomes or awards are being generated equitable?

These two interpretations may mean different things to us, but not necessarily to the Martian creature.

The Martian may wonder further if the various issues pertaining to efficiency and to equity can be separated and discussed in isolation, and whether the two sets of issues have significant impact on one another. This creature would certainly be amazed that in the field of what we call welfare economics, which presumably deals with questions about the well-being of individual human beings and of groups of human beings, there is no place for justice, ethical norms and value judgments because we wish to discuss questions of economic efficiency on a "scientific" basis!

The Martian creatures would have still other reasons to marvel at human ingenuity. In the first place, we have created a number of what, to the creature, would appear to be arbitrarily drawn borders around nation-states in which peoples have vastly different in standards of living. Secondly, we have developed a field of study called welfare economics which has no apparent theoretical apparatus to facilitate a discussion about an international economic order other than within the context of efficiency.

The Martian creatures would wonder why we cannot see that discussion about value-laden efficiency and value-laden equity within countries is relevant also to a discussion about the differences *between* countries.

Before preparing to return to Mars, our visitors might wish to tell us that while we are smart in recognizing that economic efficiency is important, we were not smart enough to recognize further that there is another important value, perhaps equally so, called economic justice. And they might want us to examine the possibility that economic justice might enhance economic efficiency, at least in theory. If the creatures were good teachers, they might explain the difference between an efficient robot and an efficient human being, i.e., that robotic efficiency need not entail a dimension of justice but human efficiency does.

I trust that my beliefs and prejudices are by now quite obvious. An economic system should not be evaluated merely on the basis of the level of per capital income and the rate of growth. Rather, it should be judged also on the basis of the proportion of people suffering from involuntary hunger and undernourishment, the proportion of people who are illiterate, the rate of infant mortality, the degree of personal liberty and freedom enjoyed by the people and similar variables. Economic activity, in other words, must serve people's needs, and should be governed by justice. For example, everyone has a duty to work. But at the same time, the economic system must provide opportunities to work for all who are able and willing to work. In addition, a laborer has the right to expect a just wage and adequate assistance in case of need.

Being Disadvantaged in the Global Market

The world trading system is not characterized by equal and mutually gainful access to markets. While it is true that international trade based on comparative advantage has helped some countries, among them South Korea and Taiwan, many other countries have found competition in international markets to be a struggle yielding few rewards. The world economy is dominated by wealthy countries. Although they repeatedly extol capitalism and free trade, these rich countries, and/or the corporations based in these countries, can and do change the rules governing trade and move capital around the world in a way which has significant adverse effects on poor countries. In general, poor developing countries have only primary products to sell in international markets. Since primary products are processed in the rich countries, the poor countries that export them do not share significantly, if at all, in the relatively high returns to the later stages of processing.

There are other reasons why the gains from foreign trade go predominantly to developed countries. Developing countries face formidable barriers to entry into developed economies, which tend to protect their own producers. Prices for primary products are volatile because they respond to changes in supply and demand to a greater degree than do manufactured commodities. Contributing to the producers' inability to control either supply or price are such variables as the difficulty of storing agricultural products, dependence on the vagaries of the weather and the undifferentiated nature of primary products. The secularly declining terms of trade faced by predominantly primary product exporters may or may not be a generally accepted hypothesis by scholars, but they certainly impose a significant burden on the affected poor developing countries.

"Brain drain" is another effect of the global market system on developing countries. Educated young men and women find that their skills are more in demand in the flourishing job markets of rich developed countries than in the poor developing countries, where they find themselves overeducated. The flow of specialized human resources from poor to rich countries is, at the same time, both a cause and an effect of the substandard living conditions of developing countries.

Private foreign investment flows in the direction where returns to those investments are highest. The poorest and neediest countries, which have relatively weak infrastructures, relatively unskilled labor forces and relatively unstable political climates, offer less than favorable conditions for such private investments. During the late 1940s and 1950s, poor countries with unexplored or underexplored natural resources in addition to relatively low-wage labor found that multinational companies in search of resource extraction and exploitation were willing to invest in their economies. In the late 1950s and 1960s, transnational corporations sought out poor countries willing to develop industries like textiles, construction and steel. More recently, however, multinational corporations are more interested in high-tech, capital-intensive industries like electronics and chemicals, and developing countries are less attractive because their workers lack sufficient education and skills.

When an individual country offers foreign aid to the developing world, it is often "tied" to specific projects, or given under the condition that machinery and inputs must be imported from the donor country even if the cost exceeds the world price. "Tied aid" may also come with political strings attached. Foreign aid often fails to reach the needy people in developing countries because wealthy, powerful interests are often in charge of implementing projects in these developing countries. Furthermore, a significant component of foreign aid is military rather than economic assistance.

Multilateral foreign aid was designed to avoid some of the limitations of foreign government-to-government aid. But, in practice, international agencies, such as the World Bank and the International Monetary Fund, are controlled to a significant degree by the rich countries. Poor developing countries have often found the policies of such institutions to be unresponsive to their needs. A case in point is the set of adjustment programs designed to bring about structural adjustment in the countries applying for assistance from the IMF. Beginning in the 1980s, the IMF has required structural adjustment programs as a condition for new loans .

During the 1980s, the total external debt of poor countries amounted to more than one trillion U.S. dollars. Not all the borrowing by the developing countries was prudent. However, it was necessary for many countries to borrow heavily to finance the purchase of equipment and supplies, sometimes when the terms of trade were not to their advantage, and when the price of imported oil increased significantly in the 1970s.

Lenders in the developed countries were only too eager to loan money to developing countries without adequately investigating their ability to absorb the new money, and without checking into the prospects for repayment. These banks had acquired huge deposits of petrodollars from the OPEC countries, and they encouraged debtor countries to borrow heavily at low interest rates. When interest rates skyrocketed at the beginning of the 1980s, many developing counries found themselves in default because they were unable to service their debt. In several years during the 1980s and 1990s, the flow of debt payments from the developing countries exceeded the flow of investments and aid into those countries.

What Has Gone Wrong?

Inequality increased both within and between countries as the rich gained income share at the expense of the poor. Let me hasten to say that we cannot, and should not, heap the blame for all that is wrong on the functioning of markets. We cannot blame markets because capitalism, loosely interpreted as free or relatively free markets, does not, and has not, existed in fact in the international economy for many decades, if it ever in fact did exist. But if international markets were actually to function freely, we would have some major problems: poverty, injustice, environmental degradation, to name just three. Furthermore, the reward structure of a free market does not necessarily coincide with the incentive structure that would generate an equitable, efficient society; efficient markets may generate outcomes that are harmful to society.[3]

It is obvious that economic activity results in changes in the levels and/or rates of growth and development as well as changes in the distribution of income. Although no one disagrees that the distribution aspect is important, the level and/or the rate of growth and development is often *the* indicator used to measure the economic progress achieved in a country. The issue of the relative weights accorded to growth as opposed to distribution is important and deserves some consideration. Although discussion of this issue is taking place with increasing frequency among economists, the impact of these discussions on economic policy has been less than signficant, especially with respect to the roles of markets and governments in shaping the nature of economic outcomes.

We need a "positive vision,"[4] perhaps even a "Grand Social Vision," that articulates the minimal aspirations of masses of people everywhere in the world to be able to afford a life with the most basic needs fulfilled. This vision must also reflect the efforts of many countries in the world to avoid default on their international debt, at the same time as their populations struggle to avoid falling below the poverty line. It is discouraging to note that even among some professional economists, there is a lack of awareness, a degree of apathy—even an attitude bordering on hostility—when the effort is made to raise people's consciousness about these issues.

We have to acknowledge that globalization has set into motion a set of forces that (1) have increased the expectations of masses of people everywhere for a better life; (2) have not decreased income and wealth inequalities (within as well as among countries), and may even have increased them; and (3) are likely to create a partial "institutional architecture"[5] that may impede a long-run, dynamically efficient outcome even as they create short-run imbalances.

For many people, stark poverty and hunger have become routine, despite the belief of many economists[6] that the price system has the ability to end poverty. Perhaps the price system has not been allowed to function properly. Alternatively, is it not possible that in order to eradicate poverty, it is necessary "that there be increased coordination among the most powerful countries, and that in international agencies the interests of the whole human family be equally represented"?[7]

Notes

1. Paul VI, *Populorum Progressio* (Encyclical Letter 1967). Reprinted in *The Papal Encyclicals,* Vol. 5, Wilmington, NC: McGrath, 1981, pp. 187-188.

2. Some readers may be familiar with the contents of this and several following paragraphs as I have written along these lines elsewhere. See, for example, Thanawala, "Toward a Just World Economy," *Review of Social Economy,* Winter 1991, pp. 628-637.

3. Frank, Robert H., and Philip J. Cook, *The Winner-Take-All-Society: How More and More Americans Compete for Ever Fewer and Bigger Prizes, Encouraging Economic Waste, Income Inequality and an Impoverished Cultural Life,* New York: The Free Press, 1995.

4. Trubeck, David M., "Social Justice: 'After' Globalization—The Case of Social Europe," Paper presented at the 8th International Conference on Socio-Economics, Geneva, July 1996, p. 21.

5. *Ibid.,* p. 47.

6. For example, Hoskins and Coons ("Notable & Quotable," *Wall Street Journal,* November 9, 1995, p. A20) observe: ". . . The new world order is one of market solutions, not government intrusion. To foster such outcomes the United States should pass legislation that eliminates the Treasury's ability to make foreign loans [through the Exchange Stabilization Fund] and that removes the ability of the Federal Reserve (through swap lines) to extend credit to foreign central banks directly or indirectly by funding the ESF. Congress should also withdraw its support for the IMF and the World Bank."

7. John Paul II (1991), *Centesimus Annus* (Encyclical Letter). Vatican City: Libreria Editrice Vaticana, p. 109.

Destroying Orissa, Fueling Climate Change: A Joint Project of the World Bank, Transnational Corporations and G-7 Governments

*Daphne Wysham**

The World Bank, transnational corporations and G-7 countries are principle actors in the destruction of the state of Orissa in eastern India. They are also proving to be principle actors in the growing instablity of the Earth's climate.

The story, in brief, goes like this: The Climate Convention gets signed in 1992 at the Earth Summit in Rio by most of the world's governments, amid much fanfare by wealthy governments and loud complaints by the fossil fuel industry. Poor countries in the global South are given more lead time to "develop their economies" before they reduce greenhouse gas emissions. Rich countries are given notice that their emissions will soon have to be reduced dramatically. Rich countries respond by funneling massive quantities of capital, via the World Bank, into fossil fuel-driven power plants in the South, and moving energy-intensive industries to the global South. Poor countries, starved for elec-

---

* The author is with the Institute for Policy Studies in Washington, D.C. For more information, write IPS for the 1996 report, "The World Bank's Juggernaut: The Coal-Fired Industrial Colonization of the Indian State of Orissa," or the forthcoming report, "The G-7, the World Bank, and Climate Change." Both reports are $7 each, shipping and handling included, checks payable to IPS. Contact Daphne Wysham, IPS, 733 15th Street, NW, Suite 1020, Washington, D.C. 20005 (tel: 202-234-9382 x208).

trical power, and eager to earn foreign exchange to pay off interest on World Bank loans, accept the new sweetheart deals for Northern TNCs, pushed by the likes of U.S. DOE Secretary Hazel O'Leary and the late Commerce Secretary Ron Brown. Privatization is pushed through at World Bank behest to ensure that foreign ownership of power production and consumption is unhindered by such sentiments as the belief that power for domestic purposes should be available and affordable. Post-privatization, power rates go up by 500 percent for the less than 20 percent of households with power; power rates plummet for industry, many of them foreign-owned TNCs, or industries producing products for export to the North. Poor people, whose only wealth is a small plot of land for crops and a clean environment, are pushed off their land to make way for mines or industry; their air and water grows steadily more polluted. Middle-income people find power unaffordable. Rich TNCs make off like bandits. Northern governments smile all the way to the Bank—the World Bank, that is—where they reinvest their profits. Global greenhouse gas emissions continue their steady climb to dangerous heights, with 3 percent of man-made global greenhouse gas emissions coming from Orissa alone.

This story of Orissa, unfortunately, is being repeated around the globe. Under the banner of "poverty alleviation," free trade and democracy, the World Bank is playing a central role in making a mockery of the Climate Convention while destroying sustainable, traditional economies in the global South. By providing private industry with such inducements as loan guarantees, low-interest loans and guaranteed access to international markets, the World Bank is ensuring that coal mining booms in Orissa. By privatizing and deregulating Orissa's power sector, by looking the other way when labor activists are beaten or tortured, by claiming the environment will "benefit" from expanded coal-fired power, as it is in Orissa, the Bank is creating a powerful magnet for chronically polluting and energy-intensive industries—many of them multinational corporations based in the G-7.

The World Bank, in Orissa as elsewhere around the globe, is not the majority source of investment capital for energy development. It supplies only 3 percent of the total finance requirements for the energy sector in developing economies; the private sector provides about four times the amount provided by official development finance. However, as the Bank admits, "the Bank plays a key role in setting the standard by which other energy projects are judged, thus exerting an influence disproportionate to the size of its investment portfolio alone." Since

1990, the Bank has approved 154 loans totaling more than $22 billion for a variety of projects in the electric power sector. Most of these loans were to non-Annex 1 countries, which do not face binding restrictions on their greenhouse gas emissions.

As in other regions of the world, the Bank has been joined by G-7 countries in financing coal-fired industrialization of Orissa. Known G-7 financiers of Orissa's industrialization include the U.S. government, which loaned $232 million toward the Ib Valley coal-fired power plant; an additional $75 million is forthcoming for further investment in Ib Valley's coal-fired power plants. France provided $607 million toward the construction of an aluminum smelting complex, Nalco, as well as the Kaniha and Ib Valley coal-fired power plants and the Ananta coal mine. Japan has invested $125 million in coal-mining expansion in Orissa. The U.K. has invested $40 million in the upgrading of the Hirakud Dam in Orissa, and an additional $75 million toward the privatization of Orissa's power sector.

This investment is not charity. For every dollar the U.S. government adds to the World Bank's coffers each year, it gets $1.3 in procurement contracts for U.S. TNCs.* It is from this perspective, of "enlightened self-interest," that the G-7 countries of France, the U.S.A., the U.K. and Japan—and other non-G-7 countries, such as Sweden and Israel—have seen gold in this impoverished east Indian state.

The biggest beneficiaries of G-7 government investments were large U.S. TNCs, such as General Electric (with annual sales larger than the Philippines), Dodge Phelps, Foster Wheeler, AES, North-East Energy Services, Spectrum Technologies and Raytheon. Stein Industries and Aluminum Pechiney of France also gained a foothold in Orissa's expanding industrial economy, as did Alcan of Canada, and Mitsui, Kakoki and Okura of Japan.

What did Orissa get out of it? In strict dollar terms, Orissa's GDP was $3.6 billion in 1993. The World Bank Group, the Asian Development Bank and G-7 loans and financial assistance, through 1996, have funneled $2.85 billion into the state, about 80 percent of its GDP in 1993. (In comparison, the combined total annual sales of the TNCs who are most benefiting from procurement contracts in Orissa's power sector is more than 80 times both figures: $290 billion.)

---

* Congressional testimony by Lawrence Summers, undersecretary for international affairs, Treasury Department, March 27, 1995.

However, when one looks beyond the GDP and into the lives of the people who live in Orissa, one sees a grim picture. The massive exploitation of coal and other mineral resources has unleashed a chaotic torrent of destruction across the state. Thousands of people, most of them participating in subsistence-based economies, many of them tribal (25 percent of Orissa's population is tribal and among the poorest in India) are negatively impacted by this energy-intensive, toxic industrial development. Some consequences:

Pollution rises: Dead rivers carry toxic effluent through villages where people still rely on the blackened rivers for bathing, drinking and washing their clothes. Choking levels of pollution from the coal-fired power plants hang in the air.

Power rates go up: Fewer than 20 percent of people living in rural Orissa (and probably closer to 4 percent) have access to electricity produced by the state's power plants, despite the fact that the state government last year declared Orissa had a power "surplus." The lucky few with electricity saw their rates go up by 500 percent after privatization. The agricultural sector will be particularly impacted by the removal of state-subsidized power. This cost will be reflected in higher farm prices, with further adverse consequences for the poorest, whose purchasing power will be reduced.

Jobs go down: While a few Orissans are employed by the coal, bauxite, chromite, and other mines and industries, many of those employed in the mines come from other regions of India. The increasing reliance on open cast—or "strip"—mining has also brought on a decline in coal-mining jobs, even while coal mining rapidly expands. India's coal production rose from 200 million to 250 million between 1988 and 1993; yet, the number of people employed in coal mining actually declined from 674,000 to 655,000.

Displacement: Many people are displaced by active resettlement programs that are clearing out "local populations" to make way for coal power-consuming steel mills, bauxite and chromite mines. Poor people are being ousted from land they have held for generations without being given comparable land or even fair compensation; World Bank internal documents urge clients to move people out before the Bank finances a mining expansion project to avoid "high visibility and [providing] oustees and their representatives with an additional platform for discussing compensation issues."

Harassment and suppression of workers rights has escalated: In Talcher, the industrial heart of Orissa, a labor organizer attempting to raise the minimum wage for poor tribals employed in the mines from 9 rupees a day to 14 rupees (or less than 50 cents a day) was beaten unconscious, and his house set on fire. Other activists working to protect the traditional way of life have been arrested, tortured and illegally jailed.

Greenhouse gas emissions skyrocket: Orissa's industries and coal-fired power plants will be emitting 164 million tons of carbon dioxide equivalent annually by the year 2005, or the equivalent of about 3 percent of the projected growth in man-made greenhouse gases anticipated globally over the next decade. In addition, Orissa's industrialization will release toxic and potent global warming agents, tetrafluoromethane and hexafluoroethane (byproducts of aluminum smelting) equivalent to eight million tons of carbon dioxide emissions, which, because they are long-lasting, will contribute to a "perpetual change" in the earth's atmosphere.

Destruction of subsistence communities: Called "an industrial drain," the Nandira tributary, once a life-sustaining river that feeds into the Brahmani River, is dead. The black water is poisoning and slowly killing people, animals, fish and plants as far away as 50 miles downstream. Agricultural productivity has dropped for farmers dependent on this polluted water; fishing communities have been wiped out.

Water supplies depleted: In addition to the contamination from industrial pollutants, groundwater in the coal mining and coal-fired power production region of Talcher-Angul and Ib Valley has dropped dramatically, forcing people to rely on the blackened river water for cooking, cleaning, drinking and irrigation.

Fluorosis: Fluoride, a byproduct of aluminum smelting, which consumes 30 percent of the power produced in the region, has contaminated the groundwater around aluminum smelters. As a result, there is a crippling outbreak of fluorosis—a disease that causes skin disease, and bones and teeth to grow brittle—among people and cattle living near the smelter and captive power plant of NALCO (a French-owned aluminum plant), where the state pollution control board tested water wells and ponds and found fluoride far in excess of the regulatory limit. In 1990, scientists from G.M.College of Sambalpur found an astonishing 67 percent of men and 64 percent of women suffered from fluorosis, with the most severely impacted being young people between the ages of 12 and 19. Cattle populations have dropped precipitously in the area due to the bone-weakening disease.

Chronic diseases soaring: The rates of cancer, bronchitis and other lung and skin diseases in the region around the World Bank-funded Talcher Thermal Power Plant, where air pollutants are heavy, are rising. These diseases are especially high among the tribal population which, because they are traditionally landless, have little choice but to live on the most undesirable land—the non-productive land closest to the mines; they have no option but to drink the water blackened by coal dust and toxic effluents.

Broken Promises: The World Bank and the G-7

Under the Climate Convention, signed at the UN Earth Summit in Rio in 1992, the task of mobilizing the financial resources needed to ensure that poorer developing countries are given the resources to develop their economies in a sustainable manner, was given to the World Bank and the IMF. The Convention states the ". . . Multilateral institutions play a crucial role by providing intellectual leadership and policy advice, and by marshalling resources for countries committed to sustainable development."

However, the standard set by the World Bank in Orissa not only contradicts its mandate under the Climate Convention; it also contradicts the original mandate of the World Bank—to alleviate poverty and promote sustainable development. As documented above, the benefits are accruing to some of the wealthiest corporations in the world.

The Bank is also pushing privatization and deregulation in Orissa. yet, privatization means less accountability and virtually no regulatory oversight of industry by government. As Union Carbide proved in Bhopal, multinationals set lower standards for their activity in developing countries; with lower health, safety and environmental standards, accidents happen. And when they do, the ones to suffer are usually those already suffering the most.

The World Bank is also downgrading its own policies, with significant consequences for its projects overseas. In April of 1996, the World Bank revised its guidelines for power plant emissions. The new guidelines are a huge step backward: They double the limit for SO2 emissions given in the 1994 guidelines, ignoring standards set by the World Health Organization and many industrialized countries regarding ambient sulfur dioxide concentrations; they do not set numeric limits for total sulfur dioxide emissions; and fail to address greenhouse gas issues. In addition to acting as agents of climate change, SO2 and NOx are also one of the main agents of severe forest damage via acid rain and soil acidification, leading to reduced crop yields. In high concentrations, SO2 and NOx also have strong negative impacts on human health.

The Bank has continued in this same deregulatory mode in a separate move to downgrade its binding 1992 board-approved "Operational Policies"on energy efficiency to non-binding "good practices" documents (GP 4.45 "Electric Power Sector"; GP 4.46 "Energy Efficiency"). These changes clearly reflect a lack of commitment to sustainable energy development—in stark contrast to the Bank's stated goals.

Saying One Thing, Doing Another: The G-7 and Climate Change

The G-7, who together with the World Bank, make destruction of Orissa possible, are equally culpable when it comes to violating commitments they have made to halt climate change. All G-7 countries are signatories to the Climate Convention, and have committed to making sustainable development a central goal of their policies and programs, and to intensifying and deepening the integration of environmental considerations into all aspects of their programs. At the G-7 Summit in Halifax, Canada, held on June 16, 1995, the G-7 countries, all of whom have signed the Climate Convention, made the following commitments:

> . . . We place top priority on both domestic and international action to safeguard the environment. . . . We underline the importance of meeting the commitments we made at the 1992 Rio Earth Summit and subsequently, and the need to review and strengthen them, where appropriate. Climate change remains of major global importance.

The actions of G-7 countries in Orissa, however, shows that their real priority is not to address climate change, but to circumvent the

Climate Convention for their own short-sighted ends while supporting transnationals from their own countries. Until this gaping loophole, intended for Southern countries to develop their own economies, is closed, the people of Orissa will continue to suffer. Meanwhile, all of us will pay an incalculably high price for what TNCs now view as an "externality" in their profit margin: the growing imbalance in the Earth's climate and the growing inequity between rich and poor.

Lighting the Path to Progress: Women's Initiatives and Assessment of Progress since Rio

Women's Environment and Development Organization (WEDO) *

Introduction

In reviewing the progress made since the Rio Earth Summit (UNCED on the United Nations Conference on Environment and Development) in 1992, WEDO has chosen to focus on the image of fire. Across religions, cultures and mythologies, fire exerts a powerful and evocative symbolism. Fire is elemental and transformative, a life-giving force that can nurture and sustain, giving warmth, light and energy. It can also scorch and destroy, turning to ashes instantly what may have taken a lifetime or a millennium to build.

Women everywhere are the users and keepers of fire. As we near the new millennium, they may well judge their progress through their relationship with and control of the flame. Women need to ask themselves, and the world, whether the last decade of the century and the years since the Rio Summit have improved their access to this basic resource.

---

* Contact the Women's Environment and Development Organization (WEDO), 355 Lexington Avenue, 3rd floor, New York, NY 10017, tel: 212-973-0325; fax: 212-973-0335; e-mail: wedo@igc.apc.org; Website: http://www.wedo.org.

Can we take the heat? Can we afford to ignore the flawed patterns of production and consumption that lead to a warming of the earth's atmosphere and deepen poverty and deprivation? Can we continue to gloss over the disparity in lifestyles between North and South that underpin the inequalities of a global division that relegates growing numbers of the poor to a life in the cold? Can the fire-eaters be allowed to produce and consume at a pace that is devouring the earth's resources? Can women protect the flame and prevent a raging blaze? The five-year review of the Earth Summit is an opportune moment for us to ask these and other questions of all committed to making the planet a healthy and sustainable one.

The Fire: The Vision of Rio

A fire was lit in Rio de Janeiro in 1992. Five years later, how hot is it? Much positive activity has been undertaken, but the spirit of Rio today seems to flicker as embers rather than blaze as a fire. The question, therefore, is how to fan the embers of progress into the flame of widespread change?

Women's initiatives have been vital to keeping the vision of Rio alive since UNCED. But, perhaps even more than five years ago, it is evident that without intensified leadership, involvement and participation of women at every level, post-Rio implementation will not achieve the pace or scope its urgency demands.

AGENDA 21 AND OTHER INTERNATIONAL ACCORDS

The importance of women to the vision of Rio is reflected in the Rio agreements, thanks largely to the unflagging advocacy efforts of women themselves. This advocacy has intensified since Rio at related international meetings, demonstrating increasing strength.

One of the more significant methodologies for consultation developed in the process was the establishment of the Women's Action Agenda 21 that became the guiding document for action for women involved in the negotiations during the preparatory meetings and in national fora. Astonishingly, the first draft document for the Earth Summit hardly mentioned the word women.

Aghast at this omission, women who were involved in the process organized to ensure that the negotiations and the documents they yielded responded to the real world. One of the most significant ways in which the deficiency of the process was addressed was the holding of the World Women's Congress in Miami in 1991, where under the auspices of WEDO and its International Policy Action Committee made up of 55 women from around the world, 1,500 women from 84 countries gathered and developed the Women's Action Agenda 21.

A women's caucus was established within the Rio conference that impacted both on the officialprocess and the NGO negotiations themselves. The final outcome, Agenda 21, was to contain not only references to women's realities within each chapter, but importantly a separate Chapter 24 on women—Global Action for Women Towards Sustainable and Equitable Development.

Chapter 24 of Agenda 21 recommended elimination, by the year 2000, of the "constitutional, legal, administrative, cultural, behavioral, social and economic obstacles to women's full participation in sustainable development and public life." This chapter made other recommendations in such areas as women's health, child care, family planning and access to credit.

Since Rio, other international gatherings have occurred that cannot be separated from an evaluation of post-UNCED progress. The International Conference on Population and Development (ICPD), held in Cairo, in 1994, and the World Summit for Social Development, held in Copenhagen in March 1995, have gradually deepened, elaborated upon and extended the recommendations of Agenda 21 and other Rio accords. Most notably, the Platform for Action adopted by the U.N. Fourth World Conference on Women, held in Beijing in September 1995, is the strongest statement of international consensus on women's equality and empowerment that has ever been agreed upon by governments. Moreover, the Beijing Platform was pivotal to moving governments from making only recommendations to undertaking actual commitments.

Underlying all the Rio and post-Rio agreements, however, is a philosophy so basic, humane and just it should go without saying. It was, nevertheless, also codified in the Rio Declaration on Environment and Development, namely, Principle 1 which states: "Human beings are at the center of concerns for sustainable development. They are entitled to a healthy and productive life in harmony with nature."

Every strategy and recommendation at UNCED was aimed at accomplishing the goals of Principle 1. Five years after Rio, though, the consensus remains imperfect and can be strengthened, an irrefutable international political foundation has been built, largely by women, to underpin the initiatives of women around the world. This stands as a major accomplishment of the last five years.

The Boiling Point: Critical Issues and Priorities

The core goal of the Earth Summit was to steer human history toward sustainable development, namely, economic development that is based on, and inseparable from, social equity, inclusion of women in policy-making, human development and environmental stewardship. But five years after Rio, global poverty, social deprivation and environmental degradation remain ongoing. Alarming statistics accumulate despite the breadth and specificity of international agreements:

- Five years after Rio, 1.3 billion people try to survive on less than $1 per day;

- The globalized market economy has deepened economic polarization between developed and developing nations. In 70 countries, average income was lower than it had been in 1980 and in 43 countries, lower than in 1970. The difference in income between the developing and industrialized world tripled from $5,700 in 1970 to $15,400 in 1993 (UNDP *Human Development Report,* 1996);

- One billion people lack access to potable water and sanitation services;

- Nearly 50,000 people, mainly children, die each day from preventable causes;

- Over half a million women lose their lives in childbirth or as a result of unsafe abortions.

The over-consumption of the North is driving many aspects of the worst environmental and human crises of the world. Over-consumption patterns of the North have dangerously begun to take root in pockets of the South, fired by the ideals of pervasive growth-oriented market-driven policies that are eroding all cultures. Equally true is the fact that the growing poverty attendant on these policies is also emerging in the north.

In debates (on sustainable development) it is often asserted that developing countries with large populations pose a greater threat to the world environment than developed countries with smaller populations. However it is well known that developed countries have higher levels of consumption than developing countries and that consumption exerts pressure on the environment (*Our Global Neighborhood,* Report from the UN Commission on Global Governance, New York: Oxford University Press, 1995).

Table 1
Consumption-Adjusted Population
Selected Countries, 1990
(figures in million)

Country	Population	Adjusted Population
China	1,139	9,329
India	853	3,907
Soviet Union	289	16,828
United States	249	22,993
Canada	27	3,159

Source: *Our Global Neighborhood, op. cit.*

Meanwhile, despite much-stated recognition that a healthy natural resource base is essential for economic health, and the increasing acceptance of so-called "Green GNP" indicators that were pioneered by women several decades ago, unbridled environmental exploitation seems to accompany most economic activity. Private sector investment, much praised in the post-Rio era as a substitute for overseas development assistance, flows only to a handful of the strongest developing countries and often to the most environmentally exploitative industries.

Five years is but a moment of time in which to overcome history's legacy. Still, since the EarthSummit—in the international women's movement as well as in many other arenas—the following have been named as key problems that require priority action:

Inconsistencies between UNCED and the Effects of the Removal of Trade Barriers and International Capital Mobility.

Under the General Agreement on Tariffs and Trade (GATT) and its successor, the World Trade Organization (WTO), most countries are being forced to open their markets to the free entry of foreign goods and, in the process, are becoming more dependent on imports for food and other essential items. Countries with large foreign debts are pried open further by structural adjustment programs imposed by the World Bank and the International Monetary Fund. The programs emphasize the increase of export earnings so that countries can service their debt and pay for imports, a debt that has been repaid in real terms many times over, claiming more than 50 per cent of government revenues. These export-oriented policies of the World Bank and IMF have wreaked havoc on many developing nations and forced women to increase their unpaid work.

The Rise of Transnational Corporations (TNCs)

As wages and working conditions suffer a downward spiral, an upward spiral fuels consumption. Private businesses exploiting natural resources, such as minerals and forests, have always been prime agents of environmental destruction. Government agencies also have been inefficient in managing and protecting public assets, such as natural resources, and are often corrupt, barely enforcing regulations where they existed. The pursuit of profit over all other objectives, all the more potent today, means that entities must exploit workers and natural resources to the limits.

TNCs are wooed aggressively by governments seeking to lure capital and investment, which compounds the power of TNCs to dictate their terms of business.

Growing Private Ownership of Natural and Biological Resources

Through the new WTO, GATT and other attempts to assign economic value to natural resources, there is now in place a very distorted notion of private property—property of the intellect and the Earth. Patents are being issued on products that could not be made at all without the ingredient of local knowledge that is centuries old. Private interests can engage in what amounts to piracy, for example, to appropriate existing local knowledge of herbal medicine, plant-based drugs or basic irreplaceable seed stocks. And very often, this knowledge is the repository of women, indeed acknowledged as special in Chapter 24 of Agenda 21 and other above-mentioned agreements.

Even the Biodiversity Convention, one of the main agreements reached at Rio to protect plant and animal resources, tends to reinforce the notion that plants and animals have an economic value and can be bought and owned by private interests. Private and semi-private organizations send ethnobotanists into rainforest areas, for example, to inventory natural assets. Sometimes, local people are employed in this process. However, the salaries they receive to share their knowledge are entirely disproportionate to the profit that will be made by the exploitation of that knowledge on the global scale envisioned.

Farmers' seeds are now declared "primitive cultivars" and "land races," suggesting no intellectual work had gone into their evolution. The Green Revolution varieties were called "elite" and "modern varieties." These varieties, themselves, evolved from a narrow genetic base and were spread throughout the world, thus displacing the millions of crop varieties that farmers had evolved over millennia (Vandana Shiva, "The Seeds of Our Future," *The Journal of the Society for International Development*, Vol. 4, 1996).

Further, under the WTO's Trade-Related International Property Rights provisions, countries are required to enforce patents on plant varieties for periods of 17 to 20 years, making traditional seed exchange between farmers illegal and resulting in higher prices based on profitability for private seed companies. As a few powerful corporations gain control of global seed supplies, farmers will be forced to abandon traditional varieties and become entirely dependent on commercial supplies.

Concentration of Power and the Exclusion of Large Segments of Global Society, Including Most Women from Government, Business, Industry, Military and Post-Military Decision-Making

Those in positions of power have always been able to shape the lives of others with less power. Today, however, small groups of people, such as boards of directors of large corporations or owners of media conglomerates, can profoundly shape the lives of hundreds of millions of people, often instantaneously. A very few economic decisions can influence the cultural behavior and consumption patterns of whole nations. These decisions can often transcend, even neutralize, the best intentions of government and non-governmental organizations.

Those who wield this degree of power are overwhelmingly male, and largely from countries of the North and in Southeast Asia. They are indeed often operating in private arenas, thus out of reach of the public through voting or other democratic means. Even in well developed democracies, they are by and large unaccountable to those over whom they have power.

The Continued Under-Representation of Women in Decision-Making

Although roughly half the population of the world, women are far from holding half of the world's power in political and economic decision-making, despite high-level and global recognition of the importance of gender equality. Five years after Rio, women hold only about 11 percent of the seats in parliaments around the world, only 6 percent of cabinet-level positions, and are virtually invisible at the highest levels of the multi-lateral financial institutions that so influence national capacity to implement Agenda 21 and corollary agreements through their activities.

The results of the gap were succinctly put by WEDO President Bella Abzug at a UN ceremony in her honor in the fall of 1996: "Unless and until women are 50 percent of the decision-makers in the United Nations and in every single country, we cannot expect any meaningful change; we cannot expect a new vision."

Persistent Pre-Eminence of Military and Nuclear Energy Activities

It is only in the aftermath of the Cold War that the true extent of the devastating environmental effects of military activity and nuclear weapons production has become apparent. Cleaning up the toxic legacy of weapons production tests the capacity of even the richest countries. And thus far no nation has truly addressed the ticking time bomb of where and how to safely dispose of tons of nuclear waste generated in conventional civilian nuclear power plants. Yet, military spending continues at approximately $800 billion per year globally, sucking vital human and financial resources away from pressing social, educational and industrial needs. Meanwhile, the prospect of increasing legal traffic in plutonium for reprocessing and use in nuclear power plants is truly frightening. It is likely to spawn an illegal traffic in the highly lethal substance, the policing of which would undermine the most basic concepts of civil liberty and freedom of movement.

Women have long been involved in global disarmament, and have been the strongest voices claiming the elusive "peace dividend" for the betterment of the human condition. Women continue to organize to draw attention to the ongoing health and environmental problems at Chernobyl and Chelyablinsk, to continued nuclear testing in the Pacific and to rapacious uranium mining on indigenous lands in the U.S. Women are in the forefront of demanding a halt to the construction of new nuclear plants in favor of other renewable energy sources. While welcoming agreements on non-proliferation of nuclear weapons and ending nuclear testing, they continue to call for elimination of all nuclear weapons.

Women have been in the forefront of these struggles. Examples include the Movement for Nuclear Safety in Russia, Mothers Against Nuclear Energy in Germany, and the Mozambican Campaign Against Landmines, which hosted the Fourth International NGO Conference on Landmines in February 1997.

Women's Initiatives in Peace and Human Rights

In Sudan, the Sudanese Women's Voice for Peace (SWVP) is working at the grassroots level with women, the church and community leaders to initiate a constructive dialogue among the warring parties of southern Sudan. Women's WORLD, an international group of women writers and publishers working on gender-based censorship, condemns the strictures on women imposed by the Taliban after their takeover of Afghanistan. In Rwanda, Pro-Femmes Twese Hamwe, a collection of Rwandan women's organizations, was named the first winner of UNESCO-Madanjeet Singh Prize for the Promotion of Tolerance and Non-Violence.

The Soldiers' Mothers' Committee of Russia was honored with the Alternative Nobel Prize for defending soldiers' rights in the Russian military and for their effort to end the war in Chechnya. And the International League for Human Rights has awarded the Carl-von-Ossietzky Medal to the Saturday Women of Istanbul in Turkey for their efforts for the human rights in Turkey.

In these and numerous other struggles all over the world, women have taken the lead in the five years since Rio in the fight for peace, human rights, and a more just and sustainable future.

Biodiversity, Cultural Diversity and Sustainability

Ignacio Peon *

Traditional and modern societies evolve together with nature, albeit at different paces. Nature and traditional cultures evolve very slowly while modern societies evolve very quickly. Spaceship Earth is suffering growing pains as it tries to harmonize natural and human entities growing at such different speeds. Modern development has a dangerously chaotic effect on nature and traditional cultures.

The equilibrium nature achieved after thousands of millions years of evolution has been seriously altered in the last 50 years. Even though the history of life on Earth includes great natural catastrophes, the present situation is unique. If current trends continue, the Earth's natural equilibrium may be permanently impaired, with grave consequences for all forms of life.

Until recently, the development of thousands of traditional cultures did not significantly alter the global equilibrium and its homeostatic adaptive mechanisms. For thousands of years, a great variety of traditional cultures proliferated all over the world. Every society had to follow a particular adaptive process to establish sustainable relations

---

* Ignacio Peon can be reached at Environmental Groups Network (Pacto de Grupos Ecologistas), e-mail: peonmex@laneta.apc.org, or the Mexican Action Network on Free Trade, tel/fax: 52-5-556-9316; e-mail: rmalc@laneta.apc.org. This article was originally printed in *La Otra Bolsa de Valores*, No. 34, Tlloc 40-3, Col. Tlaxpana, CP 11370, Mexico, D.F., Mexico; e-mail: espacios@laneta.apc.org.

with its own environment in order to survive.

When modern Western societies and their industrial technologies and short-term economic models presumed to dominate the natural world, they put environmental degradation on the fast track. For the first time, destructive forces originated within the domain of life itself. This is because the systems that make up modern civilization are not characterized by the dimensions of wholeness, synergy and viability, which are the essence of the Earth's biologically evolved systems.

The ideological origin of environmental destruction comes from the anthropocentric notion that we humans own the planet and have enough wisdom to know what to do with it. The preposterous occidental notion that science and technology should dominate nature for the benefit of man is one of the major reasons for modern environmental degradation.

Nature does not make leaps; civilization does. A new form in biological evolution will spread very gradually through genetic systems, and will become general only if the short-run advantages that allow it to survive and spread at the outset are combined with long-run viability. In cultural systems, by contrast, new forms can spread rapidly, without their ultimate viability having been demonstrated anywhere. This hyperefficiency of transmission can transform civilization into a cancer. Meanwhile, human cultural diversity has given rise to a multiplicity of ideologies or paradigms—schemata that characterize ways of thinking across the globe. Some of these ways of looking at the world, including particular views of what is the good life, may be especially conducive to sustainability. It is desirable that such attitudes become more widespread, even if cultural diversity suffers through the decline of other attitudes with more destructive consequences. The single-minded preservation of cultural diversity can engender not only paradoxes but conflicts with other development goals as well.

We are at the end of the quantitative economic century. We now know that the simple socialist and capitalist economic models of development cannot solve the world's great social and environmental problems, even if they internalize the environmental costs. In the next century, we need a new sustainable model of development beyond the economic metaphor. It has to be a qualitative model with a holistic point of view. The worldwide social and environmental problems of today will not be solved through an economic or a technological approach. These are too limited in their scope. In a post-modern pluralistic world, occidental culture cannot be the sole provider of solutions, as it has been in the past. The rich experiences of diverse cultures in every corner of the world can contribute unique solutions for every geoclimatic region of the planet. Biodiversity and cultural diversity are the qualitative cornerstones of a new sustainable model of development.

At the end of this economic century, the economic international institutions are ruling the world. National and international institutions working on environmental issues are relatively weak. The Earth's preeminent decision-makers give ecological concerns importance only in their speeches. International free trade agreements are stronger than similar environmental agreements on toxic waste, biodiversity and climate change. Funding for the implementation of the environmental programs through Agenda 21 is totally insufficient. In fact, during the past two years it has been reduced from 0.33 percent to 0.29 percent of global GNP, in contrast to the originally projected 0.7 percent.

The shift of power from government and multilateral organizations to transnational corporations with economic investments and operations in more than one country and without social and environmental accountability, is producing a void of power. Instead of a New World Order, we have a New World Disorder. The environmental problems of today are too big for the current institutional framework.

To fill this void, new social actors have gradually emerged in the last 30 years—the international grassroots development and environment networks. At the Earth Summit in 1992 in Rio de Janeiro, more than 20,000 non-governmental activists from all over the world joined together to discuss alternative environmental solutions. To deal with today's complex environmental issues, we now need to design and implement a new global institutional framework with the participation of all the social actors: governments, universities, private enterprise, multilateral and social organizations. Complex environmental problems require new alliances.

Every society, every organization is important for the solution of the complex environmental problems of the globalized world. Each one has a space and a time and multiple roles to play. We need to use our imaginations and our intuitive capacities to find our special places in the dynamic environmental puzzle. To achieve sustainability, it is necessary to achieve global unity in diversity.

The Pacific Rim area has a strategic role to play in this respect. The Asia Pacific Economic Cooperation Forum (APEC) is a force to be reckoned with as we enter the so called "Pacific Century." The region includes almost half of the population of the planet, and it is by far the most dynamic economic region in the world. A particular concern of the APEC initiative is the sheer scale of trade in goods, services, capital and labor that has become possible in a deregulated regional trading block predicated on exponential economic growth. Current patterns of industrialization and prolific energy use make East Asia and North America some of the worst performers in environmental matters.

Mexico, a Pacific Rim country, is one of the nations in the world with the greatest biodiversity. Its geoclimatic conditions produced a great variety of flora and fauna. The diversity of natural conditions favored the emergence of more than 50 cultures. Mexico has become a melting pot of races and cultures; it is a cross-road similar to the "x" in its name. It is a bridge between traditional and modern cultures, between the economies of the North and the South and between Anglo and Latin cultures and races. It is a dynamic country with a particular mixture of plural cultures.

After many centuries of hard struggle, we have learned that international and governmental policies of development do not work unless there is a real distribution of power, and that we can find most of the economic, social and environmental solutions within our own culture and territory. Mexico, like all societies, has invaluable and original experiences and solutions to offer. In a pluralistic world sustainability needs a dynamic mosaic of solutions and institutions from every corner of the world.

Sustainable America*

Peter Montague

What is a "sustainable" economy?[1] To maintain life, humans require a steady flow of physical materials and energy. We require coal, oil and natural gas for heat and transportation; wood for buildings and for paper; food for sustenance. Only nature can create all these resources. Nature's most basic process uses solar energy to convert carbon dioxide (CO_2), water and minerals into plants—the basis of all food chains.

Our economy provides us with goods and services, all of which derive from the materials and energy that nature produces. A sustainable economy uses the essential products and processes of nature no more quickly than nature can renew them. Furthermore, a sustainable economy discharges wastes no more quickly than nature can absorb them.[2]

This definition of a sustainable economy can be roughly translated into measurable quantities: how much land surface is required to produce the flows of materials and energy that sustain us? For example, our production of carbon dioxide, which is warming the planet via the greenhouse effect (REHW #429, #430), can be translated into an area of forest that would absorb the carbon dioxide we are releasing. If we set aside enough forest to absorb all the carbon dioxide we release, then

---

* This essay is adapted from *Rachel's Environment & Health Weekly* (Peter Montague, editor), Environmental Research Foundation, P.O. Box 5036, Annapolis, MD 21403-7036, tel: 1-888-2RACHEL; e-mail: erf@rachel.clark.net.

we would achieve a sustainable balance between CO_2 creation and disposal.

This approach, which is called "ecological footprint analysis," was invented by William Rees at the University of British Columbia in Canada. Ecological footprint analysis reveals some important facts about our current lifestyle. For example, on average, each person in the U.S. requires 5.1 hectares (12.6 acres) to create the flows of materials and energy that sustain our lifestyle.[3] Unfortunately, if you take all the available ecologically productive land on the planet and divide it by the number of humans living today, you find that, on average, there are only 1.5 hectares (3.7 acres) available for each person.[4] Therefore, this kind of analysis tells us that the whole world cannot ever achieve the hedonistic lifestyle of Americans. There just is not enough land to sustain it. In fact, to support the entire human population in the lifestyle of Americans (or Europeans) would require roughly three additional planets the size of planet Earth.[5]

We can learn something else from this kind of analysis. Each U.S. citizen requires 5.1 hectares of land, but if you divide the area of the U.S. by its population, you find that only 2.8 hectares of land are available for each citizen. This means that the difference, 5.1 -2.8 = 2.3 hectares per person, is land that belongs to someone else but is being used to sustain the U.S. population. Land that is supporting a U.S. citizen cannot simultaneously support another person somewhere else, so we are borrowing (or buying or stealing) someone else's current or future well-being.

If we acknowledge these facts, we are faced with several dilemmas. As William Rees points out, more material growth, at least in the poor countries, will be needed to bring people out of poverty, yet any global increase in the flow of materials and energy is ecologically unsustainable. This means that humans cannot continue on their current path. In particular, the wealthy members of the human family (in other words, the average members of every industrialized society) face an uncomfortable moral challenge: while we use up three times our fair share of the planet's resources, at least a billion people do not get the minimum number of food calories needed to sustain life. Furthermore, just meeting current demands is undermining the ability of future generations to meet their own needs. Conventional strategies for economic development seem ecologically dangerous and morally bankrupt.

Likewise, within the U.S. itself, conventional strategies for economic development seem to be working *against* the environment and *against* people. Here is an optimistic assessment from the U.S. Secretary of Labor in January 1997:

> Jobs are being created at a steady pace, but plant closings, insufficient work, and elimination of positions have caused the loss of 8% of the nation's permanent jobs every two years. Eight percent of permanent jobs were lost in 1989-91; another 8% were lost during 1991-93 and another 8% disappeared during 1993-95.[6]

What we find in place of these good jobs is temporary part-time work at reduced wages with few benefits.

Real wages have fallen more than 10 percent since 1985. Meanwhile, the gap between the well-to-do and everyone else has been growing steadily for more than 15 years: the rich are growing richer compared to the rest of us. If you divide American society into five groups, each representing 20 percent of the total, the incomes of the wealthiest 20 percent rose 26 percent between 1979 and 1995. Yet the incomes of the middle 20 percent rose only 1 percent and the incomes of the bottom 20 percent actually *decreased* 9 percent. Benefits are disappearing as well: between 1983 and 1993, the percentage of full-time employees participating in employer-sponsored health plans fell from 95 percent to 83 percent.[7] Wealth is even more inequitably distributed than income. Between 1983 and 1992, an astonishing 99 percent of the increase in the nation's wealth was scooped up by the richest 20 percent of the people.[8]

Amid this economic decline, we find that the nation's future is jeopardized by spillover effects. Here is how the *New York Times* described it in a 1994 editorial:

> America's youngest children are in serious trouble, according to a panel of experts brought together by the Carnegie Corporation. So many children are growing up without adequate medical and nutritional care, intellectual stimulation or emotional security that the nation's ability to produce healthy workers and citizens is in jeopardy.[9]

Since the 1970s, parents have worked longer hours but earned less money, leaving them less time and fewer resources to devote to their children's well-being.

One root cause of all these problems is our view of the economy. The economy was once seen as a means to an end, enabling people to enjoy a good life. Today the economy has become something different. Both people and the environment are sacrificed to maintain the economy—or, more specifically, to maintain existing relationships of wealth and power.

But it does not have to be this way. We are not helpless in the face of "the market." People—even people at the local level—can control investments that either create or destroy good jobs. By establishing "early warning" networks, we can identify firms in trouble and take steps to help them recover. Tax policy can help us or hurt us. If we come to see the environment as an essential asset, local and national policies can preserve natural resources as part of economic renewal.[10]

Now a new organization called Sustainable America (SA)[11] has appeared on the scene, aiming to tackle both the economy *and* sustainability head-on. SA held its founding convention in Atlanta two weeks ago; 85 people from 25 states and three Native American nations gathered to affirm their commitment to local economic development and to a coordinated national movement for building an economy that serves people and maintains a healthy environment.

As Executive Director Elaine Gross explained in Atlanta, SA is a national membership organization concerned about the direction of our local and national economies. SA's member groups are responding to decline by organizing locally and coming together nationally to promote policy alternatives that offer a greater degree of citizen control, economic stability, prudent use of ecological resources and a greater degree of economic equity. The membership includes both national and local organizations (and individuals), representing labor, economic development and environmental, religious, educational, policy and community leaders.

SA's national office will strengthen the infrastructure that nurtures the local and joint work of its members. The infrastructure includes:

- a Technical Assistance Bank that will allow members to share best practices and various skills among each other;

- a clearinghouse that makes available to its members publications, research results and other information;

- work/study groups that facilitate high-quality networking through collective learning, problem-solving and resource sharing;

- conferences, forums and workshops for the membership to promote cross-fertilization and to increase the knowledge base of the membership; and

- policy campaigns that alter institutional or structural barriers to SA's work.

Sustainable America has three strategic approaches:

Be Pragmatic:

- focus on high-quality networking and technical assistance among local groups doing the work;

- build an infrastructure that promotes (a) technical competence, (b) ongoing collaboration and (c) joint action; and

- seek insights into the challenges of organizing and movement-building to further this work.

Be Bold:

- pick projects that influence the mainstream economy, encourage experiments but seek to avoid marginalization by "scaling up" activities whenever possible.

Be Broad-Based and Politically Strong:

- reach out across the country and into diverse communities, across disciplines and issue areas, building a movement for sustainable economic development.

Sustainable America has four programs:

- *Community Capacity-Building.* Providing tools to understand our local economies and environments better and to create a new economic vision; strengthening our local organizations; educating local citizens; and building broad-based coalitions.

- *Democratic Control* (institutional accountability and worker organizing). Creating the framework, structures and enforcement mechanisms to ensure that communities and workers control the economic institutions that affect them—from business to government.

- *Business/Economic Development.* Getting community/labor coalitions more directly involved in job creation and retention, from the service sector to manufacturing.

- *Capital Use and Control.* Capturing our money and directing public funds toward the creation of real jobs, and using our capital resources (for example, natural resources) more wisely.

The economy does not have to work against people or against the environment. But up until now, local environmental and economic development work have gone on in a kind of vacuum—the economic development folks and the environmentalists ignoring each other. Now at last they are coming together.

If everyone piles on, this could be really big.

Notes

1. The issue of sustainability was first raised by Gro Harlem Brundtland and others in *Our Common Future,* New York and London: Oxford University Press, 1987. The "Brundtland Commission" defined sustainability as meeting "the needs of the present without compromising the ability of future generations to meet their own needs."

2. Mathis Wackernagel and William Rees, *Our Ecological Footprint: Reducing Human Impact on the Earth,* Gabriola Island, B.C., Canada: New Society Publishers, 1996, p. 7. See their discussions of "natural capital" and "weak" and "strong" sustainability in Chapter 2.

3. *Ibid.,* p. 85.

4. *Ibid.,* pp. 54, 88.

5. *Ibid.*, pp. 90-91.

6. Robert B. Reich, U.S. Secretary of Labor, speech entitled "The Unfinished Agenda," delivered to the Council on Excellence in Government, Washington, D.C., January 9, 1997; the data appear in the "Technical Appendix" to Secretary Reich's speech.

7. *Ibid.*

8. *Ibid.*

9. "Endangered Children," *New York Times,* April 15, 1994, p. A30.

10. For discussion of local economies and environmental quality, see Thomas Michael Power, *Economic Pursuit of Quality,* Armonk, New York: M.E. Sharpe, 1988.

11. Contact: Elaine Gross, Sustainable America, 350 Fifth Avenue, Room 3112, New York, NY 10018-3199. tel.: 212-239-4221; fax: 212-239-3670; e-mail: sustamer@sanetwork.org; Web: http://www.sanetwork.org.

Chapter 5: What Works to Build Sustainable Communities and Livelihoods?

Everywhere people are waking up to the realities of their situation in a globalizing economy and are beginning to recognize that their economies, resources and socio-political participations must be re-grounded in their local-regional communities. Only in reconnecting to our communities will we be able to cooperate with others to make corporations accountable and "free trade" consistent with sustainability and democracy. Such dual local/global awareness and intercooperation, what we called "Cosmopolitian Localism" in the Introduction to this book, is a new form of social connectedness and requires a new politics and a new culture.

But are sustainable communities possible in a global economy?

David Korten responds to this question by asserting that communities everywhere are on the front lines of a renewed struggle for survival. Economic globalization is pushing the maximization of profits in ways that undermine opportunities for local autonomy and self-reliance. Current racheting up so-called free trade systems, externalizing environmental and social costs by dumping them on communities, corporate extraction of resources and public subsidies, plans for a new "bill of rights for corporations" (the MAI)—all contribute to a one-sided and intrinsically anti-democratic corporate strategy for global capitalism today. For Korten, capitalism has many faces, and the one being pushed by stateless corporations is very antithetical to the interests of local communities and places.

Building Self-Reliant Communities

Michael Shuman suggests a sequenced procedure for communities to become self-reliant. The first six steps can be begun, if necessary, before involving local government. Shuman's procedure is based on a reconstruction of what many communities have done and presents a process model for what works in this area.

In agreement with other views in this anthology, Shuman sees the community visioning process as a beginning, but he stresses that these processes do not really get to the nuts and bolts of fostering community-friendly business. He proposes creating a Community Bill of Rights that identifies what is community-friendly business and what is not by assigning "good communitykeeping seals." This requires yearly information-gathering from businesses that enables local residents to make judgments about how these businesses are serving the community. This information-gathering can be extended to a survey of community assets—including unutilized resources that can become the basis for a state of the city report that civic organizations can use to build civic awareness. Entrepreneurs can be urged to take advantage of some of these opportunities and start community-rooted corporations that transform problems and dependencies into local job and capital formation processes. The relevance of learning how to run local businesses and non-profits makes learning the basics of investment and accounting essential for community activists too. Rethinking ways of getting better community banking services is the next step and this will require creating both more community-targeted banking and/or other types of credit systems, including community currencies.

Having realized these six steps, community groups and citizens can turn to the task of creating a community-friendly city hall that works to secure these self-reliance goals rather than to entice outside investors to weaken them. But all of these community-related actions will become vulnerable if communities do not become active in trying to work for campaign reform and in dispatching advocates to push for community self-reliance at state and federal levels of government. And finally, the movement for sustainable communities needs to open out through the formation of international partnerships to exchange tools and trade and initiate collaboration for opposing global capitalism.

Community Economics as Responses to Globalization

Patricia Perkins wonders if local economies are an accomodation to the global economy or an alternative to it? Reflecting on this question, Perkins interprets the rise of community economics as related to the split in OECD economies between the workers and industries that are competitive in the globalization process and those that are not. Focusing on the Toronto area, Perkins shows how a series of local economic initiatives in meeting community needs in food, shelter, transportation, money and environmental restoration have had interactive results, providing more jobs and keeping more money in the community. These enterprises often emerge from ethnic and culturally diverse communities and have been aided by well-developed community institutions that make such flexibility possible. Looking closely at some of the conditions that have permitted delinking from the global economy reveals the advantages of local knowledge and community connections that allow people to learn from each other in ways that are impossible when they become socially privatized in the dominant economic system.

It is not accidental that Toronto was also the host city for the first Healthy Cities conference that has since become a world movement now involving over 1,000 cities. Unique to this approach to sustainable cities is the inclusion of human and community health in a holistic model for planning that brings together community conviviality, environmental integrity and economic prosperity. (For an account of the Healthy Cities Movement, see Trevor Hancock's article, "Healthy Sustainable Communities," in the April/May 1996 issue of the journal, *Alternatives*.)

Funding Sustainable Livelihoods: Are There Limits to Microcredit Systems?

A major movement to extend the success of the Grameen Bank and other peer-equity, microcredit systems to more and more of the world's poor has emerged in recent years. The Microcredit Summit in Washington resulted in many international and non-governmental organizations becoming partners in moblizing donors and extending microcredit facilities to 100 million families by the year 2000 so that they can all become self-employed! Brian Hill proposes that the United Nations Commission on Sustainable Development (CSD) become the focus for bioregionally centered efforts to make micro loans that will lead to sustainable livelihoods.

But there are some dark sides to this enthusiasm for microcredit. For example, self-help groups in India have been aided by banks in increasing the microloans because of high repayment rates, but it turns out that interests rates go as high as 30 percent and loans are often used for daily consumption needs.

Will the current participation of larger banks and institutions perpetuate this treadmill of debt and end up only increasing the profits of the banks in an "underloaned" sector? Distinguishing between microlending that empowers poor people and that which is motivated primarily by profit maximization is essential. Thus the World Bank's microlending arm has declared such lending unviable where usury laws limit interest rates and is trying to force a restructuring and privatization of micro-lending that would push interest rates higher! The illusion of micro-lending is that it can be a macro-policy solution for poverty where the dominant development insititutions and the onslaut of global capitalism are sweeping aside real opportunities for creating sustainable livelihoods.

The Role of Socially Responsible Investment

Are there other ways to finance experiments in building sustainable communities? Can foundations become oriented to funding community and ecological regeneration? Stephen Viderman and Edward Tasch reflect on how the policies of the Jessie Smith Noyes Foundation have evolved in response to an awareness that it was counterproductive for the foundation to profit from investments that adversely impact on community organizations that they were supporting. Can foundations of various kinds come to an awareness that they can no longer separate the generation of investment income from the social and ecological limits of a finite Earth and vulnerable human communities? Using grant-making for small ventures and community groups, as well as asset managment that screens and targets investments, this foundation is trying to link its program goals with its investment policies.

Economic Globalization: The War Against Markets, Democracy, People and Nature

*David C. Korten**

Are sustainable communities possible in a global economy?

The answer is equally straightforward: certainly not in the kind of global economy our political leaders—both Democrat and Republican and their corporate sponsors—are crafting.

It takes us directly to an issue that had been obscured by capitalism's much touted victory over communism. Although the victory is often characterized as a triumph for democracy and the market economy, in truth capitalism has many faces and not all of them are friendly to market economies and democracy, not to mention people, communities and nature. Of particular importance to those of us who are committed to creating healthy and sustainable communities and cities is the distinction between the global capitalism that empowers stateless corporations and the local capitalism that empowers people and communities. The two are directly at odds.

It is no exaggeration to say that local communities everywhere are on the front lines of what might well be characterized as World War III. It is not the nuclear confrontation between East and West, between the Soviet Union and the United States, that we once feared.

* David Korten, founder of the People-Centered Development Forum, is author of *When Corporations Rule the World* (West Hartford, CT: Kumarian Press, 1996). This essay is based on presentations to the Third Mid-Atlantic Environmental Conference, "What Works for Sustainable Communities," Ramapo College, April 19, 1977.

It is a very different kind of conflict. There is no clash of competing military forces and the struggle is not defined by national borders. But it does involve an often violent struggle for control of physical resources and territory that is destroying lives and communities at every hand. It is a struggle between the forces and institutions of economic globalization and communities such as yours that are trying to reclaim control of their economic lives. It is a contest between the competing goals of economic growth to maximize profits for absentee owners versus creating healthy communities that are good places for people to live. It is a competition for the control of markets and resources between global corporations and financial markets, on the one hand, and locally owned businesses serving local markets, on the other.

Two things of fundamental importance to each and every one of us are now much at stake in the struggle between the global and the local. Will people and communities control their local resources and economies and be able to set their own goals and priorities based on their own values and aspiration? Or will these decisions be left to global financial markets and corporations that are blind to all values save one instant financial returns?

Will the life-sustaining resources produced by the regenerative capacities of our planet's ecosystems be equitably shared to provide for the material needs of all who inhabit this bountiful planet? Or will we allow a global economic system, now functioning on autopilot beyond conscious human control, to consume and destroy the ecosystem and our social fabric in its insatiable quest for money?

Economists, politicians, corporate spokespersons and the media have for years been touting the benefits of the global economy. They have called on us to support trade agreements, such as NAFTA, GATT and the Asia-Pacific Economic Community (APEC), that remove the constraints of economic borders and open opportunities for growth and prosperity for all in the global economy.

The failure of the global economy to deliver on these promises has become so obvious that even some of the leading boosters of economic globalization have begun to express doubts. For example, the founder/president and managing director of the World Economic Forum, a club of the world's largest global corporations, has warned that economic globalization is producing disastrous consequences that threaten the political stability of the Western democracies. They observe quite correctly that:

- Economic globalization is causing severe economic dislocation and social instability.

- The technological changes of the past few years have eliminated more jobs than they have created.

- The global competition "that is part and parcel of globalization leads to winner-take-all situations; those who come out on top win big, and the losers lose even bigger."

Higher profits no longer mean more job security and better wages. "Globalization tends to delink the fate of the corporation from the fate of its employees." Finally, they warn that unless serious corrective action is taken soon, the backlash could turn into open political revolt and destabilize the Western democracies. I could hardly have said it better myself.

NAFTA, GATT, APEC and other so-called trade agreements, which are erasing economic borders and placing global corporations and financial markets beyond the reach of the state and accountability to the human interest, are not really about trade. Furthermore, they did not happen by chance. They are the result of concerted, well-organized, well-funded and largely secret efforts by the global corporations and financial interests that benefit from them to rewrite the rules of global commerce to assure their right to go wherever and do whatever will make them a quick buck.

Unfortunately, the failures have not dampened the enthusiasm of those who benefit from the resulting global carnage. At this very moment, the Clinton administration is working in secret with these same interests in Paris to craft what could well be the most anti-democratic, anti-people, anti-community international agreement ever conceived by supposedly democratic governments. It is called the Multilateral Agreement on Investment (MAI). More accurately labeled the "Corporate Rule Treaty," its purpose is to prohibit any government or locality from establishing performance or accountability standards for foreign investors. In essence, it says that foreign investors have the right to buy, sell and move assets without restriction, and to challenge in special courts—in which they will have a standing comparable to that of nation-states—any measure that limits their freedom of action. The agreement is all about corporate rights. There is nothing about corporate responsibilities. If approved, it could well render illegal many of the activities being undertaken by communities around the United States and the world to rebuild their local economies, such as any regulation intended to favor rooted capital or firms that provide secure local employment at a living family wage. If you are interested, as you certainly should be, I have materials available for distribution from Public Citizen and the Preamble Collaborative with sample letters to members of congress, editors and state attorney generals.

As we assess the increasing power of global corporations, it is important to bear in mind that the corporation is one of the most authoritarian and undemocratic institutions ever created. The corporate CEO has the legal authority to at any time hire, fire and reassign staff, open and close plants, add and drop product lines and change transfer prices almost at will, with virtually no recourse by the people or communities affected—either inside or outside the organization.

Historically, exercise of the regulatory powers of the state was the primary restraint on the expansion of corporate power. Together the processes of deregulation and globalization have effectively removed that constraint by placing the power of global corporations and finance beyond the reach of public accountability. Day by day the largest corporations continue to consolidate that power through mergers, acquisitions and strategic alliances. The statistics are sobering.

Of the world's 100 largest economies, 51 are corporations. Only 49 are countries. The economy of Mitsubishi Trading Corporation is larger than that of Indonesia, the world's fourth most populous country and a land of enormous natural wealth. Some further statistics:

- The combined sales of the world's top 200 corporations are equal to 28 percent of the world GDP.

- These same 200 corporations employ only 18.8 million people, less than one-third of 1 percent of the world's population, even as the downsizing continues.

- In 1995, the total value of mergers and acquisitions for the world exceeded any prior year by 25 percent.

The primary accountability of these corporations is to the global financial markets, in which each day $1.4 trillion in foreign exchange changes hands in the search for speculative profits wholly unrelated to any exchange of real goods or services.

Whose Interests?

Whose interests are represented by these financial markets to which the world's most powerful corporations are beholden? In the United States, 77 percent of shareholder wealth is owned by a mere 5 percent of households. The broader population that holds a beneficial ownership through pension funds is represented in corporate governance by a few hundred fund managers, who have no accountability to the beneficial owners beyond protecting the security of their benefits.

Globally the share of the world's population that has a consequential participation in corporate ownership is far less than 1 percent. This concentration of power in corporations, accountable only to a tiny global elite, denies the most basic principles of democratic governance.

Externalizing Costs

According to market theory, a firm's profits measure its value-added contribution to the society. That is the theory. In reality, our corporations are massive cost externalization engines—privatizing the gains from economic activity while socializing the costs—i.e., passing them onto the larger community. In a global economy, the world's megacorporations gain great advantage from the processes of extortion by which they demand, in the name of global competition, ever greater public subsidies as the price of providing a community the few jobs the corporation has not yet eliminated.

Sometimes the externalization takes the form of direct public subsidies, as for example the grant given by the State of Virginia to Motorola to locate a research and manufacturing facility in the state. It included a $55.9 million grant, a $1.6 billion tax credit and a reimbursement package worth $5 million for employee training. Every dollar of this package represents a direct transfer of money from Virginia taxpayers to the profits of the Motorola corporation.

In the 1950s, taxes on U.S. corporations provided 31 percent of the federal government's general revenues. Their share is now down to just 15 percent. In 1957, corporations provided 45 percent of local property tax revenues in the United States. By 1987, their share had dropped to about 16 percent.

Then there are the costs imposed on society by the products corporations sell. For example, the health consequences of the cigarettes from which corporations profit cost the public an estimated $53.9 billion a year. Similarly society bears a $135.8 billion burden for the consequences of unsafe vehicles. Add to this the costs born by workers who suffer injuries and accidents as a result of unsafe workplaces ($141.6 billion) or die from workplace cancer ($274.7 billion).

Ralph Estes, author of *Tyranny of the Bottom Line and Corporate Social Accounting* (San Francisco: Berret-Kohler, 1995) has compiled estimates from a number of studies of the costs that corporations impose on U.S. society. He came up with a conservative total annual figure of $2.6 trillion, roughly five times total corporate profits.

The worst of it is that many forms of cost externalization involve the absolute, and sometimes permanent, destruction or depletion of the real productive capital of the society. For example:

- A corporation that hires young women in places like the Mexican *maquiladoras* under conditions that render them unemployable after three to four years due to permanent vision losses, allergies, kidney dysfunctions and repetitive stress injuries destroys individual lives and depletes society's human capital.

- A corporation that employs workers in insecure jobs with inadequate pay imposes on them and their families the stress of economic insecurity and of attempting to maintain self and family on less than a living wage. This results in family breakdown and violence that deplete society's human capital.

- A corporation that stripmines forests, fisheries and mineral deposits, dumps wastes and sells toxic chemicals that do not break down naturally in the environment depletes the earth's natural capital.

This transfer of wealth from society to the largest corporate shareholders contributes to an increasingly grotesque inequality both within and between nations. No statistic captures this obscenity more dramatically than that of the world's 447 billionaires whose combined assets roughly equal the total annual incomes of the poorest half of the world's people.

All over the world people are indeed waking up to the truth about economic globalization and are taking steps to reclaim and rebuild their local economies. Such communities face basic choices as to how they will direct their efforts. Will they concentrate on competing for a share of the declining pool of good jobs offered by footloose global corporations? Or will they work to create locally owned enterprises that sustainably harvest and process local resources to produce the jobs and the goods and services that local people need to live healthy, happy and fulfilling lives in balance with the earth.

Our experience with the real consequences of economic globalization is pointing to many important lessons. One such lesson is that economies should be local, rooting power in the people and communities who realize that their well-being depends on the health and vitality of their local ecosystem. If it is protectionist to favor local firms and workers who pay local taxes, live by local rules, respect and nurture local ecosystems, compete fairly in local markets and contribute to community life, then let us all proudly proclaim ourselves to be protectionist.

Such choices are not isolationist. To the contrary, they create a foundation for creative cooperation with our neighbors—whether they be in the United States or in other countries. Together we can share experiences, ideas and technology, and join in international solidarity in rewriting the rules of the global economy to restore markets and democracy, favor local over global businesses and encourage cooperative relations among people and communities. It is our consciousness—our ways of thinking and our sense of membership in a larger community—not our economies that should be global.

Millions of people are also making an important discovery: life is about living, not consuming. A life of material sufficiency can be filled with social, cultural, intellectual and spiritual abundance that place no burden on the planet. Living this truth helps to free us from the hold that corporations have established over our lives.

It is time to assume responsibility for creating a new human future of just and sustainable communities, freed from the myth that greed, competition and mindless consumption are paths to individual and collective fulfillment. And people are now doing that all over the world. One way to keep current and connected to these efforts is through the new journal *Yes! A Journal of Positive Futures*, published by the Positive Futures Network.

It will take millions of efforts to reclaim our power and build sustainable communities that work for people and other living things. To work together at national, global as well as local levels, these efforts must be linked together to build powerful populist political movements, on a national and global scale, aimed at radical political and economic reform.

We must press for sweeping political campaign reforms to get big money out of politics. We must establish and enforce rules that require corporations to fully internalize their own costs. We must break up the largest corporations to restore the conditions for efficient competitive market function. We must establish that a corporate charter is a privilege—not a right—and that it carries specific obligations and may be withdrawn at any time the sovereign people decide a corporation no longer serves the public interest. We must mobilize to assure the Multilateral Agreement on Investment is dead on arrival. And we must work to replace the whole range of trade agreements that place corporations beyond public accountability with agreements that protect the rights of people and communities everywhere to economic self-determination. These, by the way, are all issues on the agenda of the Alliance for Democracy, a new progressive populist movement referred to in Ruth Caplan's essay, "A General Agreement on a New Economy (GANE)."

People often ask if I have hope. I do when I remember global capital has only the power we chose to yield to it. We have both the right and the means to reclaim that power should we chose do so. We can and we will reclaim it.

Ten Steps to Community Self-Reliance

Michael H. Shuman

Your city budget is in the red, companies are skipping town, vital public services are shutting down, civic institutions are disintegrating, residents are feeling hopeless. What can you do? Where can you begin?

There are dozens of ideas working in communities worldwide: Locally owned and operated for-profits, non-profits, cooperatives and public enterprises—what I call community corporations—are demonstrating how viable businesses can be anchored responsibly in a single place. They are profitably meeting local needs for energy, food, water and materials. Special banks, credit unions and microloan funds are providing new sources of community finance.

None of these efforts is a panacea, and one undertaken in isolation from the others may have only a modest impact. It is crucial, therefore, to view these initiatives as a package, where each one reinforces the others. The watchword of the Mondragon cooperatives in Spain is "we build the road as we travel," and certainly every sustainable community must find its own way. Yet recent innovations in community economics suggest ten basic steps that can be applied almost anywhere.

---

* Michael H. Shuman is co-director of the Institute for Policy Studies, Washington, D.C. This chapter is adapted from *Going Local: Creating Community Self-Reliance in the Global Age,* which the Free Press will publish in February 1998.

237

1. A Community Bill of Rights

The principles governing economic life today are a disgrace. Throughout the country, local politicians favor cheap goods over a decent quality of life, multinational corporations over locally owned business, dependence on the global economy over independence through self-reliance and federal pork over local power. These priorities and policies thrive, not because they are what the American people want but because they are invisible.

A first step toward community self-reliance is to open up every nook and cranny of the local economy for scrutiny and discussion. The entire community, especially local entrepreneurs, should participate in a series of meetings that culminates in a statement of principles and practices—a Community Bill of Rights. This document should elucidate what constitutes community-friendly business and consumer behavior, and should be distributed to every household. A citizen board might review the performance of local business, and each year award "Good Communitykeeping Seals of approval" to responsible firms (and strip the Seals from irresponsible ones). Appearing prominently on qualifying goods, store windows or service providers' stationary, these emblems would influence people's buying, banking and investing decisions and give local business a powerful incentive to comply with the Bill of Rights.

To earn the seal, a business might be required to file a comprehensive public report on its performance each year. Ralph Estes, an accounting professor at American University, outlines the kinds of data every business might disclose in his recent book, *The Tyranny of the Bottom Line*:[1] What is the salary differential between the best and worst paid employees? Is the workforce unionized and to what extent do employees otherwise have decision-making power? What are the major inputs for production, and how many of these are imported from outside the community? What are the annual levels of discharge of pollutants and wastes, and what is being done to reduce them? What percentage of the ownership of the company rests in the community?

A Community Bill of Rights enables residents to assert that ends come before means and that businesses are only welcome if they serve the community. It creates a set of public norms about commercial behavior that protect the public and provide fair notice to corporations. A business's faithfulness to these norms, while voluntary, carries consequences. Community-friendly corporations get a commercial advantage over unfriendly ones, and unfriendly ones are pressured to leave town.

2. The State of the City Report

Virtually every community in America has a gold mine which economists have yet to discover: unemployed human resources, underused civic institutions and discarded economic assets. Many kind of human assets now lie fallow: the inventiveness of the young; the forgotten skills of retirees; the lively minds of the physically disabled; the survival instincts of welfare mothers and the homeless; the unmarketed talents of local artists. There are underutilized associations that make up civil society, especially in America's smallest communities, which can be given something better to do than adopt a mile of superhighway. Then tally the inanimate assets that have been all but written off: empty buildings, idle machinery, vacant lots, abandoned industrial sites (known as "brownfields"), wasted energy and inefficiently used water.

A community might collect this information in an annual State of the City Report. Coming together periodically to inventory local strengths can be a powerful and unifying civic exercise. If distributed to every household and business, the study can become an important political organizing tool.

What is needed is not just a snapshot of assets but a motion picture of trends. The process of preparing the State of the City Report year after year will enable a community to chart what is getting better and worse—and what to do next. Sustainable Seattle, launched in 1980, keeps track of more than a hundred indicators in surrounding King County. In Jacksonville, Florida, residents decided on 74 key indicators and have set a series of community goals to reach by the year 2000.

3. Anchor Corporations

If done well, the State of the City Report will highlight ripe business opportunities in three ways. First, unmet needs suggest new markets. The discovery of people going hungry could motivate entrepreneurs to build local greenhouses or pursue urban agriculture. Second, unused or underutilized resources suggest promising inputs for production. Piles of discarded wooden palettes provided the feedstock for Bronx-based Big City Forest, which cuts, refurbishes and polishes the wood into gorgeous furniture. Finally, every dependency is a new business opportunity for community corporations. Consumers who discover that the electricity they are using is being transmitted from coal plants hundreds of miles away may be willing to spend another penny or two per kilowatt-hour for local wind power.

The existence of even one or two successful community corporations—using local inputs, producing quality goods, operating in harmony with the environment, selling to local consumers, treating workers well, delivering profits to local shareholders—should inspire others to follow. As the late Kenneth Boulding once said, "anything that exists is possible." These new firms will create new jobs, pump up local purchases by employees and enlarge the local tax base.

Community self-reliance does not mean isolation. It means expanding the economic base to produce necessities for residents and to focus existing resources on more value-added industries. It means insulating an economy from sudden shifts in the price and supply of imports. It means striving to keep a growing share of the economic multiplier at home. As Jane Jacobs argues,

> [A]n import-replacing city does not, upon replacing former imports, import less than it otherwise would, but shifts to other purchases in lieu of what it no longer needs from the outside. Economic life as a whole has expanded to the extent that the import-replacing city has everything it formerly had, plus its complement of new and different imports.[2]

This process suggests that as one set of dependencies is met, new ones may take their place. But in a self-reliant community, each new dependency is less and less vital to its survival. Moreover, each new dependency brings new local business opportunities, provided there are local entrepreneurs prepared to seize them.

4. Community-Friendly Business Schools

Few of us have experience in running a business. But then again, neither did the Spanish priest who started Mondragon. If you volunteer for a soup kitchen or give to a local charity, consider redirecting those good intentions into starting a community corporation.

An important lesson from Mondragon is the central role of training. Many of us with only a liberal arts degree and limited resources have the potential to become good business people. You might encourage your adult-education programs and community colleges, as Milwaukee does, to emphasize accounting and management instead of bridge and tennis. High schools might be given community funding to beef up vocational training. Local non-profits might set up special schools. Two years ago my institute set up the Social Action and Leadership School for Activists, which provides night classes on running non-profits for more than 1,500 adults annually in the Washington area.

5. Community Finance

Nearly all of us have savings and checking accounts, credit cards, IRAs and Keoghs at institutions that we chose on the basis of convenience and rates of return, but not community loyalty. Anyone interested in the future of self-reliant communities who continues this practice is throwing good money away. Even if your current bank scores well by Community Reinvestment Act criteria, chances are good that it is not financing locally owned corporations.

There are many ways to rethink banking. One option is to persuade your commercial bank or thrift to set up a special division that invests locally and allows you to place your savings in that account. Another is to convince your neighborhood association to start a community credit union. If you have difficulty raising enough capital to qualify for federal insurance, you might press your city council to buy equity shares or move payrolls into the bank.

Once a community bank hangs out a shingle and announces that credit is available for community corporations, local entrepreneurs naturally will step forward. If they do not, the bank should find and train them, perhaps through microenterprise programs. Or it might set up a special community-development fund in which no-interest loans are exchanged for equity shares and some management responsibility, as Mondragon does.

As community corporations expand, so does the need for local investors. Convince your neighbors to transfer their pensions and other assets from global stocks and bonds to local ones, and from mutual funds with no preference for place to local mutual funds targeting local businesses. An important ally might be labor. The trade unions in Canada created investment funds in the provinces of Quebec, Ontario, British Columbia and Manitoba that now invest $3.1 billion in worker-friendly small- and medium-sized local business.

6. Community Currency

Local purchasing goes hand in hand with local investing, and nothing facilitates it better than local money. No business should receive a Good Communitykeeping Seal unless it accepts local currency. This requirement is not really punitive, as long as the business is permitted to accept other currencies inside and outside the community. The underlying principle is simple: Any business that refuses to take local currency is refusing to participate in a communal effort to enhance the local multiplier and deserves to be shunned.

Organizers might try to convince the local government to accept tax payments in local currency. This, in turn, would push local government to make sure that more of its payroll checks were issued in local currency, and that more of its contracts and purchases were with local businesses. Municipal employees unions might ask for wage hikes in the community currency.

The administration of a community currency system provides an important opportunity for members of the community to discuss the local economy, and plan its development. Debates over rules of entry— should the system, for example, only involve firms with the Good Communitykeeping Seal—raise important political questions about the meaning of local self-reliance. Deciding the right money supply democratizes and demystifies choices now made in secret by the economists at the Federal Reserve Board, who care far more about keeping national inflation low than creating jobs and stable communities.

7. A Community-Friendly City Hall

All of the steps above can be taken by individuals and organizations acting unofficially. There is no law in the United States that prevents citizens, working together, from framing a set of principles, awarding seals, compiling a State of the City Report, starting locally owned businesses and banks, training community-minded entrepreneurs, waging an invest-local campaign and issuing a community currency.

Still, a local government committed to community self-reliance can accelerate the rate of transformation and add expertise, legitimacy and money. It can make sure that the only beneficiaries of local investment, contracts, purchases and bond finance are community corporations. It can help match local input suppliers and workers with local producers. It can restructure taxes on income, wealth and resources to favor community corporations.

These make up the platform that local politicians should be asked to endorse. Forget the Toyota package and the Walmart deal. Do not get distracted by Jurassic stadium projects, casinos or convention centers. Stop letting politicians get away with overlooking the local economic agenda by grandstanding about crime or welfare moms. And if your mayor or city council members refuse to start making the kinds of economic stands that make a difference, consider running against them.

8. Political Reform

A community that begins the journey to self-reliance will soon encounter powerful enemies. Multinational firms that find themselves losing local markets and special governmental privileges can be expected to retaliate. They will lobby state and national governments to take away local government powers, and will continue to use trade treaties and friendly courtrooms wherever possible to circumvent the inconveniences of local democracy. But their most likely—and dangerous— reaction will be to retake municipal governments.

As long as America remains committed to a free market in political power, in which votes and influence can be sold to the highest bidder, multinational firms with huge financial coffers may be able to lobby, campaign, cajole and bribe politicians away from community self-reliance. Serious campaign finance and lobbying restrictions are therefore essential steps toward community self-reliance.

9. The Local Lobby

Communities have a critical stake in state, national and international policymaking. Local elected officials have to steer the devolution revolution so that they are given real powers over the local economy, not just more responsibilities without the revenue-raising capacity to pay for them. They need to push the national government to reorient the nation's trade policies away from the centralized autocracy of the World Trade Organization and toward the nuanced principles of American federalism. They must convince congress to abolish welfare for corporations and banks that have no loyalty to communities.

If local politicians fail to reset the federalist agenda, the captains of community-destroying corporations will. Literally thousands of lobbyists for multinationals are working the corridors of power in Washington, New York and Brussels. Every community should invest in professional lobbyists to fight for a self-reliance agenda on an ongoing basis.

10. Interlocalism

Practitioners of community self-reliance must be vigilant against parochialism and isolationism. A community that pulls back from the world cannot assume its responsibilities as a part of the world. For too long, we have equated responsible global citizenship with economic interdependence. As political scientists point out, however, the game of interdependence is constructive only if power among the players is balanced. Few communities in today's world have power over the mobile corporations driving globalization. Economic interdependence in this context ensures vulnerability and exploitation.

A more responsible course for a globally minded community is to move toward local self-reliance and to help other communities worldwide do likewise. How? By transferring innovations in technology and policy that foster self-reliance, especially to the poorest communities in the world that desperately need a new approach to sustainable development. The city-state of Bremen in Germany, for example, has been spreading biogas technology to help communities become more self-reliant on energy. Since 1979, it has co-sponsored three biogas conferences, financed a technical newsletter and supported demonstration projects through the Bremen Overseas Research and Development Association (BORDA). Over the 1980s it spent over $300,000 to spread biogas digesters in communities in Mali, Ethiopia and Tanzania.

The quest for self-reliance does not inevitably lead to isolation. Nothing will spread pro-community economics faster than collaboration among cities committed to self-reliance. Communities around the globe need to share information about what is working in community banking, local currencies, urban agriculture, renewable energy production and so forth. The International Council of Local Environmental Initiatives (ICLEI), based in Toronto, now has several hundred dues-paying cities collaborating on state-of-the-art technology and policymaking for ecological protection. The United Towns Organisation (UTO) in Paris and the International Union of Local Authorities (IULA) in the Hague are promoting interlocal collaboration on sustainable development. As more communities plug into the World Wide Web, this kind of global information-sharing and collaborating should become easier and cheaper.

The Lilliputian Strategy

Can a 21st-century economy be localized? The forces of mobile corporations seem so huge, so global, so intractable, that anything done at the local level may seem trivial, like fighting a drought with an eyedropper. But no corporation can exist without customers and investors. Take away either, and even the most powerful firm collapses.

I began my own journey in politics 20 years ago, campaigning against nuclear power for Friends of the Earth. At the time, the spread of nuclear power and its "externalities" (radioactive wastes, meltdowns, spent-fuel accidents, nuclear weapons proliferation) seemed inevitable. About 70 nuclear power plants were in operation and electric utilities were projecting the need to build as many as one reactor a day by the turn of the century. Tens of thousands of protestors tried to stop this $100-billion-plus nuclear industry. They threw themselves in front of tractors and got themselves arrested. They fought dozens of court battles challenging the health, safety and environmental analyses, insisting on modifications in design. In the end, however, these initiatives did not really matter. Something far more subtle, unexpected and powerful destroyed the nuclear industry: People stopped buying more electricity. As Americans began finding and eliminating energy inefficiencies, projections of electricity demand plummeted. Utilities were left to figure out whether nuclear reactors should be the next power plants to be shut down.

There is an important lesson in this. Why exhaust ourselves in fighting badly behaved corporations? If enough of us create our own corporations based on a new vision of community responsibility and if we choose to buy and invest only in these firms, the dinosaurs will either adapt or die. If we create even a small number of self-reliant communities in which every resident has a decent job that produces basic necessities for one another, other communities will visit, learn and follow. We have far more power than we realize.

The great struggle of the 21st century will be between those who believe in cheap goods and those who believe in place. This is a struggle that defies easy ideological definition. Advocates of cheap goods now dominate the major political parties and run nearly every city hall in the country. But most of us know in our hearts that there is far more to life than the next sale at the mall. We long for deeper connections with our families and our neighbors. We are desperate for a sense of place in which we can nurture our culture and take pride in our history. We work long hours to bequeath to our children and grandchildren the kinds of home-grown economies that can perpetually deliver prosperity. Why just wonder about what is possible in your backyard? Why just dream about a past long gone or a future far away? Why not get started today?

Notes

1. Ralph Estes, *The Tyranny of the Bottom Line and Corporate Social Accounting,* San Francisco: Berret-Koehler, 1995.

2. Jane Jacobs, *Cities and the Wealth of Nations,* New York: Random House, 1985.

Social Diversity and the Sustainability of Community Economies

*Patricia E. Perkins**

Introduction

Bioregional and "ecological economics" theory describes the growth of local economic linkages as vital to move post-industrial economies in the direction of sustainability. This involves expanding local stewardship over environmental and economic resources, so that progressively more production for local needs can be done within the community. Far from existing solely in the realm of theory, this is a pattern which is becoming more and more familiar in many parts of North America and Europe.

The blossoming initiatives to create local, community economies can be understood in light of the long history of environmental challenges faced by people living in the industrialized North, and the double economic blows of recession and trade liberalization/globalization exemplified by the passage of GATT and NAFTA in the early 1990s. Many communities in North America and Europe have been organizing

* Assistant Professor, Faculty of Environmental Studies, York University, North York, Ontario M3J 1P3, Canada, tel: 416-736-5252; fax: 416-736-5679; e-mail: ESPERK@YorkU.CA. Adapted from a paper presented to the Seventh Annual International Conference on Socio-Economics, Washington, D.C., April 7-9, 1995.

around environmental concerns for decades. Recession or trade-related layoffs in the early 1990s gave many people both time and incentives to exercise long-dormant skills for generating incomes and exchanging goods and services. Environmental awareness, community organizing and "alternative" employment creation (e.g., in environmental remediation and energy conservation activities) form a natural and dynamic synergy.

Characteristics of Community Economies

As Community Economic Development (CED) practitioners have demonstrated for decades, strong interactive multiplier effects can be generated in communities by creating jobs and needed local services, and keeping money circulating within the local area. "Green CED," as currently practiced, involves the extension of CED ideas to include financing of local economic initiatives via energy and other conservation measures, and environmental remediation as an important job-creation focus. The particulars of how this works, and the potential for "Green CED" in a given community, are, of course, closely related to the specific situation.

Toronto, for example, is home to a large and growing network of locally based initiatives aimed at creating jobs by addressing environmental problems, and increasing local control of basic economic necessities: food, shelter, transportation, money.

When Central American refugees form an agricultural cooperative, lease land outside Toronto and provide weekly food baskets of organic vegetables to urban consumers in a "community-shared agriculture" project; or when the City of Toronto provides seed loans for energy-efficient retrofits of private housing which create construction jobs and save both energy and money; or when a largely abandoned industrial area along the Lake Ontario waterfront is converted to a "green industry" center, this contributes to the development of a more ecological, less wasteful more locally centered economy.

There are countless more examples in Toronto of small-scale organizing and local economic initiatives involving people of all ethnicities and backgrounds:[4]

- Ethiopian immigrants create loan pools like those they knew in Africa, giving members of the group access to far more credit than commercial banks would provide.

- The Waterfront Regeneration Trust facilitates the growth of employment- generating "green industries," such as recycling plants and composting stations, on industrial lands bordering Lake Ontario.

- Neighborhood activists in South Riverdale and other areas work with government and industry representatives to carry out environmental clean-ups, meet the challenges posed by plant closings/"restructuring" and plan for healthy neighborhood development.

- Toronto's Local Exchange Trading System (LETS) allows people to barter a wide range of locally generated goods and services, without the need for cash.

- The Toronto Island Community Land Trust, negotiated by local residents, shows how complex land ownership and stewardship issues can be resolved, using unconventional institutional approaches.

- Pioneering eco-technology pilot projects include the Toronto Board of Education's Boyne River Ecology School and the award-winning Healthy House, both autonomous "off-the-energy-grid" buildings featuring "living machine" natural waste water treatment.

- "Green Communities" initiatives in both the East and West sides of Toronto have forged wide-ranging partnerships to create jobs by upgrading the energy efficiency and environmental quality of neighborhood life.

- The Environmental Centre for New Canadians organizes recent immigrants to Canada around environmental issues, providing a focus for advocacy and job creation.

Several factors particular to Toronto have contributed to the development of a local economy. As the largest city in Canada, Toronto benefits from ethnic and cultural diversity and a wide range of community traditions. It also has relatively well-developed environmental and community organizations and well-defined downtown urban neighborhoods. The existence of a New Democratic provincial government and Canadian federal government with clearly stated environmental priorities made some alternative projects politically feasible in recent years. At the same time, pressing urban environmental problems and an unemployment rate of well over 10 percent have placed local environmental and job-creation issues at the top of the public agenda.

The fact that similar examples of burgeoning local economies can be found all over North America and Europe, however, indicates that in many different contexts the trend persists. This raises a number of interesting research questions, especially concerning the relationship between globalization and the growth of local economies.

Globalization and Community Economies

The "restructuring" that is part of globalization inevitably leads to layoffs in some places, and laid-off workers often cannot move to where the jobs are or be retrained for them. They may either have the wrong skills or be in the wrong places for the global economy to have a niche for them. They also, however, are likely to have very important knowledge of the places where they live—and community connections—which can allow them to substitute local economic activity for whatever they formerly did.

Such a substitution:

- provides personal satisfaction and contact with others;

- furnishes basic goods and services which people need (food, clothing, shelter and personal services, such as childcare and home repairs);

- makes money less necessary at a time when money is probably less available;

- facilitates the development, "remembering," and transmission of skills necessary for personal and community self-sufficiency (such as gardening, food preparation, craft, construction and repair, music, etc.); and

- encourages thrift and efficiency of resource use, and intrapersonal specialization.

All these are things that people intuitively are attracted to and see as pleasant, worthwhile and "good." Delinking from the global economy in this way allows people to relax, depend on and learn from each other in a way that is impossible when time is precious and scarce because "time is money." When you are laid off, you can spend a week teaching your grandson how to rebuild a junked bicycle—that is, *as long as* you have got a home to live in, health care and food on the table.

The lack of basic social services in too many jurisdictions is currently the major constraint on the growth of local economies. Scandinavia and Canada, which have gone farthest toward assuring peoples' basic standard of living, also appear to have more locally focused economic activity (although statistics are nearly impossible to get).

Other factors which facilitate the growth of a local economy include the following:

- *Institutional Flexibility* in the way basic social services are provided that will allow people to switch to locally sourced food, health care and housing if they wish, and use the money saved for other things. This implies welfare payments of a "guaranteed annual income" kind, rather than food stamps, government housing, etc.

- *Acknowledgement of the magnitude of change.* Large-scale economic change happening suddenly in a local area is more conducive to development of local economic activity than protracted, smaller shifts. This is because, in the former situation, people are less likely to feel personally responsible for their being laid off. When big changes hit a community, a unified response seems easier and new institutions and lifestyles are more acceptable.

- *Good Examples.* If pilot projects or small-scale local economic endeavors pre-exist a globalization shock, this can help people to see them as a viable solution to new problems. There may be an openness to community approaches within a short time following economic unheaval, which dissipates over time as people "adjust" on their own, so a strong energy for creation of community-based economic institutions may be lost in the initial learning-by-doing phase. Pre-existing trials and "fringe" projects can reduce this. Individual adjustment and alienation are dangerous because of the high costs in depression, family violence, alcoholism and other health effects, etc. This has many gender implications.

- *Strong Community Connections.* People who know each other well, intergenerational connections and strong local institutions like churches, parents' groups, clubs and sports leagues create the fora for people to expand and develop their interpersonal ties into new areas. There is no substitute for this sort of community self-knowledge.

- *Community Stability.* The longer most people have lived in the area, the easier it is for a local economy to develop. People need to know each other as individuals, including each others' non-work related skills, strengths and needs. They need to know how the community works—its institutions and history. And they need to know the local geographical area well: What grows in gardens? Where can you get sand, or walnut planks, or locally grown apples?

To the extent that globalization depends on accelerating consumption of non-renewable resources, it is destined to be relatively short-lived. Trade in goods, which are sent long distances using fossil fuels, cannot continue at current rates. Transport prices will rise, the goods' final prices will rise and locally produced substitutes will become competitive. Anything made from metal, or which is otherwise energy-intensive in its production processes, will see a similar trend, as will goods which generate toxic or hazardous wastes as waste disposal costs rise. Production/consumption/disposal loops are already becoming shorter, and local economic linkages more important. The use of renewable energy sources is much easier in small-scale, dispersed settings. Decentralization is congruent with ecological economic development.

Environmental crises in resource consumption and waste disposal require local responses. Global capitalism needs local economies and especially local environmental management strategies or it will not be able to continue.[5] Socially, local economies can serve to "keep the lid on" social pressures arising from global economic restructuring, allowing globalization to continue longer than in their absence. The "economic rents" generated by local economic activity are, by definition, fairly dispersed and difficult for corporations to skim off, which is bad for the global economy; on the other hand, it may be worthwhile for corporate interests to turn a blind eye to local economic activity which makes possible the continuation of parallel activity in a global market.

Rising nationalism and the importance of ethnic and cultural identities underscore people's desire for diversity, not homogeneity. In the remainder of this essay, I wish to focus particularly on the issue of social diversity as it affects the growth of locally based economies.

Diversity in Community Economies

From a bioregional and ecological perspective, cultural and biological diversity is a natural response to climatic and geographical differences across the earth's surface; cultural and biological diversity have evolved together.[6] Ecologists detail the role of diversity in increasing an ecosystem's stability and chances of survival in the face of climatic or other shocks.[7] Diverse human cultures have played an important and largely unrecognized role worldwide in protecting plant and animal diversity, especially for species which are used as food.[8]

Humility vis-à-vis nature is linked to respect for other human cultures and diversity; cultural and social diversity allows for, accompanies, fosters and makes possible the growth of other ecological values.[9] "Green politics" is characterized by acceptance and embracing of functional differentiation, pluralism, decentralization and complexity; it is designed to unite diverse viewpoints in a cooperative participatory democracy leading to a deepening of community.[10] "If diversity is good for an ecosystem, it's good for a social movement as well!"[11]

New models of wealth involve wide variation in meeting ecological realities, a "new elegance" in respecting subsidiarity, anti-uniformity and a "credo of diversity."[12] Diversity must be deliberately fostered to permit adaptation to future surprises.[13]

While most CED and ecological economics literature speaks favorably of social diversity as a goal, mention can also be found of the difficulties this can pose in practice for achieving consensus in decision-making processes. For one thing, differences can make "community" hard to achieve.[14] A non-hierarchical process, "honoring what everyone can bring to the group," takes time and care, and well-developed conflict mediation skills may be necessary.[15] Moreover, decentralized communities may have the potential to become anti-woman, racist, anti-Semitic and otherwise repressive.[16] Social change may seem easier to accomplish in a group of like-minded people.[17]

Nonetheless, acceptance and welcoming of diversity in communities is a sign of their health; the skills required to mediate and develop community amidst diversity are extremely valuable for community stability.[18] Nozick points out that the crisscrossing and overlapping relationships among all the various communities that individuals may be part of—ethnic, neighborhood, arts, activist and gender affiliations—both contribute to the richness of society and reinforces the social fabric in a geopgraphic community.[19] It is a common theme in virtually all writing on CED, "Green CED," and ecological economics that social diversity, mirroring and enhancing biological diversity, is desirable, beneficial, "natural" and to be cultivated.

In conclusion, as community economies grow in response to economic globalization and global ecological realities, their characteristics and implications will become clearer. Whether they represent an accomodation to the global economy or an alternative to it, community economies seem destined to play an important role in many people's lives. Social diversity is widely recognized as a positive contributor to their stability and potential.

Notes

1. See, for example, Carolyn Merchant, *Radical Ecology,* New York: Routledge, 1992, pp. 86-87; Jeremy Rifkin, *Biosphere Politics,* New York: HarperCollins, 1991, p. 310; Kirkpatrick Sale, *Dwellers in the Land,* San Francisco: Sierra Club Books, 1985, p. 77; Herman Daly and John Cobb Jr., *For the Common Good,* Boston: Beacon Press, 1989, p. 214; and the discussion in my paper "What Is Sustainable Trade?" in Dev Gupta and N. Choudhury, eds., *Studies in Globalization and Development,* Dordrecht: Kluwer, forthcoming.

2. See, for example, Vidal Rajan, *Rebuilding Communities: Experiences and Experiments in Europe,* Totnes, Devon: Resurgence Books, 1993; Helen Forsey, ed., *Circles of Strength: Community Alternatives to Alienation,* Gabriola Island, B.C./Philadelphia: New Society Publishers, 1993; "Pathways to Prosperity: Across America, Experiments in Community Economy are Changing the Landscape," *Human Economy,* Vol. 14, No. 4, Winter 1995, pp. 12-15; Ross Dobson, *Bringing the Economy Home From the Market,* Montreal:

Black Rose Books, 1993; Marcia Nozick, *No Place Like Home,* Ottawa: Canadian Council on Social Development, 1992. Communities in the South, of course, have struggled for centuries to maintain social and economic autonomy in the face of colonialism and neo-colonialism. The focus in this paper is on the North, although many parallels exist between South and North with regard to the role of diversity in community economies.

3. An overview of this literature is contained in P. Boothroyd and C. Davis, "The Meaning of Community Economic Development" (UBC Planning Papers, Discussion Paper 25, School of Community and Regional Planning, University of British Columbia, Vancouver, B.C., 1991); see also Nozick, Pell, Fortan and others.

4. Sources on "Green CED" in Toronto include Wayne Roberts, John Bacher and Brian Nelson, *Get a Life! A Green Cure For Canada's Economic Blues,* Toronto: Get A Life Publishing House, 1993; *Community Economics,* 130 Spadina Ave., Suite 402, Toronto M5V 2L4; and *Toronto Community Ventures News,* 158 Eastern Avenue, Toronto M5A 4C4.

5. Martin O'Connor, ed., *Is Capitalism Sustainable?,* New York/London: Guilford Press, 1994.

6. Daniel A. Coleman, *Ecopolitics,* New Brunswick, NJ: Rutgers University Press, 1994, p. 126; Rajan, *op. cit.,* p. 59; F. Herbert Bormann and S. R. Kellert, *Ecology, Economics, Ethics,* New Haven: Yale University Press, 1991), p. 39; Richard Norgaard, "Co-evolution of Economy, Society and Environment," in Paul Ekins and M. Max-Neef, *Real-Life Economics,* London: Routledge, 1992, p. 79.

7. See, for example, "It's Natives vs. Newcomers, Down Under in the Worm World," *New York Times,* March 28, 1995, p. B13; Bormann and Kellert, *op. cit.,* p. 13.

8. Rajan, *op. cit.,* pp. 66, 72.

9. Coleman, *op. cit.,* pp. 150-159.

10. David Pepper, *Eco-Socialism,* London: Routledge, 1993, p. 227; Coleman, *op. cit.,* pp. 150, 164.

11. Dave Foreman, quoted in Forsey, *op. cit.,* p. 4.

12. Ernst Ulrich von Weizsäcker, *Earth Politics,* London: Zed Books, 1994, pp. 207-211.

13. Norgaard, in Ekins and Max-Neef, op. cit., p. 86; Nonita T. Yap, *Sustainable Community Development: An Introductory Guide,* Toronto: Ontario Environment Network, 1989, p. 10.

14. Forsey, *op. cit.,* p. xi. See also A. Sayer, "Radical Geography and Marxist Political Economy: Towards a Reevalution," *Progress in Human Geography,* Vol. 16, No. 3, 1992, p. 357, quoted in Pepper, *op. cit.,* p. 230.

15. "Community as Crucible," in Forsey, *op. cit.,* p. 77; Van Andruss and E. Wright, "A People of Place," in Forsey, *op. cit.,* p. 109.

16. "The More We Do, The More We Know We Haven't Done," in Forsey, *op. cit.,* p. 57; Penny Weiss and M. Friedmann, eds., *Feminism and Community,* Philadelphia: Temple University Press, 1995; George Melnyk, *The Search for Community,* Montreal: Black Rose Books, 1985.

17. Paige Cousineau, "Of Mice and Elephants: The Individual, Community and Society," in Forsey, p. 71; Sonia Johnson and Jean Tait, "A Passion for Women's World," in Forsey, *op. cit.,* p. 87.

18. Coleman, *op. cit.,* p. 121; Margo Adair and Sharon Howell, "Women Weave Community," in Forsey, *op. cit.,* p. 37, Cousineau, in Forsey, *op. cit.,* p. 71; Barbara Rose Johnston, *Who Pays the Price?,* Washington, D.C.: Island Press, 1994, pp. 229, 234-285.

19. Nozick, *op. cit.,* pp. 195-96.

References

Bell, David V.J., Roger Keil, Leesa Fawcett and Peter Penz, eds., *Global Political Ecology*, London/New York: Routledge, forthcoming.

Boothroyd, P., and C. Davis, "The Meaning of Community Economic Development," Vancouver, British Columbia: UBC Planning Papers, Discussion Paper 25, School of Community and Regional Planning, University of British Columbia, 1991.

Bormann, F. Herbert, and Stephen R. Kellert, eds., *Ecology, Economics, Ethics: The Broken Circle*, New Haven and London: Yale University Press, 1991.

Coleman, Daniel A., *Ecopolitics: Building a Green Society*, New Brunswick, NJ: Rutgers University Press, 1994.

Daly, Herman, and John Cobb Jr., *For the Common Good*, Boston: Beacon Press, 1989.

Dobson, Ross, *Bringing the Economy Home From the Market*, Montreal: Black Rose Books, 1993.

Ekins, Paul, and Manfred Max-Neef, eds., *Real-Life Economics: Understanding Wealth Creation*, London/New York: Routledge, 1992.

Forsey, Helen, ed., *Circles of Strength: Community Alternatives to Alienation*, Gabriola Island, B.C./Philadelphia: New Society Publishers, 1993.

Greco, Thomas H. Jr., *New Money for Healthy Communities*, Tucson, Arizona: T.H. Greco, 1994.

"It's Natives vs. Newcomers, Down Under in the Worm World," *The New York Times*, March 28, 1995, p. B13.

Johnston, Barbara Rose, ed., *Who Pays the Price? The Sociocultural Context of Environmental Crisis*, Washington, D.C./Covelo, CA: Island Press, 1994.

Lappe, Frances Moore, and Paul DuBois, *The Quickening of America: Rebuilding Our Nation; Remaking Our Lives,* San Francisco: Jossey-Bass, 1994.

Melnyk, George, *The Search for Community: From Utopia to Co-operative Society,* Montreal: Black Rose Books, 1985.

Merchant, Carolyn, *Radical Ecology,* New York: Routledge, 1992.

Nozick, Marcia, *No Place Like Home,* Ottawa: Canadian Council on Social Development, 1992.

O'Connor, Martin, ed., *Is Capitalism Sustainable?,* New York/London: Guilford Press, 1994.

"Pathways to Prosperity: Across America, Experiments in Community Economy Are Changing the Landscape," *Human Economy,* Vol. 14, No. 4, Winter 1995, pp 12-15.

Pepper, David, *Eco-Socialism: From Deep Ecology to Social Justice,* London/New York: Routledge, 1993.

Perkins, Ellie, "What Is Sustainable Trade?," in Dev Gupta and Nanda Choudhry, eds., *Studies in Globalization and Development,* Dordrecht: Kluwer, forthcoming.

Rajan, Vidal, *Rebuilding Communities: Experiences and Experiments in Europe,* Totnes, Devon: Resurgence Books, 1993.

Rifkin, Jeremy, *Biosphere Politics,* New York: HarperCollins, 1991.

Roberts, Wayne, John Bacher and Brian Nelson, *Get a Life! A Green Cure for Canada's Economic Blues,* Toronto: Get a Life Publishing House, 1993.

Sale, Kirkparick, *Dwellers in the Land,* San Francisco: Sierra Club Books, 1985.

von Weizsäcker, Ernst Ulrich, *Earth Politics,* London: Zed Books, 1994.

Weiss, Penny, and M. Friedmann, eds., *Feminism and Community*, Philadelphia: Temple University Press, 1995.

Yap, Nonita T., *Sustainable Community Development: An Introductory Guide,* Toronto: Ontario Environmental Network, 1989.

Funding Sustainability through Microloans, the United Nations Commission on Sustainable Development and Bioregional NGOs

*Brian Hill**

Lack of meaningful financial support has, more than any other factor, kept Agenda 21 and the objectives of the Commission on Sustainable Development as unfulfilled mandates. Now the UN itself is threatened, primarily because the U.S. prefers to default on its treaty obligations under international law. Given these circumstances, the likelihood of obtaining funding to develop sustainable ecosystems, communities and economies seems almost impossible.

This proposal is a beginning attempt to produce alternative means for funding sustainability. Three distinct components, at least, may be able to be combined to produce viable approaches for creating processes, whereby sustainability can be restored to damaged ecosystems and sustainable industries can assure local community and economic balance.

Component One

The following excerpts from the April 1995 Draft Microcredit Sum-

* Brian Hill is director of the Institute for Cultural Ecology (http://www.igc.apc.org/ice). The original document from which these quotes are taken is from William Myers (WMyers@alternatives.org).

mit Plan of Action lay the groundwork for this approach to funding sustainability:[1]

> Key to the mobilization and organization of funding will be a global system of microfinance funds. The Consultative Group to Assist the Poorest (CGAP) . . . [was] launched in June 1995. CGAP currently has over a dozen members from among donor agencies and the regional development banks. CGAP's core objectives are to: (i) strengthen donor coordination in the field of microfinance; (ii) increase learning and dissemination of best practices for delivering financial services to the poor on a sustainable basis; (iii) mainstream microfinance within World Bank operations; (iv) create an enabling environment for microfinance institutions; (v) support microfinance institutions that deliver (or are capable of delivering) credit and/or savings to the very poor on a sustainable basis; and (vi) help established providers of microfinance to assist others start such services in under-served regions.

> [Its] Policy Advisory Group Members include: Muhammad Yunus, Grameen Bank (Chair); Kamardy Arief, Bank Dagan Nasional Indonesia; Nancy Barry, Women's World Banking; Ela Bhatt, Self-Employed Women's Association; Renee Chao-Beroff, Centre International de Development et de Recherche; Martin Connell, Calmeadow; Klaas Kuiper, International Agency for Economic Development; Kimanthi Mutua, Kenya Rural Enterprise Program; Maria Nowak, Caisse Francaise de Development; Maria Otero, ACCION International; Lawrence Yanovitch, Foundation for International Community Assistance (FINCA).

> [CGAP is] . . . a multi-donor effort headed by the World Bank to address poverty through microfinance, [and] can play a vital role in persuading donors and financial institutions to cooperate in creating microfinance funds on global, regional, national and subnational levels. CGAP, paying particular attention to the recommendations of its Policy Advisory Group, should develop the organizational framework and operational guidelines for the funds. A global fund may be created at [or with the help of] the World Bank; regional funds can be created either as independent entities or as part of regional development banks. These funds can offer grant and equity financing as well as soft loans to the national microfinance funds. They can act as guarantors for loans from commercial sources, and promote various instruments for capital markets in order to raise funds for the national microfinance funds.

National microfinance funds can then offer similar services to the grassroots microcredit programs themselves.

Component Two

NGOs are known for their ability to respond quickly to new challenges. International and regional NGOs can create local counterparts to undertake the task of dispensing microfinance, while they themselves can become the source of funds, training, technical assistance and quality control services. NGOs that are not already active may be drawn into the new world of microfinance. The many organizations that have some experience of microcredit will be supported in scaling up.[2]

In order to assure and facilitate the funding for sustainability, NGOs' "local counterparts," via the CSD, can develop through consensus policies and practices for sustainable lending, industries and resource management. If an industry or lending organization is not sustainable, it will be up to the local NGO to draw sustainable practices from within the CSD pool of consensed sustainable practices. In other words, the NGOs must now take an active role in helping to develop sustainability by, on the one hand, insuring that financial mechanisms, industries and resource management policies are sustainable and, on the other hand, helping to provide or develop sustainable practices where they are needed.

Component Three

The UN Commission on Sustainable Development will, hence, become a new forum for achieving consensus on sustainable management and industrial practices for local human communities and resources. In order to assure the most complete bioregional representation possible at this time, there are proposals currently afoot to create regional or bioregional NGO councils. Kenton Miller's new book entitled, *Balancing the Scales: Guidelines for Increasing Biodiveristy's Chances through Bioregional Management*[3] is a solid step in this direction, even though he does not make an outright proposal for bioregional NGO councils. In San Francisco, California, the Planet Drum Foundation (planetdrum@igc.apc.org) has inspired the Bioregional Association of North America, which has begun to integrate bioregional efforts in Turtle

Island. And finally, the Institute for Cultural Ecology (ice@igc.org) has a specific proposal for bioregional NGO councils. According to this proposal, local NGOs will relate to their bioregional council and the council will represent them at global meetings. This would create a global community of bioregional communities funded by and dedicated to local sustainability.

The World Trade Organization's structure and policy, the plans put forth in the recently revealed Multilateral Agreement on Investment (MAI),[4] and the charge that the financial community has woken up to the fact that there is a great deal of money to be made in microlending (where interest rates can range from 20 to 100 percent) all point to the importance of distinguishing between types of microlenders. There are basically two types—those with a primary goal of empowering the poor and those with a primary goal of maximizing profit. Grassroots movements like the Global Trade Watch, which are standing up to GATT, WTO, MAI and multinational corporate control, have a vital role to play in assuring that large banking and corporate institutions actually serve the communities and ecosystems that provide their wealth in the first place.

This proposal, therefore, aims at establishing a process within the CSD, whereby grassroots groups—representing the world's bioregions and their communities—are fully integrated into financial, industrial and resouce management policy. Thus banking houses and corporations become the tools of the people and their environments as was meant in the beginning, rather than the people and the environment becoming the tools of big industry and the big banking houses as of now.

Notes

1. The Microcredit Summit Plan of Action can be accessed at microcreditsum@action.org.

2. *Ibid.*

3. Kenton Miller, *Balancing the Scales: Guidelines for Increasing Biodiversity's Chances through Bioregional Management*, Washington, D.C.: World Resources Institute, 1993.

4. See http://www.citizen.org/gtw for the draft text of MAI.

Microcredit: Band-aid or Wound?

Kavaljit Singh, Nan Dawkins-Scully and Daphne Wysham*

A global campaign to ensure that 100 million of the world's poorest families receive credit for self-employment by the year 2000 was launched at the three-day Microcredit Summit in Washington, D.C., on February 2-4, 1997. Organized by RESULTS Educational Fund, a U.S.-based non-governmental organization (NGO), this summit was supported by an array of financial and development institutions, including the World Bank, International Fund for Agriculture and Development and such transnational banking institutions as Citicorp, Chase Manhattan and American Express.

Suddenly, it appears, everyone is jumping on the microcredit bandwagon. The reasons for this are as varied as the players. Microcredit has the support of many women's advocates who view expansion of microcredit as a potential bellweather for women's empowerment as poor women gain greater access to financial resources. Multilateral development banks, in an era of budget cuts and disbursement reductions, are embracing microcredit as an opportunity for them to move away from the capital-intensive "development as charity" model to the potentially more profitable "development as business." But perhaps most significantly, the financial community has woken up to the fact that

---

* Kavaljit Singh is the coordinator of the Public Interest Research Group, Delhi. Nan Dawkins-Scully and Daphne Wysham are colleagues at the Women's Power Project, Institute for Policy Studies, Washington, D.C.

there is a great deal of money to be made in microlending, where interest rates can range from 20 to 100 percent. Microcredit is often portrayed as a "win-win" option, wherein investors profit handsomely while the poor gain access to resources that allow them to help themselves. The reality, however, is not always so rosy.

In India, a number of self-help groups (SHGs) were created in the 1980s to provide credit facilities to the poor, especially women, in both urban and rural areas. These SHGs stumbled upon a surprising finding: By targeting women, repayment rates came in well over 95 percent—higher than most traditional banks. Impressed by the repayment rates, institutions like the National Bank for Rural Development (NABARD) and Small Industries Development Bank of India (SIDBI) began increasing their lending to SHGs in India. However, the lending rates of SHGs to borrowers were not cheap. For example, SIDBI lent to NGOs at 9 percent; NGOs were allowed to onlend to SHGs at a rate up to 15 percent; and SHGs, in turn, were allowed to charge up to 30 percent to individual borrowers. Although such high-interest credit is touted as a vehicle for poverty alleviation, wherein the poor use the funds to undertake commercial ventures, various studies have found that the loans are largely used by poor people to meet their daily consumption needs.

Nevertheless, similar microcredit operations are now being established in India, with liberal grants from international donor agencies like Ford Foundation, UNDP and the Swiss Agency for Development and Cooperation (SDC). This seed money, in turn, will attract additional capital from the corporate sector and financial institutions. Loans are to be provided to borrowers through a network of subsidiary lending institutions. In order to assure investors a good rate of economic return, these corporate entities will lend at market rates. Critics charge that such microcredit, rather than resulting in poverty alleviation, will simply keep the poor on the treadmill of debt or bypass them altogether in favor of those who can afford credit at market rates.

The World Bank last year launched its own microlending arm, the Consultative Group to Assist the Poorest, (CGAP) with the goal of "systematically increasing resources in microfinance." World Bank President James Wolfensohn announced this program at the 1995 Fourth World Conference on Women in Beijing, claiming CGAP would improve access to microcredit for "the globe's poorest citizens, particularly women."

In order to evaluate whether CGAP and other microlending programs will actually achieve the goals they set for themselves, it is important to distinguish between the two types of microlenders: those with the primary goal of empowerment of the poor and those with the primary goal of profit. The field is already crowded with microlenders of the latter variety, the exorbitant interest rates of which keep the poor trapped in a downward spiral of debt. What is desperately needed are more microlenders committed to the empowerment of the poor. The laudable success of microcredit programs like the Self-Employed Women's Association (SEWA) of Ahmedabad was not won overnight, nor was it derived from a simple process of making small loans to the poor. Microlenders, such as SEWA, combine low-interest microloans with labor advocacy on behalf of women employed in the informal sector, with provision of health care, training and other services, thereby raising the wages, education and standard of living for the women it serves. Access to credit is only a small part of the picture of SEWA's success.

The World Bank's CGAP, by contrast, appears to be narrowly focused on microlending as an end in itself. And the means to that end, critics charge, may do more damage to "empowerment lenders," such as SEWA and Grameen, than good.

A recent report, produced by the Washington, D.C.-based Institute for Policy Studies, found that 46 percent of CGAP's expenditures in its first year of operation was spent on policy reforms, which may benefit lenders but end up hurting poor borrowers, particularly women. For example, CGAP views microlending as unviable in the presence of usury laws—laws which provide ceilings on interest rates. Thus its first order of business at a $500,000 conference in Mali was to get government officials to repeal their nation's usury laws. CGAP also calls on countries to completely privatize their microlending institutions, removing all subsidies for banks that service the poor. Such reforms would force banks, such as the Grameen Bank of Bangladesh that relied on subsidies for 17 years before becoming financially viable, to shut down or charge much higher interest rates to reach self-sufficiency in a shorter time span. CGAP also advocates stronger debt collection laws—specifically collateral laws—which will result in a safer environment for bankers but which could exclude the poorest, and poor women in particular, from access to small loans. CGAP is arguably a small program; its total budget approximates one-tenth of 1 percent of overall World Bank lending. Yet if past performance is any guide, this small program could prove to wield significant clout in defining the parameters and practices for microlenders.

In the current global economic climate, microcredit as a poverty alleviation tool by itself is analogous to giving a man a fishing pole, and telling him to go fish in the wake of a giant trawler with a net spanning the horizon. Macroeconomic policies of liberalization and globalization have destroyed many formal sector jobs; drastic cuts in social sector spending under the rubric of World Bank-imposed structural adjustment programs, coupled with the absence of any social safety net, has further aggravated poverty for the world's poorest. The only option for many poor is self-employment, which microcredit aims to foster. Yet the odds are stacked against the self-employed in the global marketplace. Consumer trends fluctuate nearly as wildly as the economy, which is becoming more prone to external factors as India opens its markets. Aggressive brand selling and marketing together with the strong financial clout of transnational corporations places the poor, especially poor women, at a particularly unfair advantage in the global marketplace.

In this context, microcredit, at best, can lead to micro-solutions. This is not to say that microcredit cannot play a valuable role in poverty alleviation. But any developmental strategy will require far more than the "band-aid" of microcredit on the gaping wound of poverty and unemployment. As microlenders chasing the growing ranks of the poor multiply, a proper regulatory and supervisory framework under which these entities should function must be developed in order to ensure that intermediaries, corporate bodies and others involved in microcredit come under close public scrutiny. Otherwise, these new entities may simply lend legitimacy and greater financial clout to an exploitative form of organized moneylending.

Dissonance, Responsibility and Corporate Culture in the Foundation World

Stephen Viederman and Edward Tasch*

Ours is an age of dissonance. We know that atmospheric pollution poses a significant and potentially irreversible threat, yet gasoline tax hikes are politically unacceptable and surveys show that increases of a dime a gallon for ultra-low emission gas formulations are resisted by consumers. We know that petrochemicals threaten our groundwater, yet we apply fertilizers and herbicides to our lawns and import bottled drinking water from afar. We know that cigarette smoking causes cancer, yet we value the stock of the corporations making cigarettes in the many billions of dollars and include the growth and profitability of these companies in measures of national economic health.

Reflecting this pervasive dissonance, foundations often find themselves in the position of supporting with their investment dollars activities that are antithetical to the charitable purpose of their grant-making. By accepting as axiomatic the Iron Curtain between making money and giving it away, foundations reinforce the kind of corporate culture that identifies corporate responsibility with financial management, relegating social and environmental problems to the provinces of politics and philanthropy.

---

* The authors are, respectively, president and treasurer of the Jesse Smith Noyes Foundation, New York, NY, e-mail: stevev@igc.apc.org.

At the Jessie Smith Noyes Foundation, we have found our way to such questions on both the theoretical and practical levels. In theory, we have become convinced that traditional economic models are fundamentally flawed by their failure to take into account the long-term impact of economic growth on communities and the environment. In practice, we found ourselves owning shares of a company whose environmental impact record and a lack of responsiveness to community concerns that was being contested by a coalition of our grantees.

Once recognized, this dissonance becomes undeniable on both levels. By investing with the sole aim of economic self-interest, we would endorse the market orthodoxies, in which all growth is good and any contradictions are explained away as "side effects" and "externalities." By profiting from passively holding stock of such a company, we would put our self-interest before the interests of our grantees. Once recognized, the dissonance becomes defining: the only desirable actions are those that reduce it.

But moving toward "dissonance reduction" is an uncertain process for a foundation board. The cultural barriers between finance committees and grantmakers are usually impenetrable. Many on the program side have little interest or experience in investing and do not know the language of finance. For those on the investment side, fragmentary or insufficient performance data for "social investment" seem to confirm their assumption that the introduction of so-called exogenous factors into investment decision-making reduces the universe and limits returns.

While on one level it takes considerable commitment and dedication for board members to resist falling into one or the other ideological camp, on another level the dissonance remains quite concrete. For example: Should a health funder own stock in a tobacco company? Should a foundation pursuing disarmament own stock in a munitions manufacturer? Can an environmental grantmaker own shares of a major oil company? How about the oil company that rates best in terms of compliance with environmental regulations or is the first in the industry to sign the CERES Principles?

The shades of gray multiply rapidly, and it is for this reason that many in the financial community are quick to dismiss "social investment" as subjective, difficult to quantify and unwieldy as a portfolio management tool. Yet it has been our experience that while we seldom arrive at clear-cut decisions in particular cases, the process itself is a meaningful one and leads us to central and far-reaching questions: Can companies balance the social and environmental needs of the community in which they are located with the imperatives of distant shareholders and financial markets? Is "environmentalism" something that can be "afforded" by small companies and job-starved communities?

Such questions lie at the heart of our purpose. For if we are "to prevent irreversible damage to the natural systems upon which all life depends," the goal of the Noyes Foundation, and if we believe that in the coming century economic activity will create ecological and political stresses of global proportions, then it is no longer prudent to keep philanthropy and investment separate.

While we are admittedly still early in our process, we see four principal categories of investment activity through which we can promote our purpose, complementing our grantmaking activities to achieve change. These include: screened portfolios, program-related investment, venture capital and active shareholder involvement.

The first two have been practiced in varying degrees for some time. Foundations or church pension funds with strong interests in (or aversions) to particular areas can indicate these areas to social investment money managers, who in turn screen companies in or out of their portfolio accordingly. In the case of program-related investment, foundations can make concessionary, below-market loans to or equity investments in those corporations with a mission consistent with their charitable purpose and which cannot otherwise attract investment from the capital markets. These are both areas in which foundations can enlist significant professional support as they begin the process of dissonance reduction.

We have found our own initial efforts in the areas of venture capital and shareholder activism to be particularly promising. Small, direct investments have been made in companies that make leak detection systems, enzyme-based cleaners and shoes from recycled materials, as well as in an energy services company and a person-to-person marketer of non-toxic cleaning and personal care products. We have made one indirect investment in a small venture fund utilizing investment screens broadly similar to our own, and we are currently considering additional indirect investments in small funds. The potential for venture capital to affirmatively shape the culture of young companies is enormous. Furthermore, this approach to venture investing supports the increasing number of entrepreneurs who share our concerns.

Further, we have become actively involved as shareholders of a large public company. When we discovered that we both held this company in our equity portfolio and were making grants to community groups with concerns not being addressed by the company, we considered two alternatives: divest or collaborate with our grantees to help their voice be heard. We chose the latter. First, we spoke out at the corporation's annual meeting. When the company failed to respond, we filed a shareholder resolution. As a result of our actions, a number of money managers have joined the fray; we have had a number of interactions with corporate management and there is hope that we will influence corporate behavior, albeit in a small way.

We wish to acknowledge just how small the steps we have taken are, especially when measured against the scale of the problems they seek to address. This a learning process. We are a financial institution with less than $60 million under management. Many questions remain, particularly around issues of how to measure the impact of our investments on environment and community. But we are committed to the task of dissonance reduction at the Noyes Foundation: to use asset management and grantmaking as instruments of change. This essay, written jointly by the president and treasurer of the foundation, reflects our commitment to this process.

Chapter 6: What Works for Democratizing Science and Technology?

The political, economic and scientific revolutions of the last 500 years have fragmented the coherence of Western cultural world beyond our capacity to represent its unity. Science, morality and aesthetic representations have been fragmented into specialized spheres of cognitive truth (facts), normative rightness (judgments and values) and aesthetic "expression" (beauty). Each of these disjunct spheres becomes the province of specialized professional competences, with science claiming objective truth and implying conventionality and subjectivity for the other forms of knowledge. In this sense, modern social existence is dependent upon technical information that excludes traditions in which ethical and aesthetical values are shared and forces all people to act upon knowledge that is not related to the whole. As a result, the more technically rational modern social life becomes, the less individual rational *judgment* (as the recognition of the general in the particular situation) is exercised and cultivated.

Today scientific professionals are trained in ways which are lagging culturally behind the contemporary crisis. Professional training processes as well as the academics of science continue to draw their fundamental beliefs from the middle-class ideology of the 17th and 18th centuries. They accept the fragmentation of the world into physical, socio-cultural and personal spheres and stress an abstract individualism in their perception of cognitive science separated from social contexts. This image of science, society and personhood elevates the atomistic "individual" whose performance can be evaluated in terms of the quantitative measurement of achievement and success. Until we can extend the already existing learning processes that enable people af-

273

fected by the new scientized worlds to take part in the problem-solving of their own situations, we will not able to reunite the cognitive and the social, the interrelations of scientific-technical progress and the need for public discourse about choice and responsibility.

As the following essays indicate, many who start professional careers as modernizing experts become de-professionalized partners in the construction of alternatives that affirm reuniting nature and sociocultural arrangements. In this sense, these selected essays are in partnership with those who have resisted globalizing modernity and have demonstrated critical judgement in order to find a sustainable place in the world.

Community-Based Research Models

How people learn to learn where the institutions and expert knowledge systems used for managing complexity fail is the beginning of another approach to social change. Listening to those with negative experience with the globalizing system of progress leads to many questions about Western knowledge systems . As the following essays document, people all over the world protest the reduction of human affairs to economistic rationality that further destroys the only tools and integrative social solidarities that they have to cope with the massive dislocations of the complex "new world order" forming around them.

Toward this end, Richard Sclove describes many of the current models for a democratization of science and technology that are currently being innovated. From the spontaneous learning processes that emerge from parents of children affected by leukemia in Woburn, Massachusetts, to the Dutch Science Shops, diverse models for community-based research have emerged that work to reunite the social and the technical components of everyday life. In each of these models, the learning processes are emergent from affected communities and yet include the professional communities in ways in which one essay calls "mutual learning." Comparing the institutional contexts of the Dutch community-based research methods to the "participatory action research" used more in the United States and beyond, Sclove has charted the beginning of a worldwide community research movement that is a prime example of working alternatives to the unsustainable expenditures on research and development. He is also demonstrating the capability that a more democratized science and technology releases for a world that works.

Bringing Back the Regenerative Holism of Culture-Nature

In the dominant scientistic model of nature, we interact with nature as if our secured scientific beliefs were the "unity of nature" or the "frozen habits" of nature-in-itself. Thus natural science acts upon the assumption that its cognitive abstractions are "real" and that nature is a "composite unity" where analytically separated pieces can be put back together again piece by piece. This composite unity is part of the legacy of a mechanistic image of nature that begins with Galileo's "resolutive composite method." Thereafter, causal science proceeded as if we could analyze nature into its analytically simplistic constituent parts and then reconstruct them into wholes that we can instrumentally control. However, there are reasons to believe that "wholes" may be more fundamental forms of integration than this analytic abstraction of a composite unity can represent—for example, the notion of complementarity in quantum mechanics, the idea of a non-equilibrium structure in thermodynamics or some of the concepts and methods of holistic biology. In this sense, the instrumental "unity of science," projected into nature as a realistic illusion, yields a metaphysical construct of nature that goes beyond our incomplete natural sciences.

To put it another way, the 17th-century-Western scientific revolution excluded the recognition of the interconnected diversity, holism and complexity of a living nature intrinsic to women's knowledge, traditional agriculture and non-specialized subsistence stocks of knowledge. In the 17th century and today, this resulted in a reductionist science that de-norms nature and denies the actuality of living and intrinsically regenerative processes, while at the same time transforming subjects and "citizens" into passive objects of change rather than its active participants. Denying that nature is constituted by discrete components—from atoms to genes, nor reducible to mechanistic processes characterized by single functions—arguments are that it is impossible to separate and manipulate parts of nature for unitary goals without impacts on the whole.

There are many implications of this denial of holism that are fundamental to the legitimacy of the globalization process today. To recognize the abstractive fallacy of this "building-block" world view is the beginning of another view of "A World that Works." There are many voices that challenge the interrelations of reductionist science and globalizing mal-development. For example, Bruno Latour argues that the secret of modernity and the current efforts to forcibly realize a global order are the separation of the socio-economic from the technical-natural and yet the suppression of their relation in actual practices. Hence, as Latour muses, only:

> . . . we (moderns) . . . differentiate absolutely between Nature and Culture, between Science and Society, whereas in our eyes all the others—whether they are Chinese or Amerindian, . . . —cannot really separate what is knowledge from what is society, what is sign from what is a thing, what comes from nature as it is from what their cultures require. Whatever they do . . . they will always remain blinded by this confusion, they are prisoners of the social and of language alike. Whatever we do, however criminal, however imperialistic we may be, we escape from the prison of the social or of language to gain access to things themselves through a providential exit gate, that of scientific knowledge.[1]

For example, all cultures contain nature-culture "hybrids" or quasi-objects that represent nature-culture mixtures—the human component in global warming, the 17th-century construction of "inert matter," hybrid corn and the Green Revolution, laboratory experiments and so forth. But only the dominant modern cultures assert that their biology, medicine, or telecommunications stand outside of culture and represent nature "as is." (This simultaneously makes all other cultures "relativistic" and not capable of objective knowledge of nature; they are caught in a confusion of natural and social causality!)

How cultures understand these complex hybrids or quasi-objects that they create differs widely from the pre-moderns (who are constantly symbolizing and purifying how mixtures of the divine and the natural relate to the social order) to the moderns (who completely deny that such mixtures exist while multiplying them in historically unprecedented ways). Thus while other cultures are essentially preoccupied with how interventions into nature will impact on their social-natural order, modern interventions, such as the creation of hybrid corn or genetic engineering, proceed as if only the issue is neutral "sound science."

A Return to Holism: The Model of Mutual Learning

In actuality, as the Appfel-Marglin and Addelson essay, "Mutual Learning," argues, no nature is separable from culture or culture from nature and therefore the unit of analysis for comparisons should be situated nature-cultures—and not Western science above all other nonscientific cultures. Rather than focusing on the purity of science as separated from the norms or aesthetics of culture, this approach brings into focus how nature-culture mixtures are actually everywhere and those involved in learning are responsible for its impacts on nature-culture interrelations. Such is the story they tell of the Andean Project for Peasant Technologies (PRATEC), which turned away from the model of neutral knowledge and accepted the indigenous culture and horticulture of the Andean world as a guide for a path of "mutual learning." This is not a culturologist rejection of Western science, but a regrounding of learning in situated embedded contexts where learning is "mutual" in the sense of ethically responsible for unifying place and its diverse living communities.

Mutual learning grows out the place itself as a recognition of the implicit order or design that exists, as Sean Kelly and Dave Redwood essay on "Bear River's 'Living Machine'" explicates. Turning natural orders into organic "living machines," John Todd has transformed living organisms into an organic sewage treatment ecosystem. Constructing living machines is the ecological design component of mutual learning and can be duplicated everywhere with careful study of the living order of that place.

This approach to technological innovation differs vastly to the globalization mentality of contemporary technocrats, or geocrats, who would dissolve the classic difference between nature and the artificial by the notion of "system," and therefore erase hybrids of the techno-organic, informational robotics while legitimating a self-organizing globalization process. Simulations of the "global brain," "Biosphere I" and the like are presented as geobiotic models as if they are approximating a new sensory system for the earth, rather than a hybrid that represents a specific modernizing network with particular interests and goals. As Guy Beney cautions, such technological myths are in danger of creating a Global Golem in which potentials represent a new level of totalitarian control.[2]

Notes

1. Bruno Latour, *We Have Never Been Modern*, Cambridge, MA: Harvard University Press, 1993, p. 99.

2. Guy Beney "Gaia: The Globalitarian Temptation," in Wolfgang Sachs, ed., *Global Ecology*, London: Zed Books, 1993, p. 187.

Research by the People: Building a Worldwide Community Research Network (CRN)

*Richard Sclove**

I'd take a bath and break out, like chicken pox. Take another and there's the pox again. I took a water sample to the health department; they said nothing's wrong with it. I thought they was good people, smarter than I was. But they wasn't.
                    —Victim of toxic waste poisoning[1]

Two decades ago children in the town of Woburn, Massachusetts, were contracting leukemia at alarming rates. Other childhood disorders, such as urinary tract and respiratory disease, were also unusually common, as were mothers' miscarriages. Families of the leukemia victims were the first to discern a geographical pattern in the proliferation of disease. Anne Anderson, whose son Jimmy had leukemia, began gathering information about other sick children based on chance meetings with victims' families and word of mouth. She theorized that the proliferation had something to do with the town water supply and asked state

* Richard Sclove is the author of the award-winning book *Democracy and Technology* (New York: Guilford Press, 1995). He directs the Loka Institute, a non-profit organization dedicated to making science and technology more responsive to democratically decided social and environmental concerns. For further information, or to receive periodic electronic Loka Alerts, contact: The Loka Institute, P.O. Box 355, Amherst, MA 01004, USA; tel.: 413-582-5860; fax: 413-582-5811; e-mail: Loka@amherst.edu; World Wide Web: http://www.amherst.edu/~loka.

officials to test the water. She was rebuffed.

The affected families responded by initiating their own epidemiological research. Eventually, they were able to establish the existence of a cluster of leukemia cases and then relate it to industrial carcinogens leaked into the water supply. Their civil suit against the corporations responsible for the contamination resulted in an $8 million out-of-court settlement and gave major impetus for enacting federal Superfund legislation that provides resources for cleaning up the United States' worst toxic waste sites.

Two key factors led to this outcome: (1) victims and their families organized and worked together, and (2) they were able to enlist the help of several scientists at the Harvard School of Public Health and at John Snow, Inc. (JSI, a non-profit organization), who conducted crucial research both with and on behalf of the affected families. The Woburn case is an example of what community-based research can accomplish.[2]

Presently, across the world most research is conducted on behalf of private enterprise, the military, national governments or in pursuit of the scientific community's intellectual interests. Consequently, research agendas often favor elite groups and—wittingly or not—help them maintain privileged positions. Taxpayers and consumers, such as the residents of Woburn, not only experience the consequences but also foot the bill. (And the bill is whopping indeed: annual expenditure on research and development is $145 billion in the U.S. alone—about half of that federally sponsored, and the rest corporate-sponsored.) Yet very little research is conducted directly on behalf of citizens or communities.

In contrast with this prevailing undemocratic model, "community-based research" is rooted in the community, serves a community's interests and frequently encourages citizen participation at all levels. For instance, the Woburn case involved citizens collaborating with university experts as well as with an organization (JSI) that is dedicated to helping citizens conduct research. Community-based research aims not only to advance understanding, but also to ensure that knowledge contributes to making a concrete and constructive difference in the world.

The Dutch "Science Shops": A Model Nationwide Community Research network

One of the world's most highly evolved systems for conducting community-based research operates in the Netherlands. Over the past

25 years, the 13 Dutch universities have established a network of several dozen community research centers (or "science shops") that conduct, coordinate and summarize research on social and technological issues in response to specific questions posed by community groups, public-interest organizations, local governments and workers. Each shop's paid staff members and student interns screen questions and refer challenging problems to university faculty members and students. Today the shops provide answers to about 2,000 inquiries per year.

The shops developed independently in the late 1970s, when small teams of interested professors and students began volunteering their time; as a result, they vary widely in structure, financing and operational procedures. During the shops' formative years, faculty generally performed the research, but now graduate and undergraduate students do much of the work under faculty supervision. (A few shops have the staff to conduct original research in-house, sometimes with the aid of recent university graduates.)

The students who participate frequently receive university credit, often turning their investigations into graduate theses or adjusting their career plans to reflect a new-found sensitivity to social problems. Because students are doing research and writing papers, and faculty are supervising and evaluating their work, both groups are doing what they would be doing as part of their regular workloads; thus the extra cost and time are minimal. The difference is that project results are not simply filed away and forgotten; instead, they help people in the real world address important social problems.

For a question to be accepted by a science shop, the inquiring group must show that it lacks the resources to pay for research, is not commercially motivated and will be able to use the research results productively. Some shops also accept socially relevant inquiries from organizations—such as national environmental groups or local governments—that are able to contribute to the cost of research. However, the shops do not pursue questions posed by individuals, thus avoiding idiosyncratic concerns unlikely to have broader societal relevance. Over time, many of the science shops have specialized in different areas of research and now direct clients to the center best suited to address their concerns. Thus, while a few Dutch universities share a single, generalized science shop, others, such as the universities of Utrecht and Groningen, each have up to ten specialized shops.

The Dutch system has, among other things, helped environmentalists to analyze industrial pollutants, workers to evaluate the safety and employment consequences of new production processes and social workers to improve their understanding of disaffected teenagers. One science shop conducted a study for Amnesty International to discover whether publishing graphic photographs of victims of political torture would stimulate or repel donations. Another assessed the market potential for a proposed women's radio stations. About 5 percent of the questions are posed by Dutch organizations that focus on problems confronting developing nations. (As these examples suggest, the questions addressed by the Dutch shops are as apt to involve knowledge and methodologies from the social sciences and humanities as from the natural sciences or engineering.)

Research projects generally result in a printed report, a summary in the shop's newsletter and a press release. The resulting media coverage, in turn, has benefited universities. As a result of their work with science shops, some professors have conducted follow-up research projects, published scholarly articles on new topics, developed innovative research methods, forged new interdisciplinary collaborations and modified the courses they teach. Through the shops, the Dutch university system now serves society more directly, and, inspired by the Dutch model, science shops have been crated in other European nations, including Denmark, Austria, Germany, Norway, Northern Ireland and the Czech Republic.[3]

Extending and Adapting the Dutch Model in Other Nations

The time is ripe to try something similar in the United States and in other nations. For instance, the end of the Cold War, which for decades dominated American research, presents an opportunity to think creatively about reorganizing the national research system to better serve contemporary social priorities. Establishing a U.S. network of community research centers—adapted from the Dutch model—would represent one constructive approach. Such a network would help university research become more socially responsive. During a time of austerity budget cuts in government programs addressing social and environmental problems, the new centers would provide community groups, local governments and non-profit organizations with some of the support they will need to help take up the slack. By engaging the talent and idealism of youth in social service, the centers also would help universities fulfill their responsibility to educate students for citizenship.

Furthermore, community research centers would provide a healthy counterweight to professors' deepening research ties to industry, which are encouraged by both fiscal duress and government policy. Having community organizations and public-interest groups as "clients" for their own or their students' research would help faculty members maintain a balanced perspective about both the beneficial and adverse social repercussions of research and innovation. Universities, for their part, would be likely to discover that more directly servicing communities is an excellent way to deepen popular support for higher education. Above all, societies as a whole would benefit from the constructive use of what is now a colossally underutilized resource: the vast pool of faculty-supervised college and university students, whose budding research abilities could be harnessed to aid communities at very low cost.

The budget for a typical Dutch science shop is modest; the small staff is normally paid out of the university's general budget, supplemented by government and foundation grants or the fees paid by client groups that have financial resources. In the United States, foundation and federal programs also could help support the activities of community research centers. For example, the Environmental Protection Agency's Office of Policy, Planning and Evaluation has a state-and-local-outreach program, and there are a variety of programs within the National Science Foundation, the National Institute of Environmental and Health Sciences, the Department of Housing and Urban Development, and even the Department of Defense that can support various types of community-based research projects. Universities could contribute directly by granting interested faculty members short periods of release time to help start a community research center.

Depending on local needs and funds available, community research centers could perform a variety of useful functions. Some might contribute to regional planning for defense conversion or for environmentally sustainable economic development. Others might organize community forums on public policy or help citizens participate in public- or private-sector research-and-development projects.

A Foundation to Build On: Case Studies of Community-based Research in the U.S.*

---

*Madeleine Scammell and Doug North—respectively, deputy director and intern with the Loka Institute—assisted in preparing the following case studies.

The impetus for a U.S. network of community research centers could, in principle, come from any level of government. But non-profit organizations or individual universities—indeed individual faculty members and students—can help begin one on their own. Some models already exist: the non-profit Loka Institute, which I direct, has begun compiling case studies of community-based research in the U.S. and elsewhere. These will become part of a "tool kit" of resources that we are assembling to support the creation of new community research programs in the U.S. as well as a new transnational Community Research Network:

The Policy Research Action Group Chicago, Illinois. *Determining health care needs of refugee women in Chicago.* The Policy Research Action Group (PRAG), a collection of Chicago-based academics and community activists, has built a network that connects research with grassroots activism. For example, PRAG found an intern from Northeastern Illinois University to work with a community-based organization (the Mutual Aid Associations of Chicago Collaborative) that sought data on the health care needs of refugee women in the uptown neighborhood of Chicago. In cooperation with Mutual Aid, the intern designed and administered a questionnaire that was given to 85 refugee women. As a result of the research, the Mutual Aid Associations started a women's health program that offers refugee women greater access to the health services they need.[4]

Jacksonville Community Council Inc., Jacksonville, Florida. *Assessing the fairness of public service distribution in Jacksonville.* The Jacksonville Community Council, Inc. (JCCI) is a broad-based civic organization that performs research intended to improve the quality of life in northeast Florida. In 1994, JCCI examined Jacksonville's public services—including streets and drainage, parks and recreation, and police and fire services—to determine their geographic distribution and to evaluate whether needs were being met throughout the city. Their research led to the creation of an annual "Equity Index" that assesses the distribution of public services in the Jacksonville area, and has prompted the Sheriff's Office to implement a new sector system for more equitable patrol services.[5]

Center for Neighborhood Technology, Chicago, Illinois. *Research to maintain jobs and environmental standards in the metalworking* *industry.* The Center for Neighborhood Technology (CNT) worked with non-profit industrial development organizations to help Chicago's metal finishers comply with environmental regulations that threatened this key industry and thousands of related jobs in low-income neighborhoods. CNT helped the groups to identify the problems facing metal finishers; access free environmental audits of their plants; investigate the requisite technology for compliance, determine criteria for a centralized approach that would offer economies of scale; and secure implementation financing. The effort represented a remarkable collaboration between manufacturers and environmentalists.[6]

The Urban University and Neighborhood Network, Ohio. *Evaluating computer resources and access in Ohio neighborhoods.* The Urban University and Neighborhood Network (UUNN) fosters collaborations between university researchers and urban neighborhood organizations among Ohio's largest cities. For instance, UUNN sent questionnaires to 500 neighborhood groups across seven cities to assess the computer resources available to them. The survey showed that Ohio's urban neighborhood groups have almost no Internet access. UUNN is using these results to try to secure resources to meet this unfulfilled need. In addition, they are constructing a site on the World Wide Web that will describe all participating neighborhood organizations, so that groups across the state can communicate with each other and enhance the efficacy of future research. [7]

The Dutch versus U.S. Approaches

In contrast with the Dutch science shops—which generally operate on a professional "researcher/client" model—existing community research in the U.S. is more often based on "participatory research" (PR) or "participatory action-research" (PAR) methods. In every case, a community group, non-profit organization, trade union or the like normally poses the initial problem or research question. But in PR, the group asking the question is also involved as an active collaborator in most or all stages of conducting and completing the research. Participatory action-research (PAR) is not only participatory, but intended to contribute actively toward—and also to learn from—constructive social change.

The origins of PR and PAR are largely in the developing world, where they emerged as part of popular reactions against elitist, top-down development programs.[8] But participatory approaches have also developed spontaneously "far below" in the industrialized world—e.g., by residents of neighborhoods who feared local toxic waste exposure or by HIV-AIDS activists insisting on a strong role for patient advocacy groups in designing clinical trials for new therapeutic drugs.

A healthy portion of community research in the U.S. is organized by independent, community-based non-profit organizations rather than by universities. Perhaps both this and the greater prevalence of participatory research methods, in comparison with the Netherlands, reflect the greater degree of class stratification and cultural, racial and ethnic diversity in the U.S. That is, many U.S. colleges and universities are private (i.e., not government-supported), and even the public ones sometimes have fairly large tuition fees. Universities have also often operated in the U.S. in high-handed, community-insensitive ways. Thus, when you talk with social or grassroots activists in the U.S., you find a large reservoir of scepticism or outright hostility toward universities and university researchers.[9] In this context, it is not hard to understand why independent non-profit organizations are responsible for much of the community-based research that is conducted in the U.S. It is also easy to see why participatory research methods are appealing: they are a way for those asking the question to help ensure that the subsequent research is genuinely serving their interests.

On the other hand, a major strength of the Dutch system is the extent to which students are engaged as researchers. This introduces students to socially engaged research, is very economical for society as a whole and harbors the potential over time to help transform universities to make them more socially responsive. These are central features of the Dutch system that I would like to see copied more in the U.S. Another major strength of the Dutch system is simply that is is a comprehensive, nationwide system—it can tackle virtually any qualifying research topic formulated by any community group or organization from anywhere in the nation.

Next Steps: Building a Worldwide Community Research Network (CRN)

> I learned that there was a real thirst for collaborative research, a real need for the Community Research Network.
> —CRN Conference Participant, July 21, 1996

A phrase popularized by community activists—'Think globally, act locally'—can serve equally well as a slogan for university-based scientists who want to use their knowledge to help their neighbors. . . . Two weeks ago . . . the Loka Institute . . . gathered together some 50 activists, scientists, and university officials . . . to lay down plans for a Community Research Network.

—*Science,* August 2, 1996, pp. 572-573

Although there are already organizations and programs in the United States conducting community-based research, they are few and far between, and often they are invisible or inaccessible to those who could benefit most from their assistance. And in contrast with the Dutch network, U.S. community research practitioners have frequently been unaware of each other's work and have had little sense of themselves as part of something larger—e.g., a nationwide system or social movement.

For this reason, the Loka Institute has been working for several years to establish a Community Research Network (CRN) in the U.S., modeled partly on the Dutch national network. We began by assembling a national board of advisors and establishing a community research discussion list on the Internet.[10] In July 1996, with support from the University of Massachusetts at Amherst, we organized a national conference to plan the CRN.

The four dozen participants from across the U.S. (plus one each from Canada and the Netherlands) included representatives of such grassroots, non-profit and university-based organizations as: the Southwest Organizing Project, Northeast Florida Community Action Agency, the University of Wisconsin School for Workers, Chicago's Policy Research Action Group and Southeast Asia Center, the Applied Research Center in Oakland, the Science and Environmental Health Network, and others. Our objectives in establishing a CRN include to:

- Help existing community research efforts learn from one another;

- Facilitate new research collaborations and the creation of new community-based research programs;

- Help community groups identify centers and programs that can provide research assistance; and

- Enhance the institutional acceptance, public visibility, stature and funding of community-based research.

The mission of community research centers *individually* is to provide their respective constituencies with the resources to investigate social, technological and environmental concerns, and to act on them through direct voluntary effort, legal action or public policy channels. However, we also envision that a central goal for the Community research Network *as a whole* will be to evolve into the decentralized, democratic core of a new national laboratory system. That is, rather than acquiesce to perpetuating a $25 billion-per-year national lab network that is an anachronistic by-product of World War II and the Cold War, we seek to incubate an alternative national research system that will be responsive to community and citizen concerns of the 21st century.

As an interim step toward this long-range ambition, we hope that the CRN will also function as an organizational platform for building a national constituency concerned with diverting local, regional and national research funds and research capabilities to community-based research, and thus away from military and other anachronistic or socially dubious research endeavors. This is politically ambitious, but we will try. After all, if the current research budget allocation remains intact, the established research system is sure to keep generating social problems at a much faster rate than even a mature CRN could ever respond. And besides, avoiding problems is invariably more effective than trying to fix them afterwards.

Participants in our July 1996 conference set a number of key priorities for the fledgling CRN. We accorded high priority to establishing an accessible communications infrastructure (both Internet-based and not), and to ensuring that grassroots and social change groups are fully involved in developing the CRN. A number of participants are presently beginning to create an easily accessible database through which, ideally, anyone will be able to find out who is doing community-based research, what they are studying and how to contact them. This, too, will become part of the larger "tool kit" we are developing for use by anyone interested in community-based research.[11]

Conference participants also concurred that the CRN should be transnational in scope, rather than arbitrarily limited to working within national boundaries. Indeed, the Loka Institute's efforts have inspired a related initiative by Canada's Humanities and Social Science Federation to establish a Canadian CRN as well an effort to launch a first community research center in Israel. But the idea of a transnational CRN offers further intriguing possibilities. For instance, why should not community research centers in several nations:

- Coordinate joint projects to investigate simultaneously the local activities of selected multinational corporations in each nation;

- Evaluate international agreements (such as the General Agreement on Tariffs and Trade) from community-based perspectives; and

- Conduct popular technology assessments on the evolving international division of labor, or on opportunities for local involvement in guiding the evolution of transnational technological systems (e.g., telecommunications, transportation and agriculture)?

Questions remaining include: How can we most effectively nurture a collective capacity to initiate such transnational collaborations? How can grassroots organizations remain true to their local members and constituencies, and yet participate at least some of the time in addressing translocal concerns? Can community research centers in the industrial and post-industrial worlds develop mutually beneficial and respectful collaborative relations with related community-based research institutions in the developing world (e.g., via the international network of indigenous knowledge centers)?[12] Apart from possible transnational research collaborations, what steps can we take for better transnational mutual awareness and learning among community research centers, participatory researchers, indigenous knowledge centers and the like?

The vision of a worldwide community research network upholds the promise of transforming research from an all-too-frequent enemy of the people into an organic expression of popular concerns, creativity and empowerment instead.

Notes

1. Quoted in Phil Brown and Edwin J. Mikkelsen, *No Safe Place: Toxic Waste, Leukemia, and Community Action,* Berkeley: University of California Press, 1990, p. 145.

2. *Ibid.*

3. More information on the Dutch science shops is available via the World Wide Web at <http://www.wtm.tudelft.nl/secties/Wetenschapswinkel/eghome.htm>.

4. *PRAG Report of Projects, 1991-1995.*

5. *JCCI Annual Report 1993-94.*

6. Valjean McLenighan, *Sustainable Manufacturing: Saving Jobs, Saving the Environment,* Chicago: Center for Neighborhood Technology, 1990.

7. Personal communication with Randy Stoecker, University of Toledo Urban Affairs Center, Toledo, Ohio, March 1996. More information is available on the UUNN, and other U.S. community research programs via the Loka Institute's World Wide Web page, at <http://www.amherst.edu/~loka/outreach/others.htm#comres>.

8. See, for example, Orlando Fals-Borda and Muhammad Anisur Rahman, *Action and Knowledge: Breaking the Monopoly with Participatory Action-Research,* New York: The Apex Press, 1991; and Peter Park, Mary Brydon-Miller, Budd Hall and Ted Jackson eds., *Voices of Change: Participatory Research in the United States and Canada,* Westport, CT: Bergin & Garvey, 1993.

9. See, for example, Douglas D. Perkins and Abraham Wandersman, "'You'll Have to Work to Overcome Our Suspicions': The Benefits and Pitfalls of Research with Community Organizations," *Social Policy,* Vol. 21, No. 1, Summer 1990, pp. 32-41; and Philip Nyden and Wim Wiewel, "Collaborative Research: Harnessing the Tensions Between Researcher and Practitioner," *The American Sociologist,* Vol. 23, No. 4, Winter 1992, pp. 43-55.

10. To subscribe, send e-mail to <listserv@ncsu.edu> with a blank subject line and "subscribe scishops (your name)" as the message text.

11. Further information about the CRN is available by subscribing to the scishops listserv (instructions in note 10, above), visiting the Loka Institute home page on the World Wide Web(http://www.amherst.edu/~loka) or by contacting the Loka Institute di-

rectly (see footnote at beginning of this essay).

12. Information on the international network of indigenous knowledge centers is available on the World Wide Web at http://www. iitap.iastate.edu/cikard/cikard.html#world *or* by contacting the Center for International Research and Advisory Networks (CIRAN), P.O. Box 29777, 2502LT The Hague, The Netherlands; tel: 31-70-4260321; fax: 31-70-4260329; e-mail: ciran@nufficcs.nl *or* ikdm@nufficcs.nl.

Mutual Learning: The Case of PRATEC*

Frederique Appfel-Marglin and Kathryn Pyne Addelson

In this century, the solutions for problems facing humankind and all living beings have been defined by a dominating knowledge. The dominating knowledge has been embodied in modern science, which claims to be rational and objective, producing a universal knowledge for use by all peoples. Other ways of knowing have been dismissed as superstition, traditional beliefs or mere opinion. The object of scientific knowledge is supposed to be "the real world" and the knower is any properly educated person.

This kind of knowledge is, in effect, designed for disembodied knowers, individuals who are divested of their historical, cultural and personal clothing. Objective knowledge requires that the knowers (officially at least) should have no aims other than to contribute to progress in the scientific knowledge of man and nature. But, of course, science and scientists are embodied not only in their own gendered, racialized, class-fed flesh, but in professions, disciplines, careers, university and research faculties, departments, neighborhoods, families, love affairs and on and on. Even the term, "scientist," covers up these things.

Critics have persisted in asking, "Who are the knowers?" They have insisted that the so-called "objective knowledge" is in fact produced by knowers with a politically skewed perspective. The criticism

---

*Andean Project for Peasant Technologies. The authors, respectively, teach anthropology at Smith College and philosophy at Mount Holyoke College in Massachusetts.

was that knowers were "disembodied" whereas they were actually embodied as higher-class, Western-educated men. The knowledge work itself, critics say, is integral to governing industrialized societies and to the success of capitalist markets as well as many forms of domination.

In this essay, we offer a different account of knowledge-making by arguing that notions of objective knowledge of the real world that are central to modern science are in fact those needed to legitimate the position of power, influence and authority that professionals hold. We believe this means that a challenge to the dominating knowledge requires a change in the situated practice of professionals. It requires a new understanding of what science is and a new strategy for solving serious environmental and social problems.

What we propose is a change in the relationship of knower and known, particularly a change in the relationship of professionally trained experts to the people the experts are said to serve with their knowledge. Our belief is that knowledge of nature and knowledge of society cannot be separated from the knowledge of how we should live. Ways of life are best understood by those who live them, and their knowledge must be respected. This requires a relationship of "mutual learning" in which people change themselves and each other. Mutual learning requires mutual respect, not privileging one sort of knowledge as the one truth about reality, whether the privileged knowledge belongs to Western science or so-called "indigenous knowledge."

Mutual learning requires a change in the understanding of knowledge as something that is abstracted from local practice, and so universally applicable and suited for centralized policy-making. Mutual learning requires a great sensitivity to the local situations. In our conclusion to this essay, we suggest that in trying to solve problems we place a focus first on local situations as the basis for change rather than starting out with the goal of formulating for national or global policy. We also recommend a long-range perspective rather than a quick fix or special issue approach.

Rather than talk in the abstract about mutual learning, we will tell a story of mutual learning in practice. It is the story of what a group of people has accomplished in the Andes of Peru, by the name of PRATEC. This group of people created a way of respecting each other's knowledge, a way that required drastic changes in the lives of the professionals involved. Before telling the story, we will give a little background history of the dominating knowledge and the process by which professionals came to dominate.

Issues in the Epistemologies of the Professions

Knowledge is a relation between knower and known, and an account of knowledge sets conditions on that relation and describes the character of knower and known. For example, a shaman is someone who has a spiritual relation to the sources of knowledge and who works with caution and respect, not as some distanced observer out to remake the world with his or her knowledge. The housewife has to know how to nourish her family in the situation in which they live, using the foods available in the time available, and she does it out of care for all with particular knowledge of each. In contrast, the modern sciences are supposed to contribute their knowledge to aid control of nature, human societies and even individuals.

Scientific knowledge is defined around the ideals of objectivity and value neutrality. Objectivity, in this sense, requires a detached, neutral, distanced, disinterested approach in a publicly observable space. The distance is between the knowing subject and the object of knowledge, and so the distinction between knower and known, is central—there is a knower, an object known and objectivity characterizes the relationship. In this sense, knowledge is not a reciprocal relationship. In the dominating knowledge, the knower knows and defines the object; the object at best gives feedback through test or observation devised by the knower. This is very different from the knowledge of shaman who must come to know how the object of his or her knowledge defines itself.

Equally important is the universality claimed for scientific knowledge. Although there are many objects of knowledge, there is one knowledge about those objects. The knower required by this objective knowledge is stripped of social, political, historical and even biological features. As Aristotle said millennia ago, so far as nature goes, all rational beings, if they have true knowledge of reality, have the same knowledge. This idea, of course, allows people who allegedly have the knowledge to use it to dominate others.

Of course, there are no naked, disembodied knowers of the kind that objectivity requires. All knowers are embodied in their social, biological and historical situations. All knowledge has some aim, even if that aim is said to be "knowledge for knowledge's sake." Objectivity is less a condition on knowledge than a code of ethics and politics for the professions and disciplines of the sciences. The embodiment of these purveyors of objective knowledge is indeed in science—not science, the ideal body of knowledge, but science, the real body of professions, disciplines, research institutes, careers, departments, funding agencies and the like. Even the insistence on standards concerning objective and universal knowledge of reality seem to us a justification for the powerful status of professions in modern society and, of course, the authority of the experts. Even the abstract conditions on scientific knowledge are translations of conditions on the professions. For example, one main criterion for an occupation being designated as a profession is detachment—in the sense of having in a particular case no personal interest such as would influence one's action or advice while being deeply interested in all cases of the kind (Hughes, 1984). This is the distance required between knower and known that translates into objectivity. It yields the asymmetry in the relationship between knower and known that is essential for the dominating knowledge.

The development of science as a profession, that is, as a salaried occupation, made knowledge work a commodity on the labor market, so that knowledge was also produced as a commodity. This process removed science both from the morality and the passions of civic and family life, in other words from community. This development happened in the mid-19th century along with the rise of the modern university in Germany. The idea of the autonomy of knowledge from state control was extended to the autonomy of the sciences from moral or religious questions. This served to insulate science from politics, morality, religion and passion (Proctor, 1991: 80).

Professional knowers are disembedded from community life and the constraints and meanings arising from it; they are separated from communities' purposes of regenerating themselves, that is, of continuing to live. Just as at the beginning of the industrial revolution at the end of the 18th century, production of goods became separated from communities' concerns with the advent of the factory mode of production, by mid-century a similar separation occurred with the production of knowledge in the universities. As E. P. Thompson has formulated it, work and life became separated and this was followed by the separation of knowledge and life.

The separation of knower and community led to a radically different understanding both of nature and how we humans know nature. In the late 18th and early 19th centuries, there were figures, such as Gilbert White in England, Henry Thoreau in New England and Johann Wolfgang von Goethe in Germany, who refused to be isolated from society and its moral fabric. Their science was not severed from their social affections and had not become a disinterested, abstract search for facts with no regard for their consequences or uses. These individuals, and others like them in the Arcadian or Romantic Western traditions, criticized the withdrawal of the specialized scientist from full social engagement into enclaves of professional elitism and indifference (Worster, 1977: 19).

The Arcadians related to nature with anything but detachment. Their spirit can be captured by Thoreau's famous phrase: "I to be nature looking into nature with such easy sympathy as the blue-eyed grass looks in the face of the sky" (cited in Worster, 1977: 78). Thoreau's practice was a daily intimacy with nature, smelling, touching, ingesting, looking, listening, giving his whole being to nature. For him, facts were not abstractions in a disembodied mind but sensual experiences of the whole man. Furthermore, Thoreau and the Arcadians with him rejected a Cartesian view of nature as an inert, unfeeling machine. For them, all of nature, even rocks, were one animated whole. "The earth I tread on is not a dead, inert mass; it is a body, has a spirit, is organic, and fluid to the influence of its spirit, and to whatever particle of that spirit is in me" (Thoreau, 1851 in Worster, *ibid.*: 79) For Thoreau, Goethe and others, the body and nature were not machines but part of a living interdependent whole.

Detachment was neither possible nor desirable. Humans are of nature not severed from it; there is a reciprocity between humans and the other beings: "It is not merely crow calling to crow, for it speaks to me too. I am part of one great creature with him; if he has voice, I have ears." (Thoreau in *ibid.*: 80)*

Although Darwin more than anyone else asserted the kinship between humans and animals, his theory was used to legitimize a non-reciprocal attitude toward nature and society. In this sense, the publication of *The Origin of Species* in 1859 marks a triumph of the dominating knowledge. Detached, unsituated and cold rationality becomes the tool through which order and productivity are achieved. Gone is the view of the naturalist as a humble member of nature and the human

---

* Gilbert White published in 1789 a natural history of the village of Selborne, sourth of London, where he was a curate. This book became famous (more than 100 editions by the 20th century) in the 1830s when the world he describes was vanishing under the onslaught of industrialization. For White, the natural setting of his village was not separated out from the human community. His affection and concern for his parishionners were integral to this affection and concern for the other beings sharing the same place.

community. Gone is the reciprocity and mutuality that such humility enabled. Objective knowledge emerges victorious, all other approaches delegitimized as being "romantic."

By the mid-19th century, this view of reality and of knowledge became embodied in the professions. Figures such as White, Thoreau and Goethe became increasingly impossible. Detachment, objectivity and universality were institutionalized in the professions and the modern university. Care, affection, mutuality and nurturance were relegated to the non-salaried realms of civic and domestic activities. The production of knowledge—like the production of goods—became an end in itself, severed from the continuities of particular communities and landscapes.

Now, at the end of the 20th century, it is becoming clear that the alliance between science, the market and the state has brought havoc to life on earth, be it human or non-human life—whatever short-term benefits accrue to the few. The environmental crisis needs no detailing; the regenerative capacity of nature is severely stressed. The social crisis in a country like the U.S. is deepening; the devastated inner-city communities are the harbinger of things to come. Procreative issues, understood in their broad sense of social activities that include the care and love and raising of the new generation by communities, become subordinated to economics and are increasingly addressed through the use of expertise and social engineering rather than mutual care, love and understanding.

Human procreation and regeneration, whether human or not, are inherently local, situated, particular and mutual; they require of us attachment rather than detachment; they require of us mutuality rather than a one-way observation where the professional scientist is not a participant but a judging observer who is not him or herself to be judged. Knowledge is removed from the communities and given over to the experts. Professionalization institutionalizes a one-way, non-mutual, dominating relationship between people and between people and nature. It is also a way of maintaining power. Everett Hughes, a forefather in the sociology of the professions, wrote that, "every profession considers itself the proper body to set the terms in which some aspect of society, life or nature is to be thought of and to define the general lines or even details of public policy concerning it" (Hughes, 1984: 375-376).

The difficult issue is, of course, that the ways open to us to heal ourselves and nature are entangled with Western science, the market and the state. It may be that we cannot live with them, but at this time many people in many places cannot live without them either. But that does not mean there are no creative ways to make spaces for something different. At this point, we need to relate the history of PRATEC.

The Story of PRATEC

PRATEC (Andean Project for Peasant Technologies) is a small organization in Peru. It was founded in 1987 by Grimaldo Rengifo who invited two other men, Eduardo Grillo and Julio Valladolid. These three men had spent a lifetime working for development. Rengifo was the director of a large Peruvian-Dutch development project; Grillo was the director general of the National Bureau of Agricultural Statistics and Research in the Ministry of Agriculture, and Valladolid was teaching plant genetics at the Agrarian Faculty of the National University of Huamanga in Ayacucho. Through its extension program as well as through its research and teaching, the Agrarian Faculty was deeply involved in bringing the Green Revolution to the Peruvian countryside. These three men are part of the first generation of Peruvians from non-elite peasant background to have access to university training.

All three were involved in bringing the Green Revolution to the Andean countryside. The revolution exported not only hybrid seeds and technological packages; it also exported research and curricular agendas for universities worldwide. The Green Revolution was born in Iowa in the 1930s with the development of hybrid corn. It is the story of how private enterprise broke the biological barrier to the commodification of the seed; its ability to regenerate itself had proved a formidable barrier to commodification. The development of hybrid corn in the U.S. was achieved through political machinations and the infusion of massive research funding that gave birth to Big Science two decades before the Manhattan project. No research was conducted on plant population improvement through open pollination, the manner in which peasants worldwide improve their crops (Kloppenburg 1988: 104). This development was immediately exported in the 1940s to Mexico and later to many other parts of the globe. It was one way of opening vast global markets for the commodified hybrid seeds (HYV) and the many other industrial products that the HYVs require for their very viability.

Rengifo, Grillo and Valladolid of PRATEC had devoted themselves to development in the belief that this was the way to help their people.

They lived through many phases and fashions in development: community development, participatory development, appropriate technology and sustainable development. They tried everything available, always striving to capture the reality of Andean peasant agriculture and of peasant life in general. At long last, they came to the conclusion that the problem lay in the very idea of development and particularly in the Green Revolution and the science that gave birth to it.

Development had failed. The evidence lay scattered throughout the Peruvian landscape in what some of their colleagues have called "the archaeology of development"—ruined infrastructures, abandoned to the elements after the project officials had left, uncared for by the peasants for whom they were intended and left to deteriorate. The evidence also lay in their repeated efforts to devise better methodologies and their final realization that, within their professionalized perspective and constraints, it was impossible to approximate peasant reality and therefore make development relevant to peasant lives.

They began to study other disciplines, hoping to find better knowledge of peasant reality. They devoted themselves to reading all they could about peasant life in sociology, anthropology, history and other fields. They emerged from that experience feeling that in all those studies peasant reality was being described from a position outside that reality. What they also discovered is that academic studies divided peasant reality into an agricultural domain that was the specialty of mostly agronomists and a cultural domain where anthropology, sociology, history and a few other fields of the social sciences and humanities positioned themselves.

Once they began to understand peasant reality from the inside, they realized that development consisted of a package of practices, ideas, epistemologies and ontologies that came from the modern West, profoundly alien to the native peasantry. During their extensive travels throughout the country, they became convinced that native agriculture and culture were not only adequate to the native environment but were alive and vibrant. This was so despite the efforts of development education and, before that, a long history in which native culture was the target of "extirpation of idolatry." Native agriculture and culture embodied a totally different mode of being in the world, of being a person, of relating to others both human and non-human, and of notions of time, space and nature. They awoke to the pregnant awareness that it is only from the perspective of development, which makes one wear modern Western lenses, that peasant agriculture and culture looked backward, stagnant and altogether lacking. From their new perspective, quite the opposite was the case.

What they saw was that agriculture and culture were inseparable. Cultural practices, such as rituals, festivals, ways of organizing labor and kin groups and much more, were all geared to the nurturance and regeneration of their world, both natural and cultural, the two being inextricably intertwined. They saw that the introduction of hybrid seeds and Green Revolution packages not only interrupted the regenerative cycles of the local cultivars, but of the culture as well. With irrigation, hybrid seeds, chemical fertilizers and pesticides, two or three crops could be raised where only one or two were raised previously. But this destroyed the cycle of rituals, that is to say, both the biological and cultural regenerativity transforming these peasants into individuals dependent on the market rather than on each other, nature and the *huacas* (deities). For the penetration of the Green Revolution, not only the regenerativity of the seed had to be broken through but the regenerativity of peasant communities had to be broken down. Such an assault began at the university, paving the way for the penetration of the commodification of life.

The members of PRATEC realized that the knowledge imparted to them at the university was designed to bring about the commodification of the peasant world. They also realized that this knowledge was functional to modernity and capital and inimical to the peasant way of life.

They had become aware of the richness and diversity of cultivars that are grown in this ecologically variable environment. The Andes are one of the eight world centers where agriculture first emerged 10,000 years ago. The peasants continue to grow an astounding variety of plants. Such variety is not only the result of the great ecological diversity of the Andean landscape but also of peasant practices. The members of PRATEC began to dedicate their lives to articulating these discoveries. This effort at articulating both agricultural/cultural peasant practices, as well as the epistemologies and ontologies embedded in development practice and more generally in modern Western knowledge, was undertaken as an action to "accompany" what was happening with the peasantry.

Increasingly since the 1950s, the peasantry has been engaged in what Peruvian anthropologist Enrique Mayer has called a "silent movement" (personal communication). They have taken over the lands of the large landed properties, the haciendas, in direct action without forming political parties or syndicates. With the agrarian reform of 1969 (which simply made official what had been going on for a long time), peasant reappropriation accelerated. The government tried to replace the hacienda system with government cooperative schemes. It took only 25 years to reveal the total debacle of that state scheme. Andean peasants are reappropriating these lands as well as organizing themselves in their own way.

The members of PRATEC wanted to facilitate or accompany that movement, not to theorize or lead the movement. Such a posture would in their eyes betray the communitarian ethos of Andean peasants. Being intellectuals and not farmers they found their own way of participating in the resurgence by passing on to others like themselves what they had learned. This was particularly important because, in the agrarian faculties of Peruvian universities, Andean agriculture is nowhere taught. What is taught is temperate-zone industrial agriculture. But they also helped other technicians and intellectuals come to a realization of the implications of professionalization and of development grounded in modern Western epistemologies.

The members of PRATEC speak of industrial capitalism as "the modern West" since this is how they experience it. They learned the knowledge at the university and for a long time bought its message of universality and objectivity. But they experienced it nonetheless as a foreign import. It initiated them to a world different from the one they came from. They are aware of the internal heterogeneity of "the modern West" as they are of the internal heterogeneity of "the Andean world." The contrast they speak of is one that they and many like them have experienced as university-trained persons of Andean origins. But it is only through their action of "deprofessionalizing" themselves and of acting/writing from within the Andean collectivities—an action that one of us has called a "moral passage"—that they could come to know with clarity the impossibility of participating in the Andean collective actions from within the professions. This realization brought with it a clarity as to the nature of the knowledge they were taught in school and at the university which simultaneously allowed them to see the Andean world with clarity. They speak of this double realization as a process of decolonization of the mind which has allowed them to clearly see and thus participate in the Andean world. They share this double realization with others like them in the context of a course they started teaching in 1990.

By "deprofessionalizing" themselves, the members of PRATEC rejected a location in the professions and the constraints of academic disciplines. They devote themselves to the task of writing on peasant agriculture and culture from an Andean point of view. In order to do this, they place themselves alongside the peasants who have retaken lands and have established their own way of tilling the soil and of organizing themselves. The knowledge that they make is born from sustained and intimate interactions with Andean peasants over a life time. It is a collective way of making knowledge. That process has required of them a simultaneous thorough deconstruction of modern Western epistemologies and ontologies, a process that is always ongoing since the realization that words, concepts and categories they had been using turn out to distort or blind them to some aspect of peasants' lives always arises.

The deprofessionalization meant not only that the members of PRATEC abandoned the right to know the Andean world in terms of their disciplinary concepts and methods, and thus abandoned cognitive authority, it meant a total change in their lives. Their writing emerges from their own passionate bonding with Andean peasants and the Andean landscape. Their deprofessionalization meant that there was no longer a double participation for them—namely, a participation in their professions and one in "the field." The world of which they write is the world they are making alongside the peasants, to which they are passionately bonded through a multitude of particular relations.

They quit their jobs because they realized that willy-nilly in their professions they were agents of governance, specifically the state's purpose of developing the country. They joined the collective action of the Andean peasants engaged in retaking possession of lands and re-establishing their own forms of organization and practices. They speak of the Andean world not as judging outsiders but as ones bonded to that world. They write books and articles as intellectuals not with the intent of adding to the fund of knowledge and of creating an objective account but as their chosen field of action. They write of the Andean world not primarily as a world to know but as a world to live in, to participate in, to be a part of and to collectively make.

The members of PRATEC emphatically recognize that they are situated and have partial perspectives. They insist on it. What they write about is not offered as a universal account but as an account in the Andes, valid only for that particular location. PRATEC's writings and courses are the way these intellectuals participate in collectively making the Andean world alongside the peasants and those who join their cause.

PRATEC's purpose is not the making of a more objective knowledge or the devising of an alternative science. Such purposes take for granted the nature and legitimacy of the social organization of knowledge in the university. This veils the manner in which professional knowledge, even situated knowledge, is embedded in institutions that are instruments of governance.

Objectivity and emotion free rationality can only be had in the autonomous university. To locate oneself in terms of gender, class or ethnicity—but to fail to locate oneself as a knowledge-maker in the professions and the institutions created for those professions—leads to a continuation of abstract theory-making. It continues the privileged position of such knowledge and does not challenge the "cognitive authority" of professional knowledge-makers.

What Do We Learn from PRATEC?

In their praxis and their writings, PRATEC members have created a space in which dialogue occurs with the Andean peasant through living and working among them. Within the universities, governmental and international research institutions, that peasant world may be spoken about, and it is certainly spoken to, but it is not spoken *with*. PRATEC does not approach the Andean peasant world as a problematic world to improve upon, transform or change. Nor is it approached as a changeless, native world to understand in the fashion of the old anthropology. It is approached as a world to live in and collectively fashion. What are facts to "objective observers," are their very lifestyles to Andeans.

This means a radical shift; it is a shift that entails the recognition that knowledge emerging from those other locations—the professions and their various institutional locales—is one that dominates and presses upon the Andean peasant world. However much one may rethink that knowledge, deconstruct it, criticize it, it will continue to dominate worlds lived by virtue of its being set apart, distanced and therefore privileged. It will continue to dominate, that is, unless the very practice of the professionals and other experts undergoes serious change.

Although the PRATEC experiment gives food for thought, it is situated in its knowledge and its politics, and rightly so. We cannot obtain general rules or a grand political theory and strategy from that situated experiment, but it is possible to learn from it.

First, it is important to remember that all knowledge *is in fact situated,* socially and politically, including knowledge in science and technology. No one enters a situation as a bearer of neutral knowledge. All are embedded in social, political, moral and economic webs. The political and economic bias of science and technology is well known, particularly in development work. What is important to mutual learning is that all trained professionals, paraprofessionals and professional activists should understand this and take responsibility for the outcome of their own work. Taking responsibility is not satisfied by instruments for measuring short-term project success according to scientific or other criteria, even when criteria are set in conjunction with the local people. Responsibility concerns larger, long-range outcomes for life.

Second, we believe that knowledge *ought to be situated* not in the research institutes and state bureaucracies alone, but in the communities as well. This is fundamental to mutual learning, and it requires reciprocity in making new knowledge—and, of course, understanding what reciprocity amounts to in the situation. Mutual learning is not accomplished by saying: "The community group has a question and we translated it into a researchable question, trying to define the real problem together with the group concerned." This approach may be appropriate in a small number of cases when an urgent court or legislative battle is in question, particularly at a national or global level. But with a mutual learning approach, the questions cannot be translated into "researchable questions" unless the researchers and the scientific research paradigms themselves are changed, except in the most urgent cases—and those cases are less common than politicians and activists would have us believe. Urgency is usually a short-range judgment that must be made by understanding long-range outcomes.

The PRATEC example suggests these things, but it also may help us to overcome the idea that these "isolated, indigenous cultures" are artifacts that must be protected and preserved by responsible experts and activists. The Andean peasants are dynamic peoples living in the modern world—which is why professionally trained experts could work with them. We are not demonizing science or the expertise of professionals. We are advocating mutual learning as a politics, and that requires courage to change the world. And that is why the professionals had to change themselves to work with them.

Equally important, once we give up the nostalgic, "museum" view of indigenous culture, we can see that it would be a mistake to think that mutual learning only applies in cases where we judge there is some "traditional" or 'indigenous" culture. All life knowledge is situated and even in the United States, where community is allegedly shattered and tradition is reduced to lifestyle, people still live in their places. People's lives and places must be nurtured. Places everywhere face invasion from science and its experts or from policy based on science, and also from the market (particularly the markets in employment and property). There should be no pretense that because people are citizens of a postmodern nation that there is no invasion because it is "their ideology, their science, their economy," what is characterized as belonging to "the white man" or "the West." Places everywhere are invaded and shattered. Even the U.S. and the nations of Europe are *developing* nations. Just because the communities were invaded long ago does not mean that the invasion is not still going on or that these people's questions can just be translated into problems appropriate for trained scientists to solve. Nor does it mean that professionals should come in with their knowledge to help the little people fight things out in the courts and get a fair shake under fair democratic rules. Those kinds of services may be needed in emergencies, but they need to be embedded in the long-range endeavor of mutual learning, where the changers are also the changed.

All of this means not only that mutual-learning projects have a focus on place; it means that they have a longer-range perspective than is usually given to "problems," particularly in the Western democracies where solutions are often tied to political elections or market profits. And so mutual learning requires not only a change in the non-reciprocal relationship of expert/community, but also a change from the quick-fix approach that takes for granted the permanence of the state and the global marketplace, with their abbreviated visions.

Why are long-range perspectives required? Because the past and the future of peoples are at issue. Past should be understood and preserved. Future should be worked out within a time scale that suits the place in question. Connections need to be worked out with wider circles of people to encompass as much of the regional, bioregional and global problems as need be, but always starting with peoples in places. This is an issue of strategy and method. The problems with the environment that face us cannot be solved in a piecemeal, interest-group manner, for, in the end, that is a means of maintaining the status quo. The global problems cannot be solved by fiat from on high—whether "on high" is a group of powerful nations, the United States, influential NGOs or some famous global conference on the environment. They need to be understood and solved in multitudes of situations, through mutual learning and action, and worked out over the long term. Why? Because this is where people live and act—it is not solely a moral or political question of democratic participation. In the PRATEC case, it is the situated Andean communities that provide the fire that stokes the future. In other places, it is other communities.

Mutual learning may require a change in attitude toward the state, the law and public policy, as well as the market and science and technology. Action on those fronts may be necessary from time to time, or even necessary in a long siege. But an emphasis on place means that state, markets and the professionals that run them should not be taken as fixtures of human life—neither with the goal of preserving them and acting to improve them nor with the goal of overthrowing them. Places and peoples live in the world of nations, corporations and experts, as mice live in a house with a cat, birds live in a meadow with a hawk, or deer live in a forest with packs of coyotes or human hunters. There is room to move, space to live, if we learn together in mutual respect. Professional experts and professional activists can contribute to opening that space. Given a long enough time, if we take our own places seriously enough and our own situated knowledges, it may even be that the old science, the state and the market will wither away.

References

Burt, Sandra, and Lorraine Code, eds. (1995), *Changing Methods: Feminists Transforming Practice*, Peterborough, Ontario: Broadview Press.

Code, Lorraine (1995), "How Do We Know? Questions of Method in Feminist Practice," in Burt and Code, eds., *Changing Methods*, Peterborough: Broadview Press, pp. 13-44.

Haraway, Donna (1991), *Simians, Cyborgs, and Women*, New York: Routledge.

_____ (1996), "Situated Knowledges: The Science Question in Feminism and the Privilege of Partial Perspective," in Keller and Longino, *Feminism and Science*, New York: Oxford University Press, pp. 249-263.

Harding, Sandra (1986), *The Science Question in Feminism*, Princeton: Princeton University Press.

Harding, Sandra, and Merrill Hintikka (1983), *Discovering Reality*, Dordrecht, Holland: D. Reidel.

Herrmann, Ann and Abigail Steward (1994), *Theorizing Feminism*, San Francisco: Westview Press.

Hughes, Everett C. (1984), *The Sociological Eye*, New Brunswick, NJ: Transaction Books.

Jaggar, Alison (1983), *Feminist Politics and Human Nature*, Totowa, NJ: Rowman & Allanheld.

Keller, Evelyn Fox, and Helen Longino (1996), *Feminism and Science*, New York: Oxford University Press.

Nelson, Lynn Hankinson (1990), *Who Knows: From Quine to a Feminist Empiricism*, Philadelphia: Temple University Press.

_____ (1993), "Epistemological Communities," in L. Alcoff and E. Potter, eds., *Feminist Epistemologies*, New York: Routledge.

Proctor, Robert H. (1991). *Value-Free Science: Purity and Power in Modern Knowledge*, Cambridge, MA and London: Harvard University Press.

Rorty, Richard (1991), *Philosophical Papers*, 2 Vols., New York: Cambridge University Press.

_____ (1979), *Philosophy and the Mirror of Nature*, Princeton: Princeton University Press.

Stich, Stephen (1990), "The Fragmentation of Reason" (Preface to a *Pragmatic Theory of Cognitive Evaluation*), Cambridge, MA: MIT Press.

Worsten, Donald (1977), *Nature's Economy*, New York: Cambridge University Press.

Bear River's "Living Machine"

Dave Redwood and Sean Kelly*

Build it and they will come.

On the banks of a river that ebbs and flows with the daily tides of the famous Bay of Fundy, the newest tourist attraction in the picture-postcard village of Bear River has lured over 8,000 visitors from around the world. "It's been a nuthouse, just herds of people," says manager Carol Armstrong—welcome relief to a rural Nova Scotian community hard-hit by a fisheries crisis and the closing of a nearby military base. Local inns, retail stores and the town's two restaurants have all re-ported big increases in business since the attraction was built in 1995.

So what's generating all the excitement? A theme park? The world's largest lobster statue? A casino? Would you believe a sewage treatment plant?!

Bear River (population 881) is home to an innovative wastewater treatment facility that relies on living organisms to do the dirty work. Nestled in a river valley between steep hills and located next to the town's windmill, the glass structure looks like an ordinary greenhouse. Inside however, plants, snails, protozoa and algae—fueled by the power

* David Redwood is a freelance writer living in Halifax who also works with youth and environmental groups. Sean Kelly is editor of the Sustainable Times, a Canadian newsmagazine on solutions. This piece was adapted from the article "A Living Machine," which appeared in the April 1996 edition of *New Internationalist* magazine.

of the sun—are busy breaking sewage down into clean water that flows into the tidal river. What the tourists are seeing in Bear River is a "living machine," an award-winning example of design following a natural ecosystem.

The Earth itself is the source of inspiration for the facility: the planet's ecosystems are, after all, circular, renewable, no-waste economies powered by the sun. Waste from one process becomes the raw material for another, nothing is thrown away. Nature is living testament to the truth of the adage "waste not, want not." In Bear River, even human waste is a resource that can be put to good use, if you think like an ecosystem.

Stepping through the sliding glass doors of the sewage treatment plant, one expects an odorous welcome. Instead, you are greeted with the humid, verdant-smelling air typical of any large greenhouse. Rows of clear-sided tanks are topped with an assortment of colorful vegetation, including floating aquatic plants, such as duckweed, water hyacinth and mint, and non-aquatic varieties of willow and dogwood that are suspended by netting, their roots continuing down into the nutrient-rich mixture. Snails cling to the inside of the transparent tanks, sucking up algae growth that blocks essential sunlight from reaching life in the water. A large indoor "pond" contains more plants, including banana and fig trees.

Plant manager Carol Armstrong doubles as an enthusiastic tour guide. She escorts a constant stream of visitors—many who show up unannounced, curious about this engineered ecosystem—through the voyage the waste takes before it flows into Bear River. Pumps first inject fine air bubbles into an underground tank of blended sewage and septage. When combined with the bacteria that Armstrong adds daily, this sewage becomes, quite literally, food for consumption. It enters the five-foot-high tanks where bacteria, algae and protozoa are at work detoxifying many harmful microbes in the water. These organisms find a habitat on the roots of the larger plants suspended on the water's surface, which in turn absorb toxins not broken down by the smaller species. "We tried some water lettuce and semi-tropical plants," Armstrong observes, sounding more like a farmer than a sewage treatment plant operator, "but most of them were overcrowded by other plants. Local varieties seem to do better than tropical ones, so next spring I will be planting a lot of local stuff. I am going to have fun with this." The plants are currently composted but she has plans to sell the ornamental flowers, once more residents are hooked up to the plant; the facility is only operating at one-fifth its capacity of over 50,000 litres of wastewater a day.

Gravity moves the stream of wastewater through the tanks, an indoor pond and finally to a small engineered marsh. There, grasses and irises absorb remaining toxins. A screen removes the last of the suspended solids, and an ultraviolet light completes the process by disinfecting the water. The final chemical-free product is discharged into the river clean enough to drink. It is a world of difference from most conventional methods of treating sewage which, while sometimes using a limited number of organisms to treat sewage, are not symbiotic ecosystems and have to resort to chemicals like chlorine to "clean" the water. And, making the natural treatment facility seems too good to be true, it is less expensive to build and maintain.

Dr. John Todd, the inventor of Bear River's "living-machine" process, has long advocated this kind of ecological design as the "application of natural relationships to human need and to the integration of humanity with the larger natural world around us." His ideas go beyond just mimicking nature's cyclical model; he advocates using living organisms themselves as the basis for engineering. For 25 years, he has researched living species that can form durable, self-designing and, above all, useful ecosystems. From Ocean Arks International, the Massachusetts-based research organization he established in 1980, Todd has become a modern-day prophet of the wide-ranging benefits of ecological design:

> When one is designing a living machine, you do it with a whole range of ideas in mind. You could be designing it to treat waste water as in Bear River. You might be designing a living machine for the production of foods; for the generation of fuels; for heating buildings in a cool climate; to integrate industrial activity with human settlement and agricultural activity.

> [Ecological design] grows out of the place itself—what's there now, the climate, biota, geology, topography. Whether it is urban or rural, First World or Third World . . . in fact, the opportunities for this in the tropics are just as great, or greater, than in the North. [And when you begin the work, you carry a very unique set of tools.] A wonderful example is in one of our living machines, where we use an Amazonian catfish which is very effective at ingesting sludge. How many conventional engineers would think of having an Amazonian catfish in their tool kit?

Unlike a dead machine, a living machine's parts are primarily live things. Its structure or its skeleton is inert obviously—tanks, greenhouses, things like that—but its [inner workings] are thousands or hundreds of thousands of parts made up of thousands of species. What they have is the ability to interact with each other, to self-organize, self-design, self-repair, self-reproduce.

These lessons of cyclical thinking can extend to the broader economy. Maximizing the use of non-renewable resources through durable design, reuse and recycling is one application of the philosophy. A more imaginative step is an industrial park where many businesses are integrated, symbiotic members of one common closed-loop system. The machine partsremain inert, but the natural cycle is adopted. A company's waste becomes a needed input in a second company's industrial process. The heat created in the manufacturing of one product fuels the energy needs of another.

Products can also be designed for their entire life cycle. The Environmental Protection Encouragement Agency of Germany promotes what they call "Intelligent Products"; for example, products created from sustainably managed renewable resources in a way that when returned to the earth, they biodegrade without toxic effects. "Durables" such as cars, televisions and refrigerators would not be sold but rather licensed from a company. The product would always belong to the original manufacturer, to be constructed, used and returned within a closed-loop system. When a company knows their product will end back on their doorstep, yet they cannot legally throw it away, decomposition, reuse and refurbishment soon become central pillars of design.

Back in Bear River, the living machine continues to enjoy strong grassroots support, and the community is building on this spirit of cooperation and pragmatic optimism. The town's citizens have transformed a closed school into an arts center and a recently abandoned bank building has become a community health clinic. As Carol Armstrong says, "This place is magic." You can almost smell it in the air.

Part Four

What Is Real International Security?

Chapter 7: What Works to Build International Security and Peace?

Originating in the formation of the Bretton Woods institutions in 1947 and completed in the Gulf War and the Uruguay round of GATT, a "New World Order" has split off from the international order that began with the Peace of Westphalia (circa 1648). This new order goes beyond the power of nation-states to control and has unleased a massive redistribution of wealth from the poor regions and classes to the rich and new forms of structural violence that have received little recognition in the daily media. A compelling example are the structural adjustment programs of the International Monetary Fund that impose a Westernizing economic development regime as if that is the single objective for all social evolution.

But what about security of person and place, indeed of the biosphere on which all life depends, not only from armed violence but also from structured violence which kills slowly but just as inexorably and certainly?

Just as the G-7 advocates imply that economic globalization is good for all—because it works—so the state system claims that the right to "legitimate" violence that "works." Is not military might essential to police the world and maintain law and order against the many terrorists or renegade states that would destroy peace? In the end is not the war system essential because the realties of power require it? Douglas Lummis argues that considering war to be the epitome of "what works" is absurd, the carnage-littered history of the 20th century offering overwhelming evidence that this is not so:

313

To give the state the "monopoly of legitimate violence" and ask it to keep peace—this experiment has been tried. In our time, the armed state has killed more human beings than any other institution in human history. As the century draws to an end, it is time to come up with some better ideas.

Documenting this judgment, Sidel, Shahi and Levy show how the real costs of war impact on human health, the environment and the resources needed for sustainability in incredible ways. Their essay comprehensively documents the staggering costs of the war system in ways that should put demilitarization at the top of the agenda for citizen and government action everywhere. The overall consequence of their analysis is that real security and peace does not depend on mere military might at all, but on how effectively the military is integrated into the lives of members of the community in which it operates and how effectively it is held accountable for its actions and its impacts on society and the environment. Real security will engage civil socety in various ways, such as having a largely volunteer military with professional soldiers kept to a minimum. Members of the military are also members of society who should contribute their time and energy to helping maintain and achieve social justice. But for this transformation to occur, much stronger democratization processes than we have today must prevail.

What Are the Real Conditions for Inclusive Democracy?

Jean-Bertrand Aristide points to the fact that neo-liberal economic policies dictate a sharply reduced role for government and that worldwide transitions toward democracy are occurring just as states are running out of resources and becoming saddled with debt. Never has there been such an opportunity for dialogue and democratic collaboration across national boundaries in the struggle to alleviate misery. But if democracy remains a purely formal structure—part of the window dressing of economic globalization—a historic opportunity will be lost.

Ronnie Dugger also points out that the moment is crucial for the realization of democracy in the face of a world order increasingly dominated by giant corporations larger than most nation-states. Therefore the Alliance for Democracy, which he has been instrumental in launching, is a call to reclaim and reinvent democracy and to pick up the banner carried by the 19th-century populists who denied the legitimacy of corporate domination of society. It is a call to take back the powers that have been seized by corporations but because of the global reach of corporate rule, this will also require building a global people's movement. But in this task, populist movements in the United States like the Alliance have a special responsibility; if people in the U.S. cannot get control of the corporations here, there is little hope that people elsewhere can do it either. The non-violent struggle to create an effective populist movement here must be linked to people-first organizations around the world and is the first step in the formation of a democratic, just and sustainable Earth community.

What Is the Relationship of Sustainability to Real Democracy and Real Security?

Larry Rasmussen has reflected on an appropriate ethics for a sustainable world and proposes that we think of the total earth-human process as involving an earth economics and an earth community. Indicating that the creation of sustainability has a beginning but no end, he proceeds to elaborate the virtues and ethical principles essential to make sustainability apply to environment and society together. Thus participation must be inclusive and related to both eco-efficiency and eco-sufficiency. Equity for both the natural and the human communities across time requires accountabilty, responsibility and acceptance of subsidiarity. But none of these ethical guidelines will be sufficient until the quality of life is transfomed in directions that reverse the current materialist consumer frenzy fanned by the insatiable corporate need for ever-expanding markets and promote a material simplicity and spiritual richness essential to a real Earth community.

Alternatives to War that Work

Douglas Lummis*

We will not have come up with much of an alternative to our ruling world system until we have come up with an alternative to war.

Of course, such an alternative to be an alternative form of life (not of death) must "work." Initially this may seem a formidable condition. In the United States (though not in all countries), war is seen as the very epitome of what "works." It is assumed that pacifism can be dismissed with the rejoinder, "Of course, that would be best if it were possible, but it will not work." War, brutal as it is, is the very essence of effectiveness. The surest way to mould the world into a desired shape is by direct force.

Thus any direction of "alternatives to war that work" must begin by rethinking what "working" means, and asking whether as a matter of historical fact, war has not "worked" so well, as many believe. A few obvious facts are worth remembering here. At the beginning of the modern era, the nation-state was formed, granting to itself what Max Weber called the "monopoly of legitimate violence." This right includes the right of belligerency, which means the right of the state to authorize soldiers to kill people without being considered murderers. This is the legal and moral foundation of war, the "right" on the basis of which it is carried out.

Why did the people allow this right to the states which ruled over

---

* The author teaches at Tsuda College in Tokyo. His latest book is *Radical Democracy,* Ithaca, NY: Cornell University Press, 1996.

them? Because it was believed that the states would use it to protect the lives and security of their citizens. As we approach the end of the century, it would be well to ask how this experiment has worked out in fact.

The hypothesis on which the justification for the state's monopoly of legitimate violence, and in particular of its right of belligerency rests is that it will use these to protect its citizens from violent death. In fact, however, in the 20th century more people have suffered violent death than at any other time in human history. Who has been the big killer? Not gangs. Not terrorists. Not drug dealers. Of course, it is the state. In this century the state, protected by its right of legitimate violence, has killed (according to one estimate) some 150 million people.

The majority of those people were killed not by foreign governments, but by their own.

The experiment does not seem to be working.

One might respond, no one claims that war "works" when you lose, but only when you win. But whether it works even then depends on what you mean by "work." Despite its defeat in the Vietnam War the United States has surely been the winningest of the warrior states in this century. Since the Civil War, all the wars in which the U.S. military has fought have succeeded in keeping the violence of war far away from U.S. towns and cities, its civilian citizens and their homes. This seems a great achievement. But things are not so simple.

How much of the violence of war that has leaked back in across the border? Don't we deceive ourselves in searching for the causes of violent crime in fantasies of violence (e.g. television) rather than in real violence (war and training for war). We teach our boys that being a man means being able to kill a person (i.e., being a soldier). We train millions of young people in the use of guns. We send tens of thousands abroad and give them actual experience in shooting people to death. Should we be surprised that many continue the same kind of activities at home? Thousands of our murderers and armed robbers first held a gun in the army; the founders of the L.A. gangs learned their trade in the Vietnam War; Timothy McVeigh learned his in the Gulf War—and on and on. War comes home.

In thinking of alternatives to war, then, it would be a mistake to define the situation as one in which a brutal-but-effective method is to be replaced by something less brutal but equally effective. If the aim of war was to have been the protection of the safety and security of the people, it has not been effective anywhere.

What might a "workable" alternative look like? Logically the opposite to war is understood as peace. But to say this is to say very little, not because it is a virtual tautology but rather because peace itself has come to be defined as something intimately tied up with war. Peace, we are taught, is a condition created by war, enforced by war and protected by the threat of war. Peace is achieved when the people are "pacified." So long as we continue to think in this way, peace, while the "opposite" to war, will not be the alternative to war, but its handmaiden.

The following are some of the lines of thinking that ought to be considered in any discussion of alternatives to war in our present situation, the post-Cold War period.

- *Alternative use of military force—peacekeeping:* In the United States, many view this with suspicion, especially since the Gulf War and George Bush's proclamation of the New World Order. It is true that peacekeeping can be and is used as a cover for the great powers imposing their will on the lesser powers. It is also true that peacekeeping does not escape from the old paradox under which peace is to be achieved though military force.

  But in some countries, military organizations do take peacekeeping seriously, and are seeking to develop new tactics and new ways of thinking appropriate to this end. As one Canadian officer experienced in peacekeeping put it recently, "We still use Clauswitz. The principles of military action are the same. But the enemy has changed. The enemy is combat. In a successful peacekeeping operation all sides will unite to defeat this enemy." Moreover from their actual experience in the field, these peacekeepers are discovering what peace activists have been arguing for years: that peace cannot be established by military force alone, but must be grounded in economic, social and cultural realities. Coming from military circles, this is an important new voice.

- *Progressive criminalization of war activity:* There have been laws of war for centuries; in the modern era, there has been a movement to formalize these into treaties and, after World War II, to make these laws enforceable. This movement became stagnated during the Cold War era; the effort has been revived in the establishment of the International Criminal Tribunal for the former Yugoslavia (ICTFY), which just recently got its first conviction— the first conviction of a war criminal by an international court since the Nuremberg and Tokyo trials. Many hope that by bringing soldiers, generals and political leaders to trial for war crimes, a web of legal and administrative precedent can be woven that will steadily narrow the"free hand" that armies have tended to enjoy in war zones, and eventually whittle away at the right of belligerency itself. Others wonder whether the achievement of this end might not require the construction of a Leviathan even mightier and more fearful than those ones we now have. In any case, the establishment of ICTFY is an event of extreme importance and raises vital questions that must be debated.

• *Non-violent alternatives to military force:* The representative writer here is Gene Sharp who (in *The Politics of Nonviolent Action,* Porten-Sargent, 1973, and other works) has documented the myriads of non-violent ways in which military force may be and has been subverted and resisted, and political power may be and has been brought to bear: precisely, methods that work.

• *Withdrawal of consent to the state war power:* Two of the world's constitutions—those of Costa Rica and Japan—withhold from the state the right to maintain or use military force. The Japanese Constitution's famous Article 9 ends with the sentence, "The right of belligerency the state shall not be recognized." Japan's conservative government has managed to ignore this to the extent of rebuilding its military power in the form of the Japan Self-Defense Forces, but in the half-century since the Constitution was established, no person has been killed under the right of belligerency of the Japanese state. After the Gulf War peace activist Charles Overby (University of Ohio, Emeritus) founded the Article 9 Society, raising the question of whether the principle of the Costa Rican and Japanese constitutions, hitherto considered by most as applying only to their particular historical situations, might become the basis for a new international movement. Certainly Article 9 forces us to take a fresh look at this remarkable entity, the modern state. We are so accustomed to the state enjoying the right of belligerency that we seldom ask, what is this magic touch that transforms killers into heroes and terrorist bands into armies? Certainly any discussion of alternatives to war should consider the Japanese/Costa Rican alternative.

All four of these approaches are supported in good faith by dead serious people. At the same time, there are deep philosophical contradictions among them. The first two depend upon the right of legitimate violence, which the latter two work to oppose. But all four represent real movements that operate in the world today, movements that confront each other in serious debate all too seldom. The end of the Cold War has made it possible to discuss questions of war and peace in an entirely fresh light. TOES would be an excellent forum for such a discussion to take place.

The Impact of Military Activities on Development, Environment and Health

*Victor W. Sidel, Gurinder Shahi and Barry S. Levy**

Introduction

Wars among nations or within nations (the latter often called "civil disturbances," "civil wars" or, more recently, "low-intensity wars") interfere with development by directly damaging people, land and infrastructure, by disrupting social organization, displacing people and diverting human and financial resources that might have been employed for development. Wars pollute the environment of the nation in which the war is being fought as well as that of nearby nations or even the

---

*Dr. Victor W. Sidel is co-president of the International Physicians for the Prevention of Nuclear War (IPPNW) and Distinguished University Professor of Social Medicine, Montefiore Medical Center and Albert Einstein College of Medicine, Bronx, New York; Dr. Gurinder Shahi is head of the International Vaccine Institute Project, United Nations Development Programme (UNDP), Seoul, Korea; and Dr. Barry S. Levy is president of the American Public Health Association; Adjunct Professor of Community Health, Tufts University School of Medicine, Boston, Massachusetts. This essay is abridged and adapted from the chapter by Sidel and Shahi, entitled "The Impact of Military Activities on Development, Environment and Health," in *International Perspectives on Environment, Development, and Health: Toward a Sustainable World,* published by Springer Publishing in 1997.

global environment. In addition to their indirect effects on health—delayed economic and social development, damaged environment and diversion of resources that might have been used for medical care services and for public health—wars, of course, lead directly to the killing and maiming of both combatants and civilian populations.

Even when wars are not actively being fought, military preparation and the supporting economic, social and political climate may slow or reverse development, cause environmental damage and harm health by diversion of needed resources and by psychological trauma. In this analysis, the term "military activities" will therefore be used to include (1) the active use of weapons in war, civil disturbances, civil war and low-intensity war (which we will summarize as "war"); (2) weapons development, production, testing, storage, transport and disassembly and disposal, and military training ("military preparation"); and (3) the prevalence of military-oriented attitudes and practices within a nation or in the world ("militarism").

Many societies that appear to be at peace are in fact preoccupied with the possibility of war and with preparations for war. This was the case, for example, in the United States and the USSR between the end of World War II and the fall of communism in Eastern Europe and the former Soviet Union. Although there was no official war, the era was marked by the greatest arms race that the world has ever known, with the U.S. spending approximately 7 percent and the USSR approximately 12 percent of their respective GDPs in attempting to ensure parity or superiority in conventional weapons and weapons of mass destruction and in supplying arms to the other nations (Sivard, 1993).

Even in the wealthiest countries, investment in arms diverts resources that could have been used for investments in health, education or socio-economic infrastructure instead of the economically unproductive effort of developing ever more powerful weapons of terror and destruction. Japan and West Germany, in contrast, were constrained from military spending for any purpose other than defense after World War II; their constitutions forbade the development of any offensive capability, a requirement imposed on these countries by the victorious Allied nations for their roles in initiating and continuing the war. West Germany and Japan spent less than 2 percent of their respective GDPs on the military and used resources that would otherwise have been diverted to military activities to build the second and third largest economies in the world and impressive social infrastructures.

The situation in the U.S. and the USSR described as the "Cold

War" was not unique to these countries. Recent history is full of examples of countries that lived in states of heightened tension with each other without actually going to war. Israel and the Arab States fought three short but intense wars in the last three decades, but spent much of the rest of the time building up military capability (often supported by the U.S. or the USSR). Similarly, Pakistan and India have seen similar rivalries build up, with flare-ups having occurred at least four times.

The Impact of Military Activities on Development

In addition to the extensively reported direct impact of the weapons used in war, other militaryactivities divert people, financial resources and national will from development, environmental protection and the promotion and protection of health. Indeed, in many ways the most devastating impact of military activities is the diversion to military purposes of resources that might have been used to improve the quality of life, the social and physical environment and the health of the people of the world. Between 1945 and 1992, over $20 trillion (valued in 1992 dollars) were spent on the world's military forces. Military expenditures worldwide during the 1980s climbed to almost one trillion dollars annually, an amount in constant dollars close to three times the level of 1960. These resources, had they been devoted to human welfare, would have permitted an enormous increase in economic development, in improvement in the quality of life and therefore in the preservation of world peace and security (Sivard, 1993).

Annual military spending in the U.S. rose steadily during the 1980s from $140 billion to almost $300 billion annually in current dollars. After correction for inflation and population growth, this translates to a growth in spending on the military for each U.S. resident from approximately $800 to $1,200 annually during the decade. The $2 trillion spent on the military during the decade contributed significantly to a ballooning of the Federal budget deficit, resulting in the U.S. national debt expanding from less than $1 trillion in 1980 to nearly $4 trillion today (Sivard, 1993).

The U.S. economy provides one of the world's highest standards of living, but beneath this veneer of wealth lies the reality of America's destitute. The gulf between the rich and poor has widened. Some 29 million people lived below the poverty line in 1980; by 1992 that number had grown to 36.9 million, 14.5 percent of the population (U.S.

Bureau of the Census 1993). The median income of all families with children and parents under 30 years old fell 32 percent from 1973 to 1990. One-quarter of children under six and one-fifth of those under 18 lived in poverty; nearly 50 percent of black children under 18 were poor (Sidel, 1992; *The State of America's Children, 1992*; Sidel, 1996).

Research and development is vital to improving public health and the quality of life. In the U.S., governmental funding for research on health and human services pales in comparison to funding for military research. Just as a growing proportion of the federal budget has been devoted to the military, so too has the bulk of research and development funding. Of course, along with the diversion of revenue from support for needed research, arms spending diverts highly trained people from working to improve health and the quality of life to working on military projects— in the 1980s, as many as 30 percent of U.S. scientists and engineers worked on such military projects (Sidel, 1988).

Globally, the almost $1 trillion spent on arms annually in the 1980s by the world's nations was equivalent to the annual incomes of 2.6 billion people in the 44 poorest nations, one-half the world's population (Sivard, 1991; Grant, 1992). World expenditures on weapons research alone exceed the combined spending on developing new energy technologies, improving human health, raising agriculture productivity and controlling pollutants (Brown, 1986).

UNICEF called the 1980s "The Decade of Despair." For the world's poorest people, average incomes dropped by 10 percent to 25 percent. In the 37 poorest countries, spending on health was reduced by 50 percent and on education by 25 percent. In over 50 nations, primary school enrollment fell (Grant, 1992). It has been estimated that close to one billion people (nearly one in every five living persons) live in absolute poverty, 780 million people are undernourished, 850 million are illiterate, 1.5 billion have no access to medical facilities, an equally large number are unemployed and one billion people are inadequately housed *(Report of the International Conference on the Relationship Between Disarmament and Development, 1987)*.

The Impact of Military Activities on the Environment

IMPACT ON THE PHYSICAL ENVIRONMENT

The U.S. military establishment plays a major role in the pollution of the world's physical environment (Renner, 1997). In 1986, the DOD estimated that the military produced about 400,000 tons of hazardous waste annually (*Hazardous Waste,* 1989). Since the DOD does not comply with the Environmental Protection Agency's Toxics Release Inventory, there is no way accurately to evaluate the total amounts released. Some authorities place the figure as high as 500,000 tons—more than the top five U.S. civilian chemical companies combined. In the U.S., an estimated two-thirds of chlorofluorocarbon 113 emissions, depleters of the ozone layer, are contributed by the military ("Defending the Environment," 1989; Ruff, 1992; Siegel, 1991, 1992; Shulman, 1992). Among the DOD and DOE installations that contain identified toxic waste sites hazardous to public health and the environment, approximately 100 are listed as Superfund National Priority List sites—the most dangerous hazardous waste sites—and few such sites have been designated "cleaned up" (*Military Installations,* 1992). Major causes of degradation of the environment include (1) production, testing and maintenance of nuclear weapons ("Defending the Environment," 1989; *Complex Cleanup,* 1991; Robbins, 1991; Geiger, 1992; Hu, 1992; Sidel, 1993); (2) of chemical weapons (World Health Organization, 1970; Defending the Environment 1989; Sidel 1993); and (3) of biological weapons (Geissler, 1986; Piller, 1989; Wright, 1990; Sidel, 1993).

Military bases generate large quantities of a wide variety of toxic substances, including fuels, pesticides, solvents, polychlorinated biphenyls and phenols. Tanks and airplanes are washed with caustic cleaning compounds and solvents that are drained onto the ground or into ditches. Electroplating shops that repair metal parts for military equipment generate cyanides, acids and heavy metals. Chemical propellant bags used to fire artillery shells at firing ranges are regularly burned at military bases ("Defending the Environment," 1989; Siegel, 1991; Shulman, 1992).

The examples above refer largely to the environmental impact of "peacetime" military activities. At times of war, the environment can be devastated by the impact of explosives, incendiaries and defoliants that can destroy animals and crops, crater the land, and denude vegetation. In addition, war prevents sound environmental management. The displacement of massive numbers of people may cause additional ecologic damage (Ruff, 1992; Westing, 1984A).

In Vietnam, an estimated 2.2 billion hectares of forest and farmland were denuded as a direct result of bombing, mechanized land clearing, napalming and defoliation by the U.S. and South Vietnam. Some 72 million liters of herbicides were used to destroy food crops and to deny forest cover to Vietcong forces; one of them, Agent Orange, was sprayed over 35 percent of southern Vietnam between 1961 and 1971. Dioxin contained in the spray persists, with elevated levels still found in soil, food, wildlife, human breast milk and adipose tissue. An estimated 20 million square meters of commercial timber, 135,000 hectares of rubber plantations and 124,000 hectares of mangroves were destroyed. Restoration and regeneration from this massive environmental damage is still at an early stage (Westing, 1984A, 1984B; Ruff, 1992; Allukian, 1997).

In the Persian Gulf, ecologic damage was caused by bombing and by oil-related pollution (Hoskins, 1997). The air war in the Gulf lasted for a month and a half; the ground war was over in 100 hours. Still, in this short time more weapons were reportedly used than in the protracted Vietnam war. In what may have been the most intense air war in history, it has been estimated that some 250,000 individual weapons were dropped by aircraft—or roughly 6,000 weapons a day—including some 60,000 to 80,000 cluster bombs, scattering 12 to 16 billion "bomblets." In February 1991, Iraq ignited 752 oil well fires in Kuwait; these were extinguished more rapidly than had been expected, but the health and environmental impact of the smoke produced is still largely unknown. In addition, huge pools of oil caused by leakage from sabotaged wells that did not ignite still cover large parts of Kuwait; the oil penetrates the soil and kills plants, birds and insects (Arkin, 1991; Ibrahim, 1992).

IMPACT ON THE SOCIAL ENVIRONMENT

Huge military budgets and the military's access to control of a nation's weaponry have increased military participation in social and governmental activities in many countries, aided in many cases (at least indirectly) by professional training and equipment provided by the major powers. In an analysis of 112 developing countries, the proportion under some form of military rule has shown a rise from 26 in 1960 to 52 in 1982 to 61 in 1992 (Sivard, 1993).

Military rule tends to be associated with militarization of the economy and with repression and human rights violations, with concomitant increases in the danger of war and also of domestic repression (Geiger, 1997). Countries under military control tend to have many more people under arms than other countries and have, on average, experienced six times as many years of war than have other LDCs

(Sivard, 1993).

Militarized governments appear to survive through the use of tactics of fear and repression to "subdue the opposition, bottle up change and ensure the control of resources that nourish power." In fully 58 of the 61 countries under military control in 1992, the most extreme forms of repression, including torture, brutality, disappearances and political killings were used by the authorities against their own citizens. While other LDCs cannot claim to have unblemished human rights records, at least such practices are not "institutionalized" and abuses tend to occur much less frequently in countries not under military control (Sivard, 1993).

IMPACT ON SOCIAL INFRASTRUCTURE
AND CARRYING CAPACITY

The ability of a country to provide adequately for its people requires conditions of peace and the development of necessary infrastructure (Shahi, 1994). People in developing countries are much more likely to find their lives disrupted by natural disasters, civil strife and war than are people in industrialized countries.

Such events can also reduce the carrying capacity of affected countries and territories, lead to increased migration from these trouble spots and the creation of large number of refugees. Migrating from one's home is never easy. It means disrupting oneself from one's social and cultural roots and placing oneself in totally alien and even frightening environments. The push of poverty and the pull of opportunity already draw millions of people from rural areas to urban areas within countries. Migrating across national borders can be even more difficult. But devastation of home, breakdown of social infrastructure associated with military activities and inability to provide for one's basic needs are too often the forces that push individuals over the brink.

War can be devastating on a country, with thousands of soldiers ransacking the farms and taking away the produce of farmers, their primary source of livelihood. Laying of mines, curfews and destruction of roads, bridges and infrastructure often mean that farmers have no way to get what is left of their produce to market, often resulting in its spoilage. Lack of access to fertilizers and seed often mean that farmers tend to overburden the soil and lead to depletion of its nutrients. With crop yields declining and few opportunities to earn a decent living, rural families often have little choice but to migrate from their fields in search of alternative means of livelihood. When they get to the cities, a breakdown of infrastructure—lack of communications, social welfare systems and roads, lack of access to safe drinking water supplies and lack of food in the city (due to problems in bringing it from the country-side and failure of foreign ships or planes to bring it in)—means that the urban population often starves. The haves can take their posses-sions and wealth and escape to a country that will take them. The have-nots end up as starving refugees, such as those we have seen coming out of Somalia and Ethiopia, where civil war combined with natural drought to devastate the lives of those affected.

THE IMPACT OF MILITARY ACTIVITIES ON HEALTH

The physical trauma caused by the use on human beings of weap-ons of war is obvious (Garfield, 1997). Sivard has identified 149 wars, defined as armed conflicts involving one or more governments and caus-ing the deaths of 1,000 or more people per year, from 1945 to 1992. She estimates there were 23 million deaths due to these wars, 7,500,000 deaths among military personnel and 14,500,000 deaths among civil-ians (Sivard, 1993).

Some of the other direct medical effects of use of weaponry are less clear. For example, a startling rise in childhood cancer cases (leukemia being the most prevalent) in post-war Iraq has been reported by a Harvard study team (Hoskins, 1997). The team suggests this increase may be attributed to an armor-piercing shell, commonly used during the Gulf War, made from depleted uranium.

Among all the factors that interact to cause illness, which include genetic, infectious, degenerative and traumatic factors, it is widely ac-cepted that social, economic and other environmental causes are the most important (McKeown, 1988). These factors, of course, include poverty, homelessness, hunger, lack of education and lack of family and community support. Similarly, among all the factors that lead to failure to obtain needed health and human services, the most important are social, economic and environmental. These barriers include geo-graphic maldistribution of services, and racial, sexual and economic discrimination. Studies in developing countries demonstrate, for ex-ample, that the most important determinants of infant mortality include household income and literacy of the mother. The health effects arising from the diversion of human and financial resources from health and human services to preparation for war, while less obvious, may thus be even greater than the direct physical impact of war.

Similar consequences have been seen in industrialized countries in which resources have been diverted to preparation for war. In the U.S., for example, the gap in health indices between haves and have-nots have been increasing (Sidel, 1991). Since poor children are less likely to be immunized at an early age or, are less likely to have adequate nutrition or housing or to use primary medical care in a timely fashion, their rates of morbidity and mortality are higher than for well-off children. Even before they are born, their mothers are less likely to have adequate nutrition or timely prenatal care. As a result, the rates of premature birth, of low-birth weight, of infant mortality, of infectious disease morbidity and mortality are higher for poor children (*The State of America's Children, 1992*).

Along with the impact of military activities on physical health, there is substantial evidence of their impact on psychological health. Since 1980, the American Psychiatric Association has recognized post-traumatic stress disorder (PTSD) as a specific defined diagnostic category. This diagnosis officially recognizes the psychic reactions long noted among concentration camp survivors and other victims of war on violence, replacing less precise diagnoses such as "combat neurosis" and "shell-shock" (UNICEF, 1985; Gersons, 1992; Santa Barbara, 1997).

Discussion

Despite the problems and possible devastation that military activities can cause, realities in the world as it has existed have required the vast majority of people to believe that, in the event of threat, they must be willing to fight to protect themselves, their families and their communities. We might idealistically look forward to the day when there will be no more nation-states and the associated dangers of nationalism, when we all can live in peace with each other, when no person takes up arms against another. Perhaps one day humankind will truly reach the stage when military establishments can be removed and we can start enjoying the fruits of the "peace dividend" in the form of greater social and infrastructural investment—when each individual can achieve her or his maximum potential without fear of being taken hostage by international terrorists, some of whom masquerade as national governments. Unfortunately, that day is not yet here.

Is there, then, a need for some form of military activity? The answer most people would give today is almost certainly "yes." As we increase the role of the United Nations in the aftermath of the Cold War and give increased prominence to working through the rule of international law to settle disputes and to seek justice for perceived grievances, perhaps individuals and peoples and nations will find less and less reason to take up arms against each other. This will necessarily require increasing the role of international peacemakers and peacekeepers as well as increased prominence and action on the part of international entities, such as the United Nations General Assembly and Security Council and the International Court of Justice (World Court). Until we exhaust ourselves with killing and maiming each other or have the courage to reach across age-old ethnic divides to live peacefully with each other, it seems a sad but true fact that we will need some sort of self-defense capability to cope with threats that may arise.

Clearly there is need for balance between "appropriate" military activities and peace. But what constitutes "appropriate" activities? Obviously the maintenance of sufficient weapons that could destroy the world several times over is inappropriate and excessive. Some societies may need sufficient capability to defend themselves from possible threats, internal and external. Others require stronger, possibly offensive capability, in the event that they are required to play a protective role as the world's "policemen." If, however, declaration of war is declared illegal, if countries are required to follow due process in appealing to the UN General Assembly, in getting their concerns adjudged by the "World Court," and if countries agree to abide by the decisions of the Court and General Assembly, this would obviate the need for much armed conflict.

The next step is complete abolition of weapons of mass destruction and reductions in conventional arms. But ridding the world of weapons of mass destruction will itself require a series of steps. For nuclear weapons, the steps include: total cessation of nuclear test explosions, a ban which is now verifiable by seismographic methods and required by the Comprehensive Test Ban Treaty (CTBT) negotiated in 1996; and implementation of Article 6 of the Nuclear Nonproliferation Treaty (NPT) and of the 1996 advisory opinion of the International Court of Justice, which call for expeditious elimination of nuclear weapons.

For chemical weapons, what is required is full implementation of the Chemical Weapons Convention banning development, production, stockpiling, testing, transfer or use of chemical weapons, which entered into force on April 29, 1997 and had been ratified by the U.S. Senate a few days before. For biological weapons, the major task is strengthening of the 1972 Biological Weapons Convention by plugging the loopholes that permit so-called "defensive" research and instituting verification measures. Similar curbs on conventional weapons are needed, such as the "Convention on the Manufacturing and Reduction of Arms Stockpiling, Production and Transfers," which is being prepared by a number of non-governmental organizations.

In sum, military activities must be reduced to a "sustainable" level. Here too there is evidence of some progress. The republics of the former USSR, driven by economic necessity, have begun sharply to curtail arms expenditures. Among the smaller nations, Costa Rica has consistently over the past three decades spent little on arms and has used the freed resources to spend on improvement in its health and social conditions. In the U.S., although there has been some reduction in arms expenditures, the reduction has been small. Projections of reduced global arms expenditures suggest that the United States, which in the 1980s spent 23 percent of the world's arms expenditures, will be spending 45 percent of the world's arms expenditures by the end of the millennium.

The nations of the world must also act to repair the environmental damage caused by the production, use or dismantling of weapons, which we may think of as tertiary prevention. Again such efforts have begun, as we have noted, in a number of countries.

While military activities clearly have had major repercussions for health, the environment and development, historic, social and political changes around the world give much grounds to hope that reform is already underway. The end of the Cold War, the collapse of communism, the rise of global consciousness on the need to protect the environment and to deal with such issues as abject poverty and the abuse of human rights, all point to a window of opportunity that needs to be taken advantage of for global benefit. It seems likely that the future will bring a review of the role of the military in many countries and that this will be accompanied by more rational allocation of resources to promote social and economic development.

Presidents and prime ministers from 71 nations agreed at the United Nations World Summit for Children on a series of affordable and achievable goals for the year 2000. Among these goals: the elimination of polio, neonatal tetanus and guinea worm disease; a 90 percent reduction in measles; an 85 percent immunization rate among one-year-olds; a 50 percent cut in childhood diarrheal deaths and in malnutrition of five-year-olds; and a 33 percent reduction in child deaths from respiratory infection. Reaching these goals, UNICEF estimates, would require an additional $20 billion per year. These as yet unattainable goals represent, for example, the reallocation of just 10 percent of military expenditures in the developing world and 1 percent in the industrialized world (Grant, 1992).

The International Conference on the Relationship Between Disarmament and Development has summarized the choices:

> The world can either continue to pursue the arms race with characteristic vigour or move consciously and with deliberate speed towards a more stable and balanced social and economic development within a more sustainable international economic and political order; it cannot do both *(Report of the International Conference on the Relationship Between Disarmament and Development,* 1987).

References

Allukian, M., and P. L. Attwood, "Public Health and the Vietnam War," in B. S. Levy, V. W. Sidel, eds., *War and Public Health*, New York: Oxford University Press, 1997, pp. 215-237.

Arkin, W. M., D. Durrant and M. Cherni, *On the Impact of Modern Warfare on the Environment: A Case Study of the Gulf War,* Washington, D.C.: Greenpeace, 1991.

Arms Project of Human Rights Watch and Physicians for Human Rights, *Landmines: A Deadly Legacy,* New York: Human Rights Watch, 1993.

Brown, L. R., "Redefining National Security," in L. R. Brown, ed., *State of the World 1986*, New York: W.W. Norton, 1986.

Complex Cleanup: The Environmental Legacy of Nuclear Weapons Production (Doc.#OTA-0-484), U.S. Congress Office of Technology Assessment, Washington: U.S. Government Printing Office, 1991.

"Defending the Environment? The Record of the U.S. Military," *The Defense Monitor,* Washington, D. C.: Center for Defense Information, 1989:18(6):1-8.

Garfield, R. M., and A. I. Neugut, "The Human Consequences of War," in Levy and Sidel, eds., *op. cit.,* pp. 27-38.

Geiger, H. J., "The Impact of War on Human Rights," in Levy and Sidel, eds., *op. cit.,* pp. 39-50.

Geiger, H. J., and D. Rush, *Dead Reckoning: A Critical Review of the Department of Energy's Epidemiologic Research,* Washington, D.C.: Physicians for Social Responsibility, 1992.

Geisler, E., ed., *Biological and Toxin Weapons Today,* London: SIPRI/ Oxford University Press, 1986.

Gersons, B. P. R., and I. V. E. Carlier, "Post-Traumatic Stress Disorder: The History of a Recent Concept," *British Journal of Psychiatry,* 1992: 161, 742-748.

Gorbachev, M., *Perestroika: New Thinking for Our Country and the World,* New York: Harper & Row, 1987.

Grant, J. P., *The State of the World's Children 1992,* Oxford: UNICEF/ Oxford University Press, 1992.

Hazardous Waste: DOD Efforts to Reduce Waste (Doc#GAO/NSIAD 89-35), Washington, D.C.: General Accounting Office, 1989.

Hidden Enemies: Land Mines in Northern Somalia, Boston: Physicians for Human Rights, 1992.

Hoskins, E., "Public Health and the Persian Gulf War," in Levy and Sidel, eds., *op. cit.,* pp. 254-280.

Hu, H., A. Makhijani and K. Yi, *Plutonium: Deadly Gold of the Nuclear Age,* Cambridge, MA: International Physicians Press, 1992.

Ibrahim, Y. M., "Kuwait Battling Huge Pools of Oil," *New York Times,* April 21, 1992, A1.

Klare, M. T., and P. Kornbloth, eds., *Low Intensity Warfare: Counterintelligence, Proinsurgency and Anti-Terrorism in the Eighties,*

New York: Pantheon Books, 1988.

Land Mines in Cambodia: The Coward's War, Boston: Physicians for Human Rights, 1991.

McKeown, T., *The Origins of Human Disease*, Oxford: Basil Blackwell Ltd., 1988.

Military Installations with Toxic Waste Sites, Washington, D.C.: Physicians for Social Responsibility, 1992.

Morelli, D. R., and M. M. Ferguson, "Low-intensity Conflict: An Operational Perspective," *Military Review,* 1984, 64 (11):15.

Piller, C., and K. R. Yamamoto, *Gene Wars: Military Control Over the New Genetic Technologies*, New York: Morrow, 1988.

Renner, M., "Assessing the Military's War on the Environment," in L. R. Brown, C. Flavin, S. Postel, et al., eds., *State of the World 1991* (A Worldwatch Institute Report on Progress Towards a Sustainable Society), New York: W.W. Norton, 1991:132-152.

_____. "Environmental and Health Effects of Weapons Production, Testing, and Maintenance," in Levy and Sidel, eds., *op. cit.,* pp. 117-136.

Report of the International Conference on the Relationship Between Disarmament and Development, New York: United Nations, 1987 (United Nations publication A/CONF.130/39).

Robbins, A., A. Makhijani and K. Yih, *Radioactive Heaven and Earth: The Health and Environmental Effects of Nuclear Weapons Testing In, On and Above the Earth,* New York: The Apex Press, 1991.

Ruff, T. A., "The Environmental Effects of Military Activities," *Global Security* (Medical Action for Global Security, United Kingdom affiliate IPPNW), Summer 1992, pp. 9-12.

Rush, D., "The National WIC Evaluation," *Am J Clin Nutr* 1988; 48:389-519.

Santa Barbara, J., "The Psychological Effects of War on Children," in Levy and Sidel, eds., *op. cit.*, pp. 168-185.

Shahi, G. S., "Implications of Population Dynamics and Natural Resource Use On Carrying Capacity and Sustainable Development," in A. Binger and G. S. Shahi, eds., *Proceedings of the 1st International Session of the LEAD* (Leadership for Environment and Development) Program, New York: The Rockefeller Foundation, 1994.

Shulman, S., *The Threat at Home: Confronting the Toxic Legacy of the U.S. Military*, Boston: Beacon Press, 1992.

Sidel, R., *Women and Children Last: The Plight of Poor Women in Affluent America*, Rev. ed., New York: Penguin Books, 1992.

_____. *Keeping Women and Children Last: America's War on the Poor*, New York: Penguin Books, 1996.

Sidel, V. W., "Destruction Before Detonation," *Lancet*, 1985; 2:1287-1289.

_____. "The Arms Race as a Threat to Health," *Lancet*, 1988; 2:442-444.

_____. "Weapons of Mass Destruction: The Greatest Threat to Public Health," *JAMA*, 262: 680-682, 1989.

_____. "The Health of Poor and Minority People in the Inner City," *N.Y. State J Med*, 1991; 91:180-182.

_____. "Farewell to Arms: The Impact of the Arms Race on the Human Condition," *PSR Quarterly*, 1993; 3:18-26.

Siegel, L., *Operation Ozone Shield: The Pentagon's War on the Stratosphere*, Boston: National Toxics Campaign Fund, 1992.

Siegel, L., G. Cohen and B. Goldman, *The U.S. Military's Toxic Legacy*, Boston: National Toxic Campaign Fund, 1991.

Sivard, R. L., *World Military and Social Expenditures 1993*, Washington, D.C.: World Priorities, 1991.

_____. *World Military and Social Expenditures 1991*, Washington, D.C.: World Priorities, 1993.

The State of America's Children 1992, Washington, D.C.: Children's Defense Fund, 1992.

Stover, E., J. C. Cobey and J. Fine, "The Public Health Effects of Landmines," in Levy and Sidel, eds., *op. cit.*, pp. 168-185.

UNICEF, *Children in Situations of Armed Conflict*, New York: UNICEF, 1985.

U.S. Bureau of the Census, Current Population Reports, "Poverty in the United States, 1992," Washington, D.C.: U.S. Government Printing Office, 1993.

U.S. Congress (Senate), *Report of the Majority Staff of the Senate Subcommittee on Oversight of Government Management on DOD's Safety Programs for Chemical and Biological Warfare Research*, Washington, D.C.: U.S. Senate, 1988.

Westing, A. H., ed., *Environmental Warfare: Technical, Legal and Policy Appraisal* (Stockholm International Peace Research Institute/ United Nations Environmental Program Series), London: Taylor & Francis, 1984A.

_____. *Herbicides in War: The Long Term Ecological and Human Consequences* (Stockholm International Peace Research Institute/United Nations Environmental Program Series), London; Taylor & Francis, 1984B.

World Health Organization, *Health Aspects of Chemical and Biological Weapons: Report of a WHO Group of Consultants*, Geneva: World Health Organization, 1970.

Wright, S., ed., *Preventing a Biological Arms Race*, Cambridge, MA: MIT Press, 1990.

Turning Formal Democracies into Living Ones: The Global Rules of People's Movements

Jean-Bertrand Aristide *

If someone had suggested 15 years ago that by 1996 democracy would be the rule rather than the exception in Latin America, most of us would not have believed him. But dictator after dictator fell, election after election was held and democratic governments were installed throughout the continent. More than two-thirds of the world's population now lives in countries which officially are pluralistic democracies.

Ironically, these transitions toward democracy have coincided with the most severe economic crisis of the century in the countries of the South. In Latin America alone, 240 million people live in utter poverty, an increase of more than 120 million since 1980; 1.6 billion people live in countries with shrinking or stagnating economies, with real wages often lower now than they were in 1970. The gap between the world's richest and the world's poorest grows every day, with the richest 20 percent of the world's population now absorbing 85 percent of global income while the poorest 20 percent receive only 1.4 percent.

What does the triumph of democracy mean to the poorest 20 percent? Today there is a risk that democracy might remain a purely formal structure to them. Elections may be held once every four or five

---

* The writer, former President of Haiti, now works for the Foundation for Democracy. This article is part of an address he gave at a Novib conference in the Netherlands on September 19, 1996 and is being distributed by the Third World Network.

years, but the day-to-day participation by the population in the decision-making process necessary to focus state policies on poverty alleviation may never materialize.

We may also ask: what does the triumph of democracy mean in an age of globalization? International institutions play an increasingly influential role in national decision-making in the South. And neo-liberal economic policies dictate a sharply reduced role for the state. The transition toward democracy is taking place at a time when states are rapidly running out of resources, being saddled with debt, allowing market forces to determine the economic situation and playing an ever smaller role in the provision of basic human services.

It is as if our experience in Haiti, after the restoration of democracy in October 1994, is being repeated on a global scale: after a long and difficult struggle the people arrive at the seat of power, only to find that the palace has been stripped bare. The dream of harnessing the resources of the state to serve the needs of the poor is still beyond their grasp. With states retreating from the field, it seems that the poor will enter the 21st century alone, facing a global economy in which they cannot possibly compete. But fortunately this is not the whole story.

Those of us who work alongside the poor know that even in countries suffering the severest economic crises, like Haiti, people's organizations represent a vibrant and growing force for change. These organizations offer the seeds of hope for the 21st century. Throughout the world, local church communities, peasant organizations, women's groups, grassroots environmental organizations and NGOs are struggling for human and economic rights. Their analysis and convictions are rooted in the day-to-day reality of the poor. These actors are undertaking the task of democratizing democracy: turning formal democracies into living, participatory ones. These actors are holding up alternative economic models, and offering an ethical foundation for debates on economic growth and human development.

The role of civil society has never been more critical. We must be the conscience of our age, articulating a view of development which places the human being at its center, sees economic growth as a means to human development rather than an end in itself, and advocates development which ourplanet can sustain. As others have remarked, unrestrained growth is the ideology of the cancer cell.

As the state grows weaker, and the price of globalization becomes more apparent, there are growing voices from civil society which testify to these realities. They have an increasing influence on international institutions and, perhaps more importantly, they are making contacts and forming alliances across borders—knowing that in an age when capital needs no visa or passport, so too must solidarity know no borders.

One of the defining characteristics of civil society is the high percentage of women participating. Bearing witness against human rights abuses, organizing cooperatives, creating community health projects, women have long filled the ranks of people's organizations. However, this degree of participation is not at all reflected in the number of women involved in decision-making at all levels. Worldwide, women hold only 12 percent of all the seats in parliament, and 6 percent of those in national cabinets.

By definition, democratizing democracy means both empowering the large number of women who are already participating through civil organizations, and increasing their representation at the tables of power.

We will all benefit from this. Studies have shown that when the household income is managed by women, it is more likely to be used for human development purposes: health care, education and children's nutrition. I suspect that if national budgets were in the hands of women, or if grassroots women's organizations were to participate in preparing national budgets, the results would be the same.

On the economic front, civil groups are taking the lead in addressing inequitable land distribution, giving the poor access to credit and building cooperative economic structures. In Haiti, the goal of our Foundation for Democracy is to create an opportunity for dialogue and democratic participation by the population. But this initiative has to go hand-in-hand with concrete measures to alleviate misery. To offer a hungry person only words is callous; to offer him only food is hypocrisy. The cooperative we founded, which now has more than 12,000 members, makes credit available at a low interest rate to the poorest sector and enables members to buy food at about half its market price. There are many similar, small-scale cooperative initiatives around the world, offering a seed of hope for the next century.

We can become dispirited in the face of globalization, growing economic polarization, environmental degradation and the misery one quarter of the world's population are facing each day. In Haiti, where 85 percent of the population lives in misery, it is the courage and dignity of the very same 85 percent, who continue to struggle, to speak out, to organize and to fight for better lives for their children that constantly inspires us.

In Port-au-Prince right now there is a small radio station broadcasting each day. Two hundred thousand children live on the streets of Port-au-Prince: Radio Timoun is their radio station. Children are the reporters, the announcers and the technicians. I listen every day to hear what they have to say. They interview children in the prisons and broadcast stories from the General Hospital, calling on the government to improve health care for kids. In a recent meeting, one of these young journalists told me they want to report in their daily news broadcast how many children are born and die in Port-au-Prince each day.

Our dream is that one day instead of holding out an empty hand for a dollar, kids on the streets of Port-au-Prince will hold out a tiny tape recorder and ask for an interview. This radio station is another seed of hope for the 21st century.

As citizens of the world committed to fighting poverty, we should tend these seeds where we find them, shelter them when hostile and changing conditions threaten their very existence, and plant them in other places where they may take root and bear fruit to nourish the world. So we are nourished today by the fruits of solidarity and hope.

Toward a Global Populist Movement: Accepting the Challenge of Worldwide Corporate Domination

*Ronnie Dugger and Ruth Caplan**

Creating Another Populist Movement *(RD)*

The Alliance for Democracy is a new, long-term populist move-ment—not a political party—with members that are setting forth to reject the economic and political power of large corporations as illegiti-mate in a self-governing democracy. The mission, adopted at the found-ing convention, is "to free all people from corporate domination of poli-tics, economics, the environment, culture and information; to establish true democracy; and to create a just society with a sustainable, equi-table economy.

Who are our members? We are everyday people who have come together from across the United States, listened to each other and united to end corporate rule. We are committed to true democracy, inclusion and non-violence and to building alternative democratic, human-sized economic systems and a new people's movement—first here, then around the world.

---

* The authors are co-chairs of the Alliance for Democracy and jointly con-tributed this article. Authorship of respective sections is indicated by ini-tials after section headings. They can be contacted through the Alliance for Democracy, Box 683, Lincoln, MA 01773, tel: 617-259-9395; fax: 617-259-0404; e-mail: peoplesall@aol.com; web site: http://www.igc.org/alli-ance.

341

Why do we need another organization, one may well ask. Piece-meal reform does not work any more. The corporate system will not permit us to win anything fundamental by politics as usual. We see our unique role as seeking the deep systemic change we will need to win our independence from corporate rule and replace it with true democracy.

The Alliance grew out of an article published in the *Nation* in August 1995, Ronnie Dugger's "A Call to Citizens: Will Real Populists Stand Up." Nearly 6,000 people have responded, 1,800 have joined and 53 local Alliances have formed nationwide. In late 1996, delegates from 30 states convened in the Texas hill country and the Alliance for Democracy was founded.

The populists of the 1880s arose in those same Texas hills to challenge banks and corporate trusts for control of the national wealth and spirit. Uniting farm and factory workers for the first time, they set up cooperatives, educated each other, published newspapers and books and fielded 20,000 speakers to show the way to cooperation, self-respect and hope.

Those first populists, whose numbers rose to 2,000,000, have been anathematized, in some 20th-century accounts, as marred with prejudices. They fought racism and anti-Semitism more effectively than any social movement prior to the Civil Rights movement of the 1960s, as demonstrated by historian C. Vann Woodward. Even so, a number of populists shared the prejudices of that time. We 21st-century populists are committed to the equal importance of every person, no matter the person's race, religion, gender, sexual orientation, politics or nation of origin.

One's personal plan for social responsibility and action depends on one's analysis of the real situation now. Major corporations dominate our lives, our government, our work, our health care and our food supply. Media conglomerates control the course and set the limits of public discussion, commercialize and debase our national consciousness, and manipulate mainstream public opinion.

Everywhere the natural world is threatened. Yet people worldwide are exhorted to consume more and buy more in the name of "progress" so big companies can get bigger.

- Of the world's 100 largest economies, 50 are now global corporations.

- The richest 1 percent of Americans own 40 percent of all U.S. assets.

- The combined assets of 358 billionaires equal the combined assets of almost half the world's population.

- The courts have given corporations the basic Constitutional rights of persons, but workers lose those rights on entering the workplace.

- The corporate share of U.S. taxes paid has fallen from 33 percent in the 1940s to 15 percent in the 1990s. Individuals' share of taxes has risen from 44 percent to 73 percent.

- The new World Trade Organization effectively gives corporations veto power over our U.S. environmental and labor laws, weakening our right to protect ourselves and our land by our legislation.

How does the Alliance intend to address its mission, and how does it work? We are starting carefully. In the local chapters, our basic operating units, members are educating each other, studying the corporate system and corporate power in their communities, acting against local corporate abuses and making local inventories of alternative economic and media resources. Our Annual Convention elects a national Council of 25, which oversees the organization and our national office. The chapters are self-governing in accordance with agreements with the national organization.

In 1997, our first year, we intend to:

- carry out July 4th actions around a Declaration of Independence from Corporations;

- spotlight the stranglehold transnational corporations have over our lives, as participants at The Other Economic Summit (TOES) this June in Denver, at the same time as the G-7 nations hold their summit there; and

- support family farms and local food systems and expose the transnational corporate food system with a national education and action campaign culminating during the fall harvest/Thanksgiving season.

Meanwhile, local Alliances will continue:

- networking with others locally and nationally to demand zero tolerance for private funding of the public's elections; and

- exposing corporate abuses and supporting alternatives by actions to address immediate problems in local communities.

As we come from all across the political spectrum, our beliefs vary, but most of us feel that no task is more important than taking back our democracy from the unelected corporations that, step by stealthy step, have stolen it from us.

We understand the size of this task. But we are serious in our demand for systemic change. All the changes we need and want we cannot have unless We, the People, take back our power—this time for all of us. If we do not, we will not have health care for everyone, or elections not bought by corporations or the wealthy or a just tax system. We will not have clean food and water, a healthy natural environment, or safe cities and towns. We will not have good education for our children, equal treatment for all people, full employment or an adequate safety net for our poor, weak and elderly.

The founding article that led to the creation of the Alliance, Dugger's piece in the August 15-21, 1995 *Nation*, resulted in about 1,700 letters to the author, calling for the formation of the new movement organization he had advocated there or asking for more information about it. The article laid down this challenge:

> We are ruled by Big Business and Big Government as its paid hireling, and we know it. Corporate money is wrecking popular government in the United States. The big corporations and the centimillionaires and billionaires have taken daily control of our work, our pay, our housing, our health, our pension funds, our bank and savings deposits, our public lands, our airwaves, our elections and our very government. It's as if American democracy has been bombed. Will we be able to recover ourselves and overcome the bombers? Or will they continue to divide us and will we continue to divide ourselves, according to our wounds and our alarms, until they have taken the country away from us for good?

The Alliance in Action *(RD)*

The response to Dugger's call to the "Real Populists" is now 21 months old. It is striving to revive the non-violent rebellions of the late 19th century against the robber barons of that time. The railroads, the other industrialists, the banks, the Goulds and Carnegies and Rockefellers and Vanderbilts, were using the banking and wage systems to oppress the producing classes, that is, the farmers, the workers. Answering them were the Knights of Labor, a million strong, and the Farmers' Alliance, two million. We go back to that time for our model of rebellion. So far we have formed 53 local Alliances, and have about 5,500 people in our database. Our chapters range from 10 or 12 in Southern California to half a dozen in Texas, to half a dozen in Massachusetts and many in between. Most recently we formed chapters in Baltimore and Philadelphia.

We have three medium-term objectives: the end of corporate domination of our democracy; the restoration and enhancement of our economic and political democracy; and we seek to help precipitate, among the plethora of people-first organizations in the country, a new national people's movement.

It may be said fairly accurately that we are proceeding on six principles. First, as long as we struggle only over single issues (national health care, peace, campaign finance reform) or only in single configurations (as environmentalists, people of color, union people, feminists, gays and lesbians, and so on), the corporations will continue running every aspect of our lives. As populists we believe that, although the democratic forms are still intact, the oligarchy now buys and owns the content that is permitted to pass through the system into law. The issues are not the issue, the issue is the system, and to the extent that we can, we must unite to change it.

Second, we therefore seek not coalitions in governance—which may threaten separate organizations' turf, leaders or sources of money—but rather coalitions in action against our common adversary. We believe that only as we act together and learn to trust each other do we become the national movement. We do not oppose identity politics; we seek, by these coalitions in action, to finesse it while helping to realize its goals with joint action from which will emerge and grow the overarching solidarity of people as people.

Third, we do not compete with consanguine organizations. When they succeed, instead of carping we rejoice. If they are doing a good work, we offer to help them do it. Who gets the credit does not matter. We seek joinder, too, with the socially conscious churches, synagogues and mosques. (It is very important not to omit the mosques.) Above all, we seek a joinder of the union movement and all the rest of the reform movement in the United States. The French unions, with only 9 percent of the French workforce, brought the Chirac government to its knees with a general strike, because in France the other social movements act with labor and labor acts with the other social movements. In my opinion, time is a-wastin' for just such a general strike in the United States.

None of this can work without the fourth principle, what we in the Alliance call the alternative approaches theory. Ideally, we would all be working in a multi-ethnic, multicolor coalition. That's a given. But groups of us arise in different contexts and take different tacks. We have the Green Party, the New Party, the Labor Party. We have single-issue stresses on health, the environment, peace, campaign finance. We have tendencies toward organizational separatism on the bases of race and religion. We believe that we start where we are. We do not insist that the others follow our approach. As long as we share common values and are moving in the same direction, free of control by the government, corporations and the two major parties, we can work and act together.

Fifth, even a strong people's movement in the United States cannot bring the global corporations back down to democratic earth. They are cybernetically international, insatiably selfish and voraciously destructive. Only a global people's movement can stop them, and so we stitch together, as we build our local and national movement, an active alliance of democratic people-first organizations around the world.

We want to end the overconcentration of wealth and power and we want institutions that decentralize wealth and power. We also must invent enough democratically governed central power to deny corporations any right to govern us and any presence of any kind in our democratic politics.

Sixth, and finally, the Alliance for Democracy is committed to nonviolence. We believe that all the humanly decent means for seeking social change, from demonstrations to civil disobedience, will need to be used. This is a large subject that can be touched upon here. However, most elementally, we will not enter coalitions which include some members or organizations favoring violence to cause social change in the U.S. now. Those who use violence preempt and therefore define the movements they are in and render democracy within such movements a farce.

As we set forth, in honesty we should specify such limits to unity. For another example, a real commitment to democracy, to self-governance, is not rhetoric. Are the organizations we work with democratically organized and run, or are they controlled at a center? Do we know what shape of governance they seek for society—democratic or run from the top? We the people are not going to win this long struggle against autocracy and oligarchy by papering over differences that set people onto basically opposite courses. In due course, then, when we are reorganized together, celebrating and helping each other, we will have a national political party worthy of the people, and we will take the country back, and figure out together what we want our new democracy to be.

In the Alliance, we set forth arm in arm with our sisters and brothers for democracy and justice, to fight and win—first locally, then nationally, then in the world—a non-violent, democratic rebellion against the corporations that are ruining our lives, our democracy and our earth.

Democracy and Economic Justice: Forging the Link *(RC)*

This is indeed the challenge to democracy in North America and around the world: When political power is in the hands of the wealthy who can buy political favor—whether they be giant corporations or persons who have accumulated their wealth through control of such entities—there can be no true democracy. Campaign finance reform is essential but not sufficient to rout the ability of the wealthy to curry favor with ambitious politicians. This understanding is reflected in the mission of the Alliance.

Populism grew out of farmers' efforts to free themselves from the shackles of the company store which kept them forever in debt. When the price paid for their farm produce fell, their situation became desperate. As the populist movement gathered momentum, it shifted from an effort to achieve some justice within the larger system to recognizing fundamental flaws in the system itself. In pursuing "A World that Works," we have much to learn from the idealism, determination, incredible success and ultimate failure of their effort.

The movement first focused on circumventing the company store by setting up their own cooperative warehouses where seed and equipment could be purchased on credit until the crops came in. Within a few years, they realized the critical importance of avoiding the large cut taken by the middleman and so established cooperatives to sell their produce directly to buyers. But as these cooperating farmers set out to compete against the rapidly consolidating agricultural sector and the monopoly of the railroads, they found that small, local cooperatives were insufficient. When they sought to establish large-scale credit cooperatives, they were unable to obtain the necessary loans from private banks. Even when they pooled their resources and could show sufficient collateral to secure the needed loans, they were still turned down cold by the banking establishment. This deepened their understanding of the economic power they were up against.

As Lawrence Goodwyn details so powerfully in his book, *The Populist Moment* (New York: Oxford University Press, 1978), it was this major barrier to their success, even as their cooperatives were growing by leaps and bounds, that caused the populists to delve deeply into the fundamental ways in which the economy was structured.

Their proposed solution, the sub-treasury system, was developed by Charles Macune, one of the populist leaders. Macune proposed to overcome the withholding of loans by private banks by turning to public financing. Federal warehouses termed "sub-treasuries" would be "erected in every country in the nation that annually yielded over $500,000 worth of agricultural produce." The farmers would be able to store their crops to wait for higher prices and at 2 percent interest rates would be able to "borrow up to 80 percent of the local market price upon storage, and could sell their sub-treasury "certificates of deposit" at the prevailing market price at any time of the year" (*Ibid.*, p. 109).

Goodwyn makes clear how this sub-treasury proposal went to the heart of the economic system:

> In effect, Macune had replaced the high-interest crop-mortgage of the furnishing merchant with a plan that mortgaged the crop to the federal government at low interest. It thus provided the farmer with the means to escape, at long last, the clutches of the advancing man and recover a measure of control over his own life. For the farmers of the South, both black and white, the sub-treasury plan was revolutionary (*Ibid.*, p. 110).

One of the lessons to be gleaned is the need to accumulate capital in differing amounts depending on the enterprise. All too often in proposing our alternatives, we ignore this need despite the fact that the economy is far more centralized today through the transnational corporations than it was in the late 19th century under the robber barons. Instead, we focus on small-scale, community-based enterprises. Nor has there been much focus on the question of where poorer communities can get the financial resources needed to move toward sustainable enterprises and full employment with liveable wages.

A second lesson is that the populist movement collapsed when it proved unable to translate their cooperative movement into a political movement that could garner the power to get their sub-treasury plan enacted. They started off strong by forming the Peoples Party, an independent third party, but were sold out by ambitious politicians fusing with the Democratic Party to ensure the votes they needed to get elected. Goodwyn tells this story in brilliant detail.

Today workers are becoming increasingly bound to the stock market through their pension fund investments and the shifting of their personal savings from insured savings accounts to uninsured mutual funds. If social security goes to private investment, rather than remaining in the public sector, the noose will tighten dramatically. Workers' economic security will be fully identified with a system that is becoming increasingly unequal and unjust.

The time has come once more to return to the fundamentals of our economy. How can we be freed from the corporate domination of our lives, our communities and our workplaces without looking to the economic system which allows these corporations to increase their power globally without limitation? It is time to learn from the populist movement.

We must dig deep together and find the clear aquifers of analysis and action that will inspire and sustain us together and allow us to build a new populist movement. It is time to take back our power from the corporations and the wealthy, joining together as workers, as members of our communities, as citizens and ultimately as part of a global peoples' movement.

Reaching Out to the World *(RD)*

In a sidebar story that ran with the founding article in the *Nation*, Dugger wrote in 1995:

Once we are formed, in my opinion, we should at once connect with other democratic workers' and citizen movements and people-based non-governmental organizations around the world, because the only hope for turning giant corporate fictions into fundamentally subordinate bodies is direct and cooperative international citizen action.

The large national and transnational corporations have stolen a march on the people of the world and formed a world government of the super-rich and the super-powerful. Their first name for it is the World Trade Organization. They are hollowing out national governments, and under the suicidal mantra of endless growth, they are deploying the resources and people of the world to make themselves ever richer and ever more powerful. If this continues, we will all be ruled by an international aristocracy in the one global marketplace the oligarchy owns and controls, on a planet the corporations will finally ruin.

To the undeniable reality of corporate world government-gutting and commanding of nations, we believe that the logical answer is a global people's movement—that the only convincing reply to international aristocracy is international democracy. If we the people here in the U.S. do not get control of the corporations here, then there is little hope that people can do it in the rest of the world.

Unmistakably, the large national and international corporations and the invisible kings of superwealth behind them are the people's common adversary. The subtle corporate sell is that democracy is the same as capitalism dominated by the transnationals. It is not. The large corporation is top-down, hierarchical and anti-democratic, dedicated to sucking wealth up from people and communities into the already obscenely rich corporate aristocracy. A command world economy is just as deadly for democracy as the command communist economy was, and now we know it. Self-government is the one fatal vulnerability of the structurally dictatorial corporation.

We are called to struggle for self-governance. The corporate oligarchy's common cause against us, and our own democratic humanity, are our common ground. Our first tasks are to return to our democratic roots and to join together the forces we already have.

A Final Word (RD)

The computer and the Internet, its worldwide incarnation (in combination with the computerized power of large corporations) are among the reasons the transnational corporations and financial institutions are so rapidly perfecting their ideology and strategies and coordinating their structures for the incorporation of the human race. To achieve a comparable set of strategies and structures for transnational economic and political democracy, we have to keep the Internet open and uncensored and form a human alliance for democracy before we are permanently shut out of the governance of our own species. Computers and the Internet are the transnationals' central nervous system, but computers and the Internet can also quickly become the nervous system of the people ourselves as we counter-build a humane and human-scale society where we safely produce and fairly share the world's goods and services and live together peacefully.

Some relatively few of us in many movements may care to venture now into the foothills of a quest for a global democratic people's movement through which we can learn and teach each other and act together across all borders and eventually in every country.

Toward an Ethics of Sustainability

Larry Rasmussen*

Sustainability is a process with a beginning but no end; and in considerable measure, it is a social construct. It requires, absolutely, recognizing and respecting ecological integrity. It also requires a human vision for nature's duration, on terms hospitable to us and millions of other creatures. It is thus a matter of human imagination and dreaming as well as concrete technologies, tasks and policies.

Among other things, this means that all those questions of participation in the play of human power are crucial to sustainability: who gets to sit at the table, whose knowledge and experience count, who casts what kind of votes, who represents future generations and those of the present gernations who cannot speak for themselves, whose values and character carry the day. These questions are vital because "sustainable" modifies "environment" and "society" together. Both environment and society, together, are dynamic processes without foreseen ends, processes depending heavily upon human constructs of both heart and mind, indeed upon some modicum of justice and peace, together with sober respect for the integrity of creation.[1]

Such processes as these, and questions of power and its play in society and nature together, mean the ascendancy of ethics in matters of sustainability. So we finish by lifting the implicit moral norms from the

---

*The author is a faculty member of the Union Theological Seminary in New York. This essay is adapted from his *Earth Community, Earth Ethics,* Maryknoll, NY: Orbis Books, 1996.

discussion to this point, as norms of and for sustainability.

- *Participation* as the optimal inclusion of all involved voices in society's decisions and in obtaining and enjoying the benefits of society and nature, together with sharing their burdens. All primary "stakeholders" have opportunity to articulate their needs, propose and consult on projected solutions, and be part of considered implementation.

- *Sufficiency* as the commitment to meet the basic material needs of all life possible. This means sufficiency for both human and other kinds of populations. For humans it means careful organization of the economics of borrowing and sharing, with both floors and ceilings for consumption. A sufficiency revolution must accompany the eco-efficiency one called for by the United Nations and business. Eco-efficiency is a first step into sustainability. Eco-sufficiency is a basic requirement.

- *Equity* as basic fairness is the cousin of sufficiency. Both distributive and procedural justice are needed as means to ensure global equity among nations and societies, biotic equity among species, equity across generations stretching into the future and equity between women and men. Such equity is necessary to assure that sufficiency levels are attained and sustained.

- *Accountability* as the sense and structuring of responsibility toward one another and earth itself, carried out in ways that prize openness or "transparency." (Accountability is sometimes considered a dimension of participation, but here the character of that participation is made clear. Please know who and how decisions are made, and there are structures and procedures for holding decision-makers accountable.)

- *Material simplicity and spiritual richness* as markers of a quality of life that includes bread for all *(sufficiency)* but is more than bread alone. Negatively stated, major disparities of wealth and poverty generate instability and unsustainability. So do soul-barren cultures.

- *Responsiblity* on a scale that people can handle. This is an argument for actions commensurate with workable community. It is also an argument for technologies whose consequences are more apparent rather than less, are smaller in their range of impact than larger and are subject to alteration and correction without vast disruption.[2]

- *Subsidiarity* as the means of participation most attuned to Earth and the scale proper to *responsiblity.* Subsidiarity states that problems should be resolved at the closest level at which decisions can be taken and implemented effectively. Negatively stated, one should not withdraw from persons and their communities and commit to larger entities that which they can accomplish by their own enterprise and means. Larger and higher bodies should not perform and provide that which can be performed and provided by smaller and subordinate bodies.[3]

Adding these moral requirements to preceding discussions, we might summarize the whole by recognizing that sustainability necessarily involves the total earth-human process. It encompasses the requirements of sustainable environments, sustainable societies, and livelihoods, economies, and ways of life. While the full range of human activities is thus engaged, together with a certain set of moral values, virtues and obligations, *all must function as a phase of earth economics and earth community.* Any millenial drive of human power, married to the conviction that we somehow transcend the natural community of earth and need not worry overmuch about other kind's claims, can only be deadly for all.[4] Earth community is basic.

With a view to the human task, all this points to whole-systems approaches that address overconsumption, population numbers and inequality simultaneously. These are interlinked, and ways must be found to bring human society into balance with the earth and its economy— household by household, locale by locale, region by region.[5] If we turn to the planet's three socio-ecological classes, the 1.1 billion desperate, the 3.3 billion managing poor, the 1.1 billion overconsumers, sustainability means huge shifts. Roughly 80 percent of environmental damage is caused by the overconsumers and lives organized around cars and planes, high-caloried meat diets, prepackaged and disposable products, single-family dwellings and wasteful ways. This must shift in a direction more in keeping with the 3.3 billion who occupy more modest, but adequate, quarters, whose diet is a healthy one of grains and vegetables and some meat, whose travel is via public transport and bicycles, and who use unpackaged, local goods while practicing extensive recycling. Above all, the lot of the 1.1 billion absolutely deprived must be addressed, with their nutritionally inadequte diets, contaminated water, rudimentary shelter, scraps for clothing, endemic disease and daily insecurity.[6]

Notes

1. This paragraph is indebted to the paper of Stephen Viederman, "The Economics of Sustainability: Challenges." (The paper is available from the Jessie Smith Noyes Foundation, New York City.) Used with permission.

2. This listing of norms is a composite drawing from World Council of Church discussions as well as the Presbyterian Church (USA) draft of "Hope for a Global Future: Toward Just and Sustainable Human Development" (report of the Task Force on Sustainable Development, Reformed Faith, and U.S. International Economic Policy, August 8, 1995).

3. This paraphrases the wording in the encyclical of Pope Pius XI, *Quadragesimo anno* 79, as cited by J. Philip Wogaman, *Christian Ethics: A Historical Introduction,* Louisville:Westminster/John Knox, 1993, p. 213.

4. The discussion echoes Thomas Berry's in "The Meadow across the Creek" (unpublished manuscript), pp. 152-159.

5. David C. Korten, *When Corporations Rule the World,* San Francisco: Berret-Koehler/West Hartford, CT: Kumarian Press, 1996, pp. 35-36.

6. All this is elaborated in some detail by Alan During, "Asking How Much Is Enough," in Lester R. Brown, et al., *The State of the World, 1991,* New York: W. W. Norton, 1991, pp. 153-169.